Displaced
    Homemakers

Displaced Homemakers

ORGANIZING FOR A NEW LIFE

by LAURIE SHIELDS

Epilogue by TISH SOMMERS

McGraw-Hill Book Company

NEW YORK   ST. LOUIS   SAN FRANCISCO   AUCKLAND
BOGOTÁ   JOHANNESBURG   LONDON   MADRID   MEXICO
MONTREAL   NEW DELHI   HAMBURG   PANAMA   PARIS
SÃO PAULO   SINGAPORE   SYDNEY   TOKYO   TORONTO

1 2 3 4 5 6 7 8 9 FG FG 8 7 6 5 4 3 2 1 0

First McGraw-Hill Edition, 1981
ISBN: 0-07-056802-2

LIBRARY OF CONGRESS CATALOGING IN PUBLICATION DATA

Shields, Laurie.
Displaced homemakers.
Bibliography: p.
Includes index.
1. Displaced homemakers—United States.   I. Title.
HQ759.S4627   305.4'3   80-15336
ISBN 0-07-056802-2 (pbk.)

Book design by Andrew Roberts

This book is gratefully dedicated to my parents
and my daughter, Christine; to Tish and Barbara,
who opened doors to a new future for so many;
and to thousands of women who took up a cause
for themselves and others and turned it into
the Displaced Homemakers Movement.

CONTENTS

INTRODUCTION   IX

CHAPTER ONE
Expectations versus Realities   3

CHAPTER TWO
Genesis of a Movement   25

CHAPTER THREE
Laboratories of Hope   71

CHAPTER FOUR
Where There's a Bill There's a Way   113

CHAPTER FIVE
Organizing for a New Life   147

Epilogue by Tish Sommers   190

Appendices   217
VOLUNTEER CONTRACT   219
SENATE BILL NO. 825   223
RESOURCES   229
DISPLACED HOMEMAKERS
   PROGRAM DIRECTORY   231
HELPFUL PUBLICATIONS   261

INDEX   265

INTRODUCTION

Who are "displaced homemakers"? West Coast feminist and advocate for older women Tish Sommers, who coined the term in 1974, saw them as persons caught in the middle—in the middle of changing family structure, in the middle of new divorce laws and changing societal mores, in the middle of life. She saw the analogy between displaced persons "forcibly exiled" through social upheaval or war and a whole generation of women caught in the 1970s, "forcibly exiled," displaced from a role, an occupation, dependency status, and a livelihood.

By definition, according to Sommers, a displaced homemaker is an individual who has, for a substantial number of years, provided unpaid service to her family, has been dependent on her spouse for her income but who loses that income through death, divorce, separation, desertion, or the disablement of her husband.

As a group, displaced homemakers fall through the cracks of federal income security programs. They are frequently too young for Social Security, and many will never qualify because they have been divorced from the family wage earner. (Prior to 1978, any woman divorced short of a marriage of twenty years was ineligible for benefits on her ex-spouse's record. The amended law dropped the figure to ten years.)

They are also ineligible for federal welfare assistance if they are not physically disabled and if their children are eighteen. They are ineligible for unemployment insurance because they have been engaged in unpaid labor in the home. Considered too old for the traditional job market, they frequently wind up in low-paying, part-time jobs which carry none of the fringe benefits other workers enjoy, such as health insurance or pension plans.

When we began in 1974 there were no official statistics on the number of women who fit the definition "displaced homemakers." Traditionally, the woman's role wasn't (and isn't today) counted as labor; therefore, former homemakers weren't and aren't counted. An unofficial study commissioned by Sommers in 1975 placed the figure between three and six million women who matched the definition and disclosed an additional fifteen million women as potential displaced homemakers. But in 1978, in order to allocate its funds between regions, the Department of Labor needed "official" figures. Using data based on the *Survey of Income and Education,* March 1976 (the most comprehensive national survey of marital status, labor force participation, and income), the Women's Bureau of the Department of Labor estimates that there are four million displaced homemakers, three million of whom are between the ages of forty and sixty-four. Thus, four years after the

Alliance for Displaced Homemakers (ADH) study, the Women's Bureau repeated the process in a more sophisticated manner and came up with comparable figures for CETA (Comprehensive Employment Training Act) use. Since 1976, as legislated state displaced homemaker programs developed, needs assessment studies were done in several states. (Those interested can check their State Commission on the Status of Women to find out if such a study has been done.)

"Things don't turn up in this world until somebody turns them up," observed James Abram Garfield. One reason the issue was picked up and spread so rapidly across the country—"it was as though we struck a raw nerve," Sommers says—is that nearly everyone recognized the displaced homemaker as someone they knew, but hadn't known the individual problems were common to millions of other older women.

Using legislation as a tool (not only to organize other older women but also to focus attention for the first time on the economic needs of older women), Sommers, in 1975, proposed pilot training programs designed to prove that homemakers do, over the years, develop skills that are transferrable to the job market and that they have natural skills as well which can be utilized in opening up new careers.

My path crossed hers shortly after the first bill, the California Displaced Homemakers Act, was filed in April 1975. I was a displaced homemaker (although I didn't know it at the time), a fifty-five-year-old widow trying desperately to re-enter the job market after fifteen years as a full-time homemaker, wife, and mother. I became involved in the "cause" and, as one of the cofounders of the Alliance for Displaced Homemakers, served as its national coordinator, helping to direct the political strategy that moved the issue across the country and up Capitol Hill to a federal program in a fast-paced three years of grass roots action.

Crisscrossing the country in my "tennies" (deliberately chosen for comfort but also as a not so subtle protest against the notion that little old ladies in tennis shoes are flaky), I met thousands of women who, with disquieting unanimity, greeted the message of the legislation with a teary "My God, I thought I was all alone." I met still more through letters generated by media attention.

In an exchange of correspondence, I built up a relationship with many of these women that transcended our shared problems. I came to know them as friends; I found myself deeply moved by their quiet courage in the face of real adversity. Sharing their lives, however briefly, and observing their battles against loneliness and despair gave new meaning to the importance of the legislation and the work we were collectively doing.

What we found was that displaced homemakers exist in every state, in every community (large or small), belong to no one political party or religious denomination, and are of every race. What binds all of us together is the commonality of our age and experience, our struggle to move to economic self-sufficiency in the middle of our lives—caught, as columnist Ellen Goodman put it, "between the expectations of one decade and the realities of another."

This book is not an academic treatise on a "new social phenomenon," as *U.S. News & World Report* referred to displaced homemakers, but it is hoped it will be useful to professionals serving this newly defined segment of the "economically disadvantaged." Nor is it the intent of the author to chart the step-by-step development of the displaced homemaker movement or to tell in its entirety the political history of the legislation, despite the fact that some readers might be interested. It will, however, document the extent to which discrimination against older women, consciously or unconsciously, prevails in both the public and the private sector and is arrogantly practiced by some elected and nonelected members of government and perpetuated by some self-serving agencies with an eye to expanding departmental or organizational budgets.

The displaced homemaker movement, which officially began in 1975, owes its existence to some feminist activists but also overwhelmingly to the collective action of thousands of women who thought and spoke of themselves as "just housewives." Despite our inexperience, we were able to break through the "system" and establish a toehold on effecting change. Several became leaders within their own states—women such as Marguerite Davis of New York, Margaret Garvue of Florida, Doris McAtee of Washington, and Charlotte Stewart of Texas, who, along with others, played a substantial role in getting displaced homemaker measures enacted in their states.

By late 1979 there were approximately three hundred programs, most minimally funded, serving displaced homemakers. The term itself is increasingly becoming a "buzz" phrase in both the private and public sectors. Hopefully, all of this should mean more and more older women will be helped in their transition from dependency to self-sufficiency. But it must be admitted that it will continue to be an uphill struggle.

Our demand for a fair share of jobs is only a beginning for older women. In the years ahead we must join with others—if not lead the struggle—to have homemaking and child-rearing recognized as a viable occupation for both sexes based on an economic partnership. Dependency must be phased out, but only with adequate protections (Social Security credits, unemployment insurance, disability) solidly in place for the homemaking spouse.

More than anything else, it is the author's hope that this book will encourage other older women to take a new lease on life, to work toward building new and satisfying careers, and to do so with the firm conviction that all the past years of homemaking can and will provide a valuable foundation for the future.

It will also serve a purpose if the book helps to expose the wasteful bias of ageism that pervades our society today. It is particularly urgent that women—*all* women—understand the meaning of that bias because aging *is* a woman's issue. The cold sobering fact to keep in mind is that in just twenty years—by the end of the 1990s—thirty-six million women in this country will be forty-five years of age and older. What a force for change we can be!

Those of us in the adolescence of aging today should be gearing up for our own geriatric revolution. The words of abolitionist Frederick Douglass are no less true now than they were in 1857: "Power concedes nothing without a demand. It never has and it never will."

LAURIE SHIELDS

Oakland, California

Displaced
Homemakers

CHAPTER ONE

Expectations versus Realities

The opening of the 1970s marked the explosion of the women's movement with growing demands of feminists for equal rights for women in employment, education, sports, politics, and for options in lifestyles. Expectations ran high, commitment was intense, and the race to gain the "freedom to be me" swept past millions of women who clung to what they were and wanted to be—full-time homemakers, wives, and mothers. The reader who wrote in 1971 to the editor of one of the leading women's magazines spoke for more women than herself: "As a homemaker and mother of four, I find being at home all the time the most rewarding experience of my life. Planning for my family instead of planning for someone else is heavenly." Clearly, all hands that rocked the cradle were not yet ready to rock the boat.

In the ten short years of the '70s feminists and traditionalists learned some hard lessons. Feminists who had demanded the right did open the doors to more paid jobs, but only a tiny fraction of those were in the higher wage bracket in fields previously considered "men's work." Working women discovered they weren't "superwomen." As Betty Friedan, first president of NOW and early leader of the women's movement, confessed to a New York audience late in 1979: "The choices we sought in the '70s are not as simple as they seemed. Indeed, some choices women are supposed to have won by now are not real choices at all. And even the measure of equality we have already achieved is not secure until we face these unanticipated conflicts between the demands of the workplace and professional success on the one hand, and the demands of the family on the other."

Conversely, traditionalists (married women who had scorned the women's movement) got caught up in the push for economic security as inflation eroded the salary of the male breadwinner. By the end of the '70s, 5.5 million wives had entered the labor market, and three out of five American families had at least two wage earners.

With the structure of the American family under assault, a large percentage of older women are caught in a terrible bind. Millions of middle-aged and older women have emerged as part of a new phenomenon—a group of women composed of the "old poor" and the "new poor," former dependents outside the poverty ranks. For them, the cultural changes that grew out of the '60s and the erosion in the '70s of the roles and expectations of women in the world in which they had grown up is confusing enough. But the compounding impact of ageism, being made to feel useless and of little value to themselves or society, imposes a heavy psychological toll on such women.

Most women who are today forty and older bought the social contract of "man the breadwinner, woman the homemaker." They may not all have heeded St. Paul's admonition "Wives be subject to your husbands as to the Lord"; but they paid it at least lip service because it was "expected." Men were providers and protectors; women were supportive and nurturing. Consequently, it was men who worked in the salaried world while women wholeheartedly, if not always happily, accepted the charge that she "looketh well after her household" as a labor of love in the home which was their world.

Father is the head, mother is the heart, and home is where the heart is. In their maturing years, the message was threaded through fiction, movies, popular songs, and was heard most persistently from the pulpits where the faithful worshipped. Whatever her husband's income level, most of these homemakers assumed that retirement benefits, health insurance, and economic security flowed from their marriage. If women worked outside the home, it was likely to be supplemental, irregular, and mostly part-time. In one period of national emergency they stepped in as Rosie the Riveters and took over the jobs of men who had gone off to war. All but a small percentage just as obediently returned to the kitchen when the emergency ended.

Among the cultural changes of the '70s that affected older women adversely was the increased frequency of divorce, which Dr. Robert Weiss of the University of Massachusetts calls "one of the most important changes in American social life in the past generation." Nationally, in 1975 divorces soared over the one million mark—an increase of 5 percent over the previous year. In 1979 the million mark was reached in just over ten months.

The rise in no-fault divorces accommodated the taste of the '70s for multimarriages but wreaked havoc on women who had viewed marriage as "till death us do part." In Nebraska, for example, six months after no-fault divorce went into effect, sociologist Ellen Sim, testifying before the state legislature, reported a 59.6 percent increase in divorce after thirty-one years of marriage! No longer under the restraint of community disapproval, dissolution on demand of one spouse worked against older women—especially those who neither wanted nor expected a divorce.

Additionally, former dependent wives are seldom in a position to engage attorneys who can protect their interests. As Rianne Tennenhaus Eisler points out in her excellent book *Dissolution:*

> ...except in cases of substantial community or jointly held property, the attorney for the wife is primarily dependent on a court award for fees; whereas the attorney for the husband usually gets paid up front, or at the very least, has the assurance of direct payment from the client.

And she continues:

> There are a number of consequences flowing from this situation. In lower-income families, the wife may simply not be able to afford a good attorney.... In higher-income situations the problem is more subtle, since it usually involves the personal and psychological relationship between the opposing counsels. If they are friendly and move in the same circles, the wife's counsel may, by gentlemen's agreement, have little opposition from the other side about the size of the attorney's fees. However, since the purse strings are under the control

of the husband's counsel, there is a certain conflict of interests inherent in the situation which might set unconscious limitations on the effectiveness of wife's counsel.

Women who have written to relate horrendous stories of their divorce experiences put it less tactfully. More than one reports "We used the same attorney in order to save money." "My attorney told me if I didn't cooperate I'd wind up with nothing. I wound up with not much more than that anyway." "I found out later I was entitled to half of his pension but my lawyer said I wasn't."

At least part of the problem for these displaced homemakers again stems from their dependent role. If they know a lawyer, it is usually because of their husband's contact with one. They tend to trust the lawyer who "drew up our wills" and will turn to him/her assuming he/she can equally represent both parties. There is a reluctance to "shop" for a lawyer as we might seek a second opinion from a doctor. The lawyer is the "expert"—a figure of authority older women, in particular, accept with few questions. But as Eisler notes:

> The proper role of the attorney . . . is to sufficiently educate the client so that she or he can understand each problem and its risks. It is the lawyer's job to give advice . . . not to give orders. It is the client's job to decide what course of action to take.

She recommends "shopping" for a lawyer just as you might take care before buying expensive appliances, and she warns against trying to economize by hiring a mediocre lawyer or none at all because

The wife's attorney usually has more of a job to do than does the husband's. The husband not only has control of the assets, but has all the information about them. The massive effort of discovery and analysis of the financial picture, as well as the task of persuading the court of the wife's needs, falls to her attorney.

The poor and the low-income person may be able to draw on free legal-aid services; and since child support could be an important factor, legal help is essential. But as Eisler notes, for such services "the waiting period for a divorce case can be as long as a year or more."

Paula, who is fifty, is representative of an increasing number of older women whose expectation of togetherness in the sunset years of their marriage is shattered by husbands turning to divorce and remarriage to younger women.

After 30 years of marriage and working in the home as per my husband's demands, I am being forced to get a divorce or get out as he says. I have no social security, no pension, no retirement, all things that he has. Nowadays it seems that when a woman is through raising her family her life is finished.

Her assessment of her financial situation is underscored by the thinking of jurists like the California judge who stated "when a marriage is bankrupt, the wife is bankrupt." Too few on the bench in family courts are as sensitive to the needs of older women as is Justice Robert Gardner (California Court of Appeals). Holding favorably for a forty-four-year-old wife divorced after twenty-five years of marriage, he commented:

Wife's employment picture is bleak. She is 44 years of age and has not even completed high school. She has no apparent job skills. She has made eight efforts for employment as a salesperson, all of which were unsuccessful. She is attending a two-year junior college class which she describes as a "guidance class for someone my age that has not had any employment, and I would like to try for something if I do lose my eyes completely." This latter comment refers to the fact that the wife testified that she suffers from an incurable iritis in both eyes with the possibility of becoming blind in the near future. Furthermore, she is an arthritic.

The notice of the appeal filed by the ex-wife addressed the spousal support granted upon dissolution. The court had ordered the former husband to pay spousal support of $200 per month for two years, $150 per month for two years, $100 per month for two years, $50 per month for two years, and $1 per month for four years. Thereafter, support would terminate.

Judge Gardner correctly saw this as a "dreary picture" in which an "unemployed and currently unemployable woman, 44 years of age" faced the possibility of going blind and who was also "confronted with a court order which reduces her spousal support to a mere pittance for the next 12 years" when, of course, if she lives, she would be 56 and face a "substantial likelihood that she will become an object of charity."

In explaining his decision to overturn the lower court's spousal support ruling, Judge Gardner stated:

A woman is not a breeding cow to be nurtured during her years of fecundity and then conveniently and economically converted to cheap steaks when past her prime. If a woman is able to support herself, she certainly should do so. If, however, she has spent her productive years as a housewife and mother and has missed the opportunity to compete in the job market and improve her job skills, quite often, when divorced, she becomes a displaced homemaker.

It took California's legislature until late in 1979 to enact legislation which mandates that all jurists in divorce proceedings must consider the employability of the nonworking spouse in assigning support decrees. Much remains to rectify another injustice. Justice Gardner included in his comment on this case:

> Domestic relations litigation, one of the most important and sensitive tasks a judge faces, too often is given the low-man-on-the-totem-pole treatment, quite often fobbed off on a commissioner. One of the paradoxes of our present legal system is that it is accepted practice to tie up a court for days while a gaggle of professional medical witnesses expound to a jury on just how devastating or just how trivial a personal injury may be, all to the personal enrichment of the trial lawyers involved, yet at the same time we begrudge the judicial resources necessary for careful and reasoned judgments in this most delicate field—the breakup of a marriage with its resulting trauma and troublesome fiscal aftermath. . . . The handling of this case, which involved the breakup of a 25-year marriage, the custody of two teenage girls, the disposition of all of the property accumulated during that marriage, and the plotting of the fiscal future of the entire family is illustrative. Judged by the brevity of the record, not more than 15 minutes of the court's time on a busy Friday afternoon short-cause calendar were involved.

Demographic changes have also contributed to changing the expectations of former homemakers. The greater life expectancy of women over men has continued to grow, and the gap is widening. By 1979 the

Census Bureau, while cautioning that its long-range assumptions were contingent on "no large-scale war, widespread epidemic, or other major catastrophe," was predicting a life expectancy of up to eighty-one years for women as opposed to 71.8 for men. According to the same report, there were, in 1978, 644 widows for every 100 widowers, and their average age was fifty-six. Widowers, like divorced men, tend to remarry more often than widows and choose younger women when they do. Although some older women marry younger men, the practice is far from common; and the gap in ages between the bride and groom is far less than that between older men and younger women.

Displaced homemakers in their job search are not infrequently asked (by male personnel staff), "Why not remarry?" It still takes two to tango! The option is illusory even if the woman is willing. Divorced women appear to have more opportunities, and the younger they are, the better their chances. Of those in their twenties, 76 percent remarry. At thirty, the figure drops to 56 percent; at forty, it's down to 32 percent; and only 12 percent of divorced women fifty and over will remarry.

What, then, happens to women without an income, too old for men to care and too young for Medicare? Like Anne, a widow from a small town in Pennsylvania whose husband dropped dead of a heart attack when he was fifty-four and she was forty-six, these women find themselves up against some frightening realities.

> In the seven years since his unexpected death, I've had trouble finding a decent job. I get only a small veteran's widow's pension. I have no skills and have had to scrounge around for odd jobs—cleaning offices three nights a week and taking care of the elderly two nights

a week. These are all minimum wage jobs with no health insurance. I've had a hard time making ends meet, and I'm scared of the future. I don't want charity or welfare.

Because she and millions of others like her believe she has "no skills," she and they will continue to "scrounge up odd jobs," doing what they can to survive. Unless all of them are given an opportunity to prove to themselves as well as to others what they do have, skills which can be turned into salaried jobs, welfare will be in their future—like it or not.

Poverty for women in old age is a progressive matter—the older, the poorer. A 1979 Health, Education and Welfare Department report shows that unmarried (widowed, divorced, or never married) older women account for 72 percent of all poor elderly people. A 1978 Department of Labor study on single heads of households reported that of the approximately ninety-two million single heads of households, forty-three million were older Americans; and of these, 41.5 percent, mostly women forty-five and older, were welfare recipients.

In San Antonio, Texas, in July 1979, a ninety-one-year-old widow who described herself as "desperate" was arrested for stealing $15 in food. Her monthly income amounted to $125 in Social Security benefits and $113 in veterans benefits, her late husband having served in World War I. She had to spend $75 for rent, which didn't include utilities. She told the police she stole the food because she was starving. Not surprisingly, she added that she "wished God would close my eyes. I'm tired of living." Stories like this are picked up by the press and trigger the compassion of the general public. Among today's women in the adolescence of aging, such stories scare displaced homemakers witless.

In ending her letter, Anne asked why there weren't "some training programs for older women to help us get jobs that will let us live in dignity in our later years?" It's a good question. Part of the answer lies in America's enchantment with youth. We are constantly urged to "stay young," to "look young" as though it were possible physically to live forever in Yeats's "Land of Heart's Desire," "where no one grows old or godly or grave." In our brutally youth-oriented society we are reduced to employing defensive cop-outs as we tell one another, "Age is a state of mind" or "You're only as old as you feel." Until very recently, we saw ourselves portrayed negatively in the media, peddling the products the advertising world thought we needed most— Exlax, Geritol, and Preparation H. (Lately, judging by the models being used in some TV commercials, it now seems younger women, but not men, share our problems of irregularity, tired blood, and hemorrhoids.)

The main reason Anne's search for a job-training program will be futile lies in the ageism that prevails in the marketplace, which in turn infects the headset of those who serve it. Despite the fact that middle-aged women today have almost as many years still to live as they have lived, those who run job-training programs, especially in the public sector, serve the young on the assumption that younger workers have many more years ahead in which to contribute to the labor force. The planner of one state jobs program, testifying before the U.S. Civil Rights Commission during an eighteen-month study on age discrimination in federally assisted programs, said, "The highest priority is placed on serving young primary working age individuals" because "the marginal return on the investment is greater." Younger workers are more readily placed, and the commission found that persons difficult to place were screened out of programs. "Agencies administering the programs limit participation of some age groups so their program will be considered successful when measured against the Department of Labor's performance standards," which raises the question of how much the governmental push for "cost-effective" programs (successfully serving a large number of participants, thereby reducing the cost per person) by funding agencies contributes to a lack of interest in those "difficult to place."

It is hard enough for an older man who loses a job to find another, but the older unemployed male at least has a work record. Since homemaking isn't considered work, displaced homemakers are often turned down in the private sector because of lack of a record of recent paid employment.

Many displaced homemakers who would profit from public job-training programs not only get shot down because they are older women but also because their eligibility for these programs is predicated on the family income of the previous six months.

> I have been trying to get a job since my husband became disabled. He does not get unemployment insurance, and Social Security has turned him down on disability payments. I have found the only marketable skills I seem to have so far are selling door-to-door and cleaning other people's homes. I have been tested and found capable of being trained for better jobs; but my problem is I need an income now, and I don't qualify

for CETA because our income last year—money paid to my husband from disability insurance—was $7,000. My husband is 60 and I am 51. We have been married close to 35 years. It seems to me our future looks pretty bleak.

Their prospects *are* bleak; and she, no less than her husband, feels trapped. Belatedly, he probably shares the opinion she expressed in a P.S. to her letter. "I wish now that I had chosen a profession along with homemaking so that I wouldn't be in the bind I'm in today; but he didn't want me to work, and to be honest, I felt my job was in the home."

Tying the displaced homemaker's eligibility to the family income also excludes many divorced older women who may or may not have shared in their ex-spouses' income of the previous six months. It should be pointed out that practice has thoroughly debunked the theory that every divorced wife "takes her 'ex' to the cleaners"—spousal support (alimony), if granted at all, is usually limited to one or two years. Studies indicate that only 14 percent are awarded such support; and of that figure, only 46 percent get their payments with any degree of regularity. Widows, presumed to be "well taken care of," in practice benefit on the average from approximately $5,000 in insurance; and some, but not all, inherit small savings accounts. Such monies would affect their eligibility negatively. They are, consequently, put into the Catch-22 position of having to spend down to meet the poverty guidelines without any assurance that an income-providing job will materialize at the end of the training course.

Ironically, one job in the private sector increasingly offered to "mature women only" has evolved from the advances made by younger women moving into the labor force and the erosion of the extended family. Live-in housekeepers, once a status symbol of the financially successful, are replacing the occasionally engaged baby-sitter to meet the demands of working women, often single heads of households who no longer have access to the free services of mothers, grandmothers, or aunts. Babysitting has moved from part-time work to full-time jobs, living in or out of the house.

On the face of it, these seem reasonable jobs for older former homemakers, providing them an opportunity to be part of "family" life again, using nurturing skills gained during their own years of motherhood; and some older women will be attracted to such jobs.

The problem is that those who accept such positions, out of desire or desperation, too often find themselves in low-paying jobs without any fringe benefits other than the one some advertisers seem to feel outweighs all other considerations—"a room of her own and TV."

A spot check of offerings listed in a San Francisco Bay Area paper in 1979 turned up examples that can probably be found anywhere in the country. One ad called for the services of a "babysitter, live-in, mature lady, rent-free, salary neg." for which room and board plus a weekly salary of $50 to $75 was offered to "an older women who wants a home and will be a nanny to two girls, 4 and 7." "Light housekeeping, light cooking for the girls and preparation of dinner" was expected for a six-day work week. The seven-year-old was to be walked to and from school, as was the four-year-old who attended preschool twice a week. The advertiser was a working mother whose hours "were hectic" and who sometimes "managed to get home by six, but not often." It apparently didn't cross her mind that while many women might love children enough to want the job, few at any age, let alone older women, would possess the physical stamina required to take care of two lively youngsters from dawn through dinner six days a week.

Even less sensitive to the needs of older women was the advertiser who wanted only a "mature" woman's services from 8:00 A.M. to 6:30 P.M. three days a week, explaining, "My mother comes twice a week, and I'm here on weekends." The salary offered was $2 an hour for a thirty-and-a-half-hour work week. Besides caring for a sixteen-week-old infant, the "babysitter" would be required to dust, pick up, and prepare dinner. She was expected to provide her own transportation without reimbursement, although she "could eat whatever was available for lunch." Daily shopping for dinner was expected "because the baby should get out in fine weather." At best, it was a job paying $61 a week without benefits or reimbursement for expenses that might serve an older woman desperate to supplement a fixed income.

Such jobs do fill a need, though it might be asked whose need. They also perpetuate the image of women as servants to the family. The charge would undoubtedly be denied, but these are typical of exploitive jobs offering minimum pay without any fringe benefits such as health insurance, pensions, or an opportunity to build a Social Security record to women who have never worked outside their own home.

There are, of course, other jobs available to older women—jobs they have traditionally filled, often because it was the only thing they thought they could do: waitress, hospital aide, retail sales clerks (mostly part-time). In a later chapter we will discuss other options opening up in the service field that hold more hope for older women workers.

Two "new" jobs we hope will never catch on were reported by John Balzar, Sacramento correspondent for the *San Francisco Chronicle.*

> The California Manufacturers Association, voice of progress for the state's industrial concerns, has an idea how to continue producing those lucrative but dangerous chemicals and pesticides in factories here, even though they render workers sterile. . . . In testimony to the government recently, association lobbyist Al Libra explained the effect of recent findings about reproductive damage to chemical workers. . . . "Where someone is beyond the age of childbearing, then the question of exposure (to chemicals) on that ground is no longer a particular problem."

Shocking as this suggestion seems, consider the following item in Balzar's story:

> Arthur Cherkin, director of geriatric research at a Los Angeles Veterans Administration hospital, wrote a letter recently in the same vein. . . . He said it might be a good idea to create Gray Panther SWAT teams to clean up after nuclear power plant accidents. "Older people have less time to live, so they're less likely to live long enough to suffer the ill effects of radiation," Cherkin reasoned. "I think we could make these teams into national heroes."

Balzar later commented on the reaction to his article (most of it highly critical of both statements) but added that he also had some calls from people who thought they were good ideas. But then if the above is an example of the thinking of a professional in the geriatric field, who can fault the ordinary lay person for exhibiting genocidal ageism?

A number of factors combine to make it difficult for the older former homemaker to break into good paying jobs, not the least of which is her attitude about herself as a potential candidate.

Sandra Smith Moore, then director of the Research Center for Women at Alverno College in Milwaukee, Wisconsin, spoke of the differences in counseling younger and older re-entry students in testimony at a state legislative hearing:

> It's one thing to talk with an eager, energetic, under-40 woman whose consciousness has been raised and whose aspirational level is at its peak . . . who is seeking meaningful employment because she wants to fulfill her potential. It's quite another thing to talk with a woman who has committed 20 or 25 years or more of her life to raising a family and being a helpmate and partner to her husband . . . who suddenly finds herself without financial support, whose emotional level has also collapsed and whose needs level is considerably lower on Maslow's hierarchy. She needs training and counseling programs to help her appreciate herself again.

Even if they know where to look—and most are unaware of available resources other than the classified section of the daily newspaper—neither the woman who has been a full-time dependent homemaker nor the older AFDC (Aid to Families with Dependent Children) mother whose support is about to be terminated is in any way job-ready. As one woman said, "The last time I worked was twenty-five years ago. How does one write a résumé when I haven't held a paying job in years and years? . . ." Another: "I'm a divorced woman of fifty-five. I have no talent whatsoever. A high school graduate but very poor in math. What do I do? Where do I start?"

The low self-image is reinforced by the negative view industry has of homemaking as a "career." A survey of both large and small firms in a Florida county in 1979, which found that overwhelmingly "a large majority of firms do not accept homemaking skills as having a market place value," led to the researcher's observation that it was "small wonder" an older displaced homemaker lacks self-confidence and is reticent even to seek employment, "considering the skills and experience of her lifetime are at best disregarded by prospective employers."

Women, especially those seeking to re-enter the job market, generally face the "over the hill" syndrome earlier than men. Because it is difficult to face aging, most of us don't recognize age discrimination when it hits us. It's often only after repeated rebuffs that the message seeps in and forces us to deal with it. When letters to want-ad box numbers remain unanswered, when countless applications are accepted with a terse "We'll let you know" and then they don't, or being told you're "overqualified, underqualified, overeducated, undereducated," it reinforces the lack of self-confidence and drains away any you might have had.

One stares in utter frustration at pages and pages of help-wanted ads that call for experience which can only be gained by an investment of time to learn—a high-risk venture for the over-forty bunch. The conviction that we are unemployable takes root, giving rise to the temptation to stop looking. A fifty-four-year-old West Virginia woman confessed the reason she began staying in her apartment all day was not as she had said, "because with all the applications I had out, I was afraid I'd miss a phone call," but "because I just couldn't take any more turndowns."

Testifying before the U.S. Civil Rights Commission hearing in 1977, Secretary of Labor Ray Marshall confirmed that persons forty-five or over make up a large number of discouraged workers—the majority of them women workers who said they wanted jobs "but were not looking for them because they believed no work was available; that they could not find work; that they lacked education or skills; that they were too old."

In my own case, whatever doubts raised by my unsuccessful attempts to resume the career in advertising which I'd abandoned when married, the idea of being "too old" wasn't one of them. The manager of a small San Francisco employment agency broke the news, putting it to me tactfully and, all things considered, gently. She had studied my résumé and portfolio. Folding her hands over both, she said it was a good record but added as her smile faded, "Given today's competition, I'm afraid it's not recent enough." She must have sensed I disagreed; years out of advertising, particularly if spent as a homemaker-consumer, should have added to my employability. Dropping her eyes to the material on the desk, she continued. "Perhaps I shouldn't say this, but I'm forty-eight [long pause]; and unfortunately, in this city, maybe in the whole Bay Area, that's pretty much over the hill for most jobs. Not that anyone would come out and say so because it's against

the law, but I know that if I had to start looking for a
job today . . ." Her voice trailed off, but her meaning
was quite clear.

I was stunned. So I was fifty-five. So what? I exploded. "What's age, for God's sake, got to do with
creativity? With being able to create an ad or direct
merchandising efforts?" Her reply was a sad smile and
a sympathetic shrug of her shoulders. I left the office
still enraged but also somewhat shattered by the new
knowledge that if she was correct, there was little or
nothing I could do. I was what I was—fifty-five.

Over the years I've recalled that interview as I met
not some but many women who felt their situations
were so helpless that suicide seemed the only way out.
It is not by chance in our society that the suicide rate
for women peaks at age forty-five. I know of at least
one forty-seven-year-old Los Angeles woman who did
take her life because, as she said in the note she left behind, "I'm hemmed in by debts and a sense of failure.
There's no other way out." She left no family.

Was her act the end result of an overload of self-
pity—the act of a person unwilling to be self-respon-
sible, capable only of seeing herself as a victim? We'll
never know. A real, imagined, or imposed sense of pow-
erlessness to cope with mounting problems does breed
desperation and reinforces a feeling of inadequacy to
effect change. One does not have to condone suicide to
recognize that for that woman who was alone, "hemmed in," and felt she was a failure with "no other way
out," it was a desperate act of a desperate woman.

In the early days of the women's movement, feminists put down the role of the full-time homemaker, cit-
ing dependency as demeaning. Few saw the correlation

between dependency and aging as a woman's issue that would have special implications for formerly dependent women. Some were totally impatient with displaced homemakers. Even today the harshest critics are women who have long been responsible for their own support.

> My only complaint about displaced homemakers is that they are always shown as victims.... Many women were absolutely too lazy to hold jobs. I don't know where all those martyrs were, and I resent the implication that all women fit the category described.

As is true of most sweeping generalities, there is an element of truth in the remarks of this twice divorced, older, professionally successful woman. Not all women do fit the category. Some, born self-starters as she is, and equipped with a high degree of self-worth, can and will move to new careers with ease. Since she admits she was never comfortable with the role of a home-maker and doesn't consider it labor, it is natural for her to assume that nonsalaried homemakers were "too lazy to hold jobs." The reality of the homemaker's role has escaped her. As a popular poster of the '70s proclaimed, "Every mother is a working woman," to which might be added, "and always was."

That is the point society has missed. Homemaking *is* work; but as long as the "pedestal principle" pertains to marriage, the in-kind contribution the homemaking spouse makes to the family unit will never be properly assessed. Pedestals leave very little room for individual action, let alone joint ventures. Marriage must be recognized as an economic partnership, and a monetary value on the homemaker's labor must be established. It has been facetiously stated that if the traditional roles of marriage partners had originally been reversed and men were the "nurturers," both goals would have been reached long ago.

Organizations working for women's rights are rarely attuned to age discrimination. Those in the field of aging are seldom conscious of the effects of sex discrimination or of the particular problems of women as they grow older. Consciousness must continue to be raised in both camps so that significant progress can be made by older women which will lead to institutional changes to give them the leverage they lack today.

The feminist call for equal rights rings hollow unless it is accompanied by a concerted attack on ageism, the last common bias that shames us as a nation of free people and denies older women the freedom to *be* older women with options and choices for self-sufficiency.

What Tish Sommers and a handful of older women began in Oakland, California, in 1974, has made it possible for many older women to realize theirs were not singularly unique situations they were powerless to deal with; they were not inescapably victims of individual circumstances.

As will be seen in a later chapter, the vast majority of displaced homemakers do not remain "victimized" if given an assist and the opportunity to take responsibility for the rest of their lives. For them today, and others tomorrow, there is a new awareness of the truth and hope spelled out in Doris Lessing's words: "Any human being anywhere will blossom into a hundred unexpected talents and capacities simply by being given the opportunity to use them."

CHAPTER TWO

Genesis
of a Movement

While former homemakers wondered uneasily if there was a scrap heap in their future because there was no husband in their present, Tish Sommers said even if there was, the answer should be "Hell no! I won't go!" "Organize, don't agonize," she told the women she was the first to champion.

Sommers had learned at first hand the barriers faced by older former homemakers who fell through the cracks of all social programs. They were too young for Social Security and considered too old in the job market. Her interest in the special problems of older women predated her activities as a feminist advocate on their behalf. It was triggered by her experience when, at age fifty-seven, she was divorced after twenty-three years as a homemaker, wife, mother, and volunteer community activist.

She immediately became aware of the problems former dependent homemakers encounter when they lose their "job." Her health insurance, for example, like that of most wives, had been tied into her husband's job health plan. Following her divorce, she applied for but was ruled ineligible for policy conversion because of a history of breast cancer many years earlier. She was too young for Medicare. Since she was healthy at the time and had some personal resources, she decided to gamble and wait until she would be eligible for Medicare. (She lost. Just six months before her sixty-fifth birthday and automatic coverage under Medicare, she had a recurrence of cancer, twenty years after her first bout.)

"Believe me," she says today, "I know what 'catastrophic costs' means. I also know that a health-care system tied to employment excludes a large number of persons, mostly older women, who are neither part of the work force nor eligible for welfare or Medicare. One can be virtually out of the system even with the ability to pay."

With no Social Security record of her own, she was years away from receiving benefits on her ex-spouse's record, particularly since she was ten years older than her former husband. Despite an inheritance from her mother which left her financially secure, her first attempt to get credit in her own name for a gasoline charge card proved difficult and came about only after a series of letters, in the last of which she threatened the company with legal action.

In brief, nearly all of the issues the newly organized women's movement was identifying as sexist Sommers found compounded for older women in a youth-oriented society, simply because they were older women.

In his insightful book *Leadership*, James MacGregor Burns explains that "the essence of leadership . . . is the recognition of real need, the uncovering and exploiting of contradictions among values and between values and practice, the realigning of values, the reorganization of institutions where necessary." "Essentially," he adds, "the leader's task is consciousness raising on a wide plane."

Curiously, public attention to the aging problems of women did not come, as might be expected, from academic institutions, from those concerned with women's studies or gerontology; and the plight of older former homemakers was certainly not a concern of the early founders and followers of the women's movement. But Sommers quickly sensed the potential within the women's movement. In 1973 she founded the first national Task Force on Older Women within NOW and served as its coordinator. Having identified the "real need" of a constituency of her own generation, she became a full-time volunteer advocate for all middle-aged and older women.

"I never guessed, when I became coordinator of the Task Force on Older Women, how timely the cause. I couldn't know how great the need, and I certainly didn't expect the enormous response." So wrote Tish Sommers in a quarterly newsletter sent to the growing numbers of Task Force supporters.

But she also worked to bridge the gap between so-called traditional women and feminists. Her first public appearance in Oakland found her addressing a large audience of Presbyterian women curious about the emerging "women's movement." She reached out and built ties with other church women. Unitarian women were among the earliest financial supporters of her efforts. She wrote a book, *The Not So Helpless Female,* and plowed the profits back into organizing work. Experimenting with her changed lifestyle, she found living alone too lonely and joined with three other feminists to buy an old house in Oakland, one room of which she turned into an office. Communal living, with shared responsibilities and alternate turns of duty, gave her a new freedom to pour more energy into community outreach.

Sommers gave herself a title for her new "career"—"free-lance agitator"—and adopted as a logo for her cards a witch astride a flying broom, a tongue-in-cheek attack against stereotyping older women as hags and old witches. The caption below the logo left no doubt as to her view of aging: "Me, retire? I've just begun to fly!"

With wit and style, she attacked the issues of her concern; and a light touch of humorous irreverence became the hallmark of her advocacy. On one occasion, in 1975 shortly after the first federal Displaced Homemakers bill was filed, she was invited to address a distinguished forum of national government figures to present "in five minutes" all of the recommended changes in social policy which would help older women. She met the ridiculous request by offering ten commandments for them to ponder:

1. Thou shalt honor thy mothers and thy fathers—all of them. As long as social policy toward the elderly is based upon the cheapest way to keep an old person alive, there can be no honor. The U.S. is the only country in the world to care for frail elderly persons as a business.

2. Thou shalt not devise fine programs for thyselves alone. If full medical coverage is good for legislators, it

is good for the rest of us. If comfortable retirement income is just for public servants, we your employers would like it, too.

3. Thou shalt not design painful social policy for everyone but thyselves. If Social Security taxes are compulsory for the rest of the work force, considered in part as income transference, this principle should apply to those in government as well. When affirmative action is a requirement for others, it should also apply to the employment policies of lawmakers. If belt-tightening is in order, those in public office should lead the way.

4. Thou shalt not program for failure. You pass fine titled laws costing billions, then tie them up with layers of bureaucracy so that little money is used to address the problems the laws were designed to alleviate. Then you point to the failures and call for reductions. There is a third alternative to cutting the necessary social services and breaking the bank. It is called: eliminate the middle man.

5. Thou shalt not balance the budget on our backs. Granted, the budget needs considerable trimming. We would be glad to organize an advisory commission of experienced budget-balancers from the homefront to assist in making a few economies. But we would not begin by reducing Social Security benefits, food stamps, or medical benefits. To achieve some values, others must be forfeited; but the forfeit part has been too heavily weighted on those on the bottom, where most older women are to be found.

6. Thou shalt not ignore us. As yet, we homemakers seldom appear in statistics. How many homemakers have been displaced from their jobs because of widowhood or divorce, for example? If something isn't

counted, it doesn't exist. But displaced homemakers *do* exist, and we are currently working for passage of legislation. We've learned "where there's a bill there's a way!"

7. Thou shalt reward us on earth as well as in heaven. If staying home and taking care of children is so important to the fabric of American society that we are denied child-care centers for that reason, why are we not entitled to retirement benefits like other workers?

8. Thou shalt not judge our value by two standards. When we are your wives and helping you up the ladder, our services are priceless, impossible to define in monetary terms. But when we no longer serve you, our past labor is deemed worthless. The homemaker receives no Social Security credits for her work, and the pitfalls of dependency are legion. If she is disabled on the job, she receives no disability benefits; if she is divorced, her past labors are seldom counted; and if her husband worked for the government, the retirement benefits she helped produce are lost to her forever.

9. Thou shalt not put us in double jeopardy. It is patently unfair to exclude us from jobs and then lament the growing number of persons who are not producers. We *can* create new jobs using our nurturing skills to provide urgently needed services while at the same time earning Social Security credits for our own futures.

10. Thou shalt not try to understand all women through thy wife. The man who relies solely on his domestic relationship for input on women's issues is likely to fall into the same trap as the white person who explains blacks by saying, "My maid says . . ."

She concluded, saying that "in reviewing alternatives of social policy, the problem is not to fit human needs into the status quo but to change the status quo to fit human needs."

It was a basic premise she had consciously embraced as a volunteer community leader for most of her adult life. She credits a three-year residence in Germany in the early thirties for the awakening of her social conscience. "It was an historic time," she says. As a young student of modern dance studying under Mary Wigman in Dresden, she boarded with a Jewish family and, "watching Hitler's rise to power, saw at first hand the step-by-step destruction of human beings in the name of racial superiority."

In all of her work to change the status quo, she was a staunch advocate of self-help. "No one *sets* you free, so stop agonizing and start organizing!" That was what she told the handful of older women in Oakland that she brought together early in 1974 in the Jobs for Older Women Action Project. Reminding them that "each group that has emerged on the civil-rights scene has come out of invisibility by making a public fuss," she encouraged them "to rattle a few cages." An opportunity arose that year when some two hundred West Coast businessmen were scheduled to attend a two-day conference at the elegant Fairmont Hotel in San Francisco to learn what they would be expected to do to comply with new government regulations on affirmative action.

One of the speakers was to be Carin Clauss, then serving in the Department of Labor's Fair Labor Standards Division, charged specifically with handling age-discrimination and equal-pay cases. Better enforcement of the Age Discrimination in Employment Act was one of Jobs for Older Women's goals since age discrimination was keeping older women out of the labor market. Sommers wrote and requested five minutes on the agenda to make a case for older women "who also need access to equal employment opportunities." She was advised the agenda was closed. Even a session on bias was apparently biased against older women.

Excluded from participation, Sommers suggested the members of JOW make their case by staging a public demonstration. Given the traditional orientation of the women involved, it is not surprising the suggestion frightened them. One former member recalls, "It really scared us. Taking to the streets as the young people had done didn't seem proper to us." In the end though, they agreed to develop a position paper and hold a press conference at the hotel during the conference. Two things may have swayed them: Sommers' reassurance that demonstrations need not be confrontations and the fact that it would be the "first older women's action in the country."

The story of the Fairmont Caper, as it came to be known, is a classic example of how effective well-planned collective action can be in rallying support for a cause. It's also a story not without humorous aspects.

For those who may not know it, the Fairmont is a prestigious hostelry where, as their brochure unblushingly proclaims, "style, elegance, and tradition reach a pinnacle." Out-of-town visitors leave their hearts along with Tony Bennett's in its beautiful Venetian Room. Its plush lobby and the tasteful display of rare jade, imported gifts, and expensive jewelry in its shops suggest that the 700 rooms and suites above, with their super percale sheets, Irish linen hand towels, and evening maid service, are not for those who have to ask the rates. It was probably the least likely target in San Francisco for a demonstration.

JOW added members of the Gray Panthers, NOW, and the National Women's Political Caucus to their numbers and on the scheduled day, when public transport was shut down by a strike, turned to Synanon, another community service organization, which cheerfully loaned them a bus. On the ride across the Bay the women lustily rehearsed their theme song, "The Old Gray Mare," with new lyrics: "The Old Gray Mare/She's better than she used to be/With many more years to go."

Today, it's clear from Sommers' retelling that she relished the occasion.

> The problem began with the bus. It had been loaned to us by Synanon, then widely known in the Bay Area for their work with drug addicts. When that Synanon bus pulled up to the Fairmont to discharge 35 older women, all neatly dressed but singing their theme song with gusto, I guess it was too much for the doorman. He alerted the manager, who called the security chief; and he, in turn, phoned the police before he even came out to see what we were all about.

The radioed police call alerted TV crews who were nearby interviewing President Ford; and they rushed over to see, as one of them told Sommers later, "what the hell the little old ladies from Synanon were up to."

> The security chief refused to allow us to hold the press conference in the lobby as we had planned, and we were moved to the parking apron near the entrance.

From our point of view, it couldn't have been better! The arrival of the police and the press drew a sidewalk crowd, many of whom applauded our statement which Milo Smith, JOW's first director, read and reread for press. Some even joined in the singing.

The harried security chief finally agreed to ask Carin Clauss to leave the meeting and meet with the women. She did and accepted their prepared paper, agreed to let one of the group address the afternoon session of the conference, and, in response to questions from the by then well-informed press, admitted enforcement wasn't all it should be and promised to do more in the future. Sommers concluded:

> To our great delight, the story was carried by all the local radio stations, the major TV stations, and the San Francisco and Oakland papers. That raised a lot more awareness than we'd been able to generate in our own community. The success, of course, had the greatest impact on the women themselves. It showed them that political actions can be put to good use, that focusing on one issue can be productive, and that media will respond if you can give your action a creative twist. Just the idea of older women staging a protest demonstration was enough; the bus was a fillip we hadn't planned, but it worked for us.

One of the stories caught the eye of a young attorney, Barbara Dudley, who was interested in public service legal aid. She volunteered her services to Tish, who immediately snapped up the offer. Dudley's sharp analytical mind and legal expertise brought a new dimension to Sommers' work. Despite the differences in their ages, twenty-seven and sixty, the relationship between them was as equals. Possibly because Dudley, no less than Sommers, was committed to changing "the status quo to fit human needs."

When by the end of 1974 they made the decision to go the legislative route to address the unmet job needs of older women, it was Dudley who drafted the measure. The opening clause was vintage Dudley—a succinct statement of the cause of the problem, a challenge to the system to correct it: "Homemakers are an unrecognized and unpaid part of the national work force who make an invaluable contribution to the welfare and economic stability of the Nation, but who receive no health, retirement, or unemployment benefits as a result of their labor."

They knew what they wanted the legislation to provide: multiservice centers where older women could get the necessary training, peer counseling, and job placement which existing programs failed to give them. But foremost, they wanted these centers to explore the needs of the community with an eye to creating new jobs that would utilize the skills of former homemakers.

Sommers felt something was missing. "We needed a handle, something that would immediately identify these women as being different from other job seekers." One of her former housemates recalls Sommers pacing back and forth one night searching for that "handle." "Finally," relates Tanis Walter, "she asked me what I thought about 'displaced homemakers.'" "As in refugees?" Walter asked. A quick check of the dictionary provided the rationale for Sommers' choice. "Means forcibly exiled," she reported to Walter, "and that's precisely what these women are." The others agreed; and on April 15, 1975, when the California bill was filed, the term entered the public domain for the first time.

Each of us have days, dates, and events that are special to us, some that hindsight later reveals as being turning points in our lives. May 7 and 8 of 1975 loom large as benchmarks in my life. They almost weren't.

A few days earlier, quite by chance, a friend of my daughter's suggested that I get in touch with Tish Sommers. She knew I was having trouble finding a job and knew, too, that Tish "was doing something for older women." I had no trouble dealing with the classification, having been firmly put in my place as an older woman the day before. Ready to grab at any straw, I phoned that evening. It was not the most encouraging conversation I've ever had.

Sommers confirmed the existence of widespread discrimination against older women, pointing out that employers tended to look for qualities in female employees which had no bearing on the job per se; hiring younger women most often reflected a sexist interpretation of the job. I mentioned the demand for recent paid work experience, and she concurred that it eliminated older women from many job opportunities.

She seemed to sense my deepening depression and asked suddenly if I'd be interested in attending a meeting of a self-help group, Jobs for Older Women. She said it was even possible someone there might have some job leads for me. I said I'd go, and she gave me the address.

But the next day I wavered; I seriously doubted that anyone in a group of old ladies meeting in a church basement could turn up a job in advertising or merchandising. I wasn't yet ready to lower my expectations of getting one in my chosen field. That's what I said to myself; but perhaps, like the woman from West Virginia, I just didn't want to face another disappointment. I recall flipping a coin. Luckily for me, it came up heads and I went.

Seated around a long, wide old-fashioned dining-room table in what had probably been a social room when the building served as a Presbyterian Church, I found eight or nine older women. The thought flashed through my mind that these were, indeed, *older* women. It may have been the setting, but I had the uneasy thought that I'd wandered into one of my mother's Altar and Rosary Society meetings where the ladies had tea or coffee and homemade cookies while they discussed the forthcoming parish dinner. The impression locked in place when one woman with a welcoming smile invited me to help myself to coffee, adding, "Be sure to try the cookies; they're homemade."

I was convinced nothing would come of this meeting for me, but I couldn't think of an excuse to leave. Tish hadn't arrived but, along with Barbara Dudley, was expected "momentarily." The woman who offered that bit of news turned out to be Martha Gresham, a transplanted Southerner, a retired federal employee who had worked in D.C. and never married. She identified herself as a "feminist" who, when she moved to California, teamed up with Tish because of their mutual concerns for older women; and she volunteered information on the other members. Two had helped their husbands in small offices and now were widowed. One was a retired nurse, another a trained counselor. There was a retired teacher, and at least two had worked full time during the early years of their marriages. Two had

even been Rosie the Riveters during World War II
when women had to fill the jobs of men drafted for
service.

Upon her arrival, Tish walked over and introduced
herself. She was wearing tailored slacks and a colorful
blouse, a combination that emphasized her slimness
and made her seem taller than she actually was.
Martha had told me she was sixty, but I couldn't believe it—there was an unmistakable vitality about her,
generally presumed to be the mark of the young. Her
eyes were brown, and thick glasses made them seem
enormously large. Her voice was low-pitched but not
deep; and together with precise diction, graceful ges-
tures, and a smile that literally lighted her face, it all
added up to an attractive, openly friendly woman. Yet
there was a sense of reserve that suggested her personal
space had perimeters no one would violate.

In contrast, Barbara Dudley was informal, relaxed,
given to dotting her conversation with the verbal short-
hand of college campuses of the day—"far out," "right
on." She seemed the epitome of the liberated female
student. Her greeting, "Hi, kiddoes," was as casual as
her attire, a plaid cotton sports shirt tucked into a blue
denim wraparound skirt. Her hair was blond, short and
curly, capping her head without any pretense of style.
Her legs were bare and she wore sandals. There were
laughter lines at the corners of her gray eyes, which
were flecked with green. Her smile was more of a grin
that frequently dissolved into hearty laughter. Neither
woman wore make-up. Each carried a yellow pad on
which, when they later made notes, Sommers' were
large and haphazardly scrawled across the page and
Dudley's were neat entries quickly outlined. That

fooled me. I would have guessed it would be the other way around.

Except for the exercise in people-watching which always fascinates me, I found the meeting dull and uninteresting. Later that night as I was writing to thank Tish for the invitation, she phoned. She went directly to the point. "JOW didn't grab you, did it?" Apparently I wasn't the only people-watcher. I confessed it hadn't but hoped no one else suspected it. She changed the subject. "Are you interested in politics?" "All my life" was my quick reply, adding, "That isn't exactly unusual for someone born in Chicago." "Good!" she said. "I've invited some feminists to my house tomorrow evening to discuss some legislation I think you might find interesting. It's a bill we've just had filed in Sacramento—a bill to help displaced homemakers. It's part of our advocacy action for older women." "A bill to help whom?" I asked. "Women like you," she replied. She then briefly outlined the purpose of the legislation. I laughed self-consciously. "That does sound like my bill," I told her and agreed to go as we concluded our conversation.

My interest in politics was avocational. True to the thinking of my generation, I didn't think of it as an interest to be pursued by women for personal gain. For all that I casually studied the art and avidly followed the careers of specific politicians, my participation in any part of the process had been limited to an occasional tour of duty—a turn on the district election board because a friend of my mother's invited me, envelope stuffing and telephoning voters for a local candidate I admired, driving seniors to the polls on election day.

A lifelong Democrat, I hadn't missed a vote since becoming eligible, with a record of only one fall from grace: I liked Ike. As a child of the Depression, I shared my parents' reverence for Franklin Roosevelt and developed my own for his wife.

As a senior in an all-girls high school, our class went to Washington, D.C., during Easter vacation. It was a sacrifice for most of our parents to send us. President Roosevelt, then in his second term of office, was just beginning to turn the country around, but it would take another three years before he would implement nearly all of the economic and social reforms of his New Deal. Money was tight, but pride in the country was running high; and our parents viewed the opportunity to visit the nation's capitol (never an option for them in their youth) as a learning experience not to be denied their offspring. (Not all my classmates' parents shared our enthusiasm for either the trip or the President. The Republican father of one friend reluctantly acquiesced to his daughter's tearful pleading; but he made it clear to the two nuns, the teachers who were to chaperone us, that "under no circumstances is my daughter to come in contact with *that man* in the White House!")

Actually, none of us did; but urged on by Sister Terence, our history and civics teacher, we tramped up all the worn steps of the national monuments she thought it was important for us to visit. She took her chaperoning duties to mean more than seeing we all stayed in our rooms at night; and with professional zeal, she made the trip an extension of her classes. She briefed us before, during, and after each visit to every site. What Sister said, she believed passionately. As we grouped around her, wearing our ankle socks and brown-and-white saddle shoes purchased new for the trip and powdered dazzling white every night, it mattered not that our legs were turned blue by the cold, raw spring winds. Her passion for the people and places of importance in America's history warmed us, and awe overwhelmed our pain.

There wasn't anything new in her words. Anyone who took Sister Terence's classes had heard them repeatedly. Wise students incorporated them into term papers as religiously as we all offered those efforts to Jesus, Mary, and Joseph with a JMJ inscribed at the top of the first page. It was hearing all those familiar statements in Washington that made it different.

How many times had we heard Sister say of Lincoln, "More than any other man, Lincoln gave new meaning to democracy. Ours is a country of the people, governed by the people, for the people. He wanted us to truly be a nation of free people." Her classroom tirades against racial discrimination—long before it was a popular cause—took on new meaning as I looked up at Lincoln's face. "He's so sad," I thought. That face haunted me; and so the night before we were to leave D.C., I sneaked out of the hotel with two friends to go back for a final visit. Whether it was the effect of different lighting or one of those unexplainable flashes of insight, there was suddenly more to the expression than just sadness. It seemed a sadness imposed upon the features of a deeply compassionate man who really cared for other human beings. It dawned on me that "he's sad because Negroes really aren't free, and that's what racial discrimination is all about."

My feelings about government were influenced by Sister Terence but also by other factors. Growing up in

Chicago in the heyday of ward politics instilled a faith that the Democratic party was the hope of the poor. We knew with the same degree of certainty that the Republican party championed the affluent and favored business. Those were years of appealing simplicity; in politics as in life, there were the good guys ("us") and the bad ones ("them"). As for the federal government, Sister's words rang in our ears as we hung over the rail in the galleries of Congress:

> The men who sit in Congress make the laws of the land. People get the kind of government they deserve, so respect the men you elect to office as you respect yourselves. Women didn't always have the vote, so use yours seriously when you get it. As voters, demand of candidates conduct that merits respect. Good government meets the needs and protects the rights of all Americans, but citizens have the responsibility to see that it does.

As with all her pronouncements, it was followed by her admonition to "Remember that, girls!" I did, even though as I grew older I sensed that the business of Washington had less to do with civics and more to do with politics. I felt that, more often than not, the two were mutually exclusive. Still, the prospect of discussing legislation that would do something politically positive about age discrimination struck me as something Sister Terence would call a civic responsibility.

I was ready to accept that, but I had some reservations about the women I'd be working with the next evening. "Feminists," Tish had called them. All I knew about feminists was what I'd read in the papers or seen on TV. Granted, neither Tish nor Martha Gresham seemed to fit the image I'd formed; but then, there were exceptions to all rules. Feminists, or rather "women's libbers" as I'd heard of them, were pushy, rowdy women given to demonstrating in large numbers, carrying placards, and wearing buttons with messages at odds with all I'd been taught about women's role.

"Act like a lady" had been my mother's constant reminder.

"Speak softly and carry . . . the right gloves," said Sister.

Somehow I'd managed to survive skillfully all the admonitions without totally conforming and, happily, married a wonderful man who couldn't have cared less about my being anything except myself. But I *knew* how ladies should act. When I had to, I could play the part. Now here were all these women—what was their phrase?—"letting it all hang out." They had made it clear "unliberated" women were, at best, dumb; at worst, blind to reality. My whole experience as a full-time homemaker, wife, and mother had been traditionally oriented; but it had been freely chosen. I never had thought of myself as oppressed, nor did I refer to myself as "just a housewife." I was Mrs. Arthur Shields, an equal half of a whole; and there had never been any reason to muddy up the waters of my very happy marriage with concern for women's rights. Advocacy, feminism, activism were not only new words to me; what they identified was foreign to my past—or, at least, I'd never known them under those labels. Thinking of the meeting the following evening, I wasn't certain I wanted them in my future either. I phoned Tish back to express my concern that I might be out of place at that meeting. I told her why: "I'm not happy with the whole idea of feminism. I never felt oppressed as a woman, so what's to liberate?"

She laughed. "Would you believe," she asked, "that's exactly the way I felt some years ago? I mean, the feminist movement was just beginning; but I wasn't interested. I felt as you do, that I hadn't been oppressed." She went on to explain that she had long been involved in community organizing in behalf of poverty programs and against racial discrimination. "But," she added, "there's only so much an individual can do. It was when I realized that the women's movement offered an opportunity to act creatively and collectively to root out the causes of all oppression and I could be a contributing part of that movement that I joined NOW."

"Well," I responded, "NOW probably suits you, but I find it somewhat frightening. Besides, I'm not overly keen on *any* woman's organization. One dutiful stint as the president of Christine's school's Mothers Club turned me off forever." The comparison apparently amused her because her laugh was long and hearty.

I sensed the wave of her hand as she dismissed my fears of feminism. "Look, you don't have to join NOW to be a feminist, and you don't have to hate men to join NOW. You don't have to repudiate the years of a good marriage to admit that society offers poverty, loneliness, and neglect as the pay-off for a lot of older women who have performed the traditional homemaker role as women." I agreed and later hung up feeling somewhat better about the meeting.

The next evening, some of the stereotyped images flew out of the window of my mind. None of the forty was rowdy, although there was an excited pitch to their conversation, snatches of which I overheard as I walked through the rooms of Tish's house. There was a high level of energy being expended on matters I'd never thought of as women's concerns.

"Elderly shut-ins don't have the money to take cabs to doctors' appointments. . . . I just went straight to the drivers union, and they voted to give five percent out of their pockets to a senior program. Now I'm going to hit the cab companies for matching funds."

"Class-action suits *will* work; and I say, if we have to sue the Governor, let's sue him!"

"How is the Women's Commission doing on the sex equity drive?"

"Tish and Barbara aren't sure the bill has a chance to pass, but I agree with them; it sure is going to be a great consciousness raiser."

Class action suits? Consciousness raising? Sex equity drive? It was as though I'd dropped onto another planet. If their conversations were different, their appearance wasn't. Most were middle-aged or older women comfortably, if not fashionably, dressed. A sprinkling of younger women were wearing sweaters and skirts; one or two wore jeans. There wasn't but one button in sight, and that (Senior Power) was worn by a sweet-faced elderly lady who looked like everybody's grandmother should.

Everyone participated, and the meeting moved along smartly. By 9:45 we had thoroughly discussed the legislation and had agreed that since Jobs for Older Women had just received a grant of public monies which precluded their doing any official lobbying for the bill, a new organization had to be formed. We voted, after some discussion, to call that new body the Alliance for Displaced Homemakers.

It was a beginning—in more ways than one for me. When I stepped over the threshold of Tish's house that balmy May evening, I crossed another that led in a very short time to a brand-new career—one I never would have sought. Perhaps more importantly, it marked the start of personal growth that led eventually to a new awareness of my personhood as a woman.

I was indeed to become a "late-blooming feminist," but the process of change was slow and gradual. Instead of the "click" most feminists speak of—the sudden acknowledgment of what being a woman is all about, individually and collectively—my awakening was more like a series of buzzes, tiny signals that screamed "tilt!" when the reality of life didn't match the game plan I'd been taught.

If dependency in marriage was so wonderful, why were there displaced homemakers? Buzz! If men and women worked at the same job, why did women earn less? Buzz! If the "old boys network" was used by men to their advantage, why couldn't an "old girls network" benefit women? Buzz! Buzz!

It took time, but the seed of that late-blooming feminism was planted the night the Alliance was formed. I came to agree with Tish that "a feminist has a particular perspective which helps to reveal the roots of oppression, such as sexism or ageism, and provides another handle to get out of the mess we're in." In time, I could more fully appreciate Gloria Steinem's observation that ". . . older women may take up feminism less frequently, but are activists for life when they do."

The Alliance for Displaced Homemakers was formed to work only on getting the legislation enacted (the California bill that had just been introduced) and, as soon as possible after that, a federal measure. Sommers and Dudley, on an earlier trip to Washington, had left a draft with the staff of Representative Yvonne B. Burke (Democrat, California). Burke subsequently filed the measure, May 15, 1975; but it was clear nothing would happen on the Hill before the fate of the California bill had been decided.

There was a need to build grassroots support for both bills. Shortly after our meeting, Tish asked if I'd consider assuming the leadership of the Alliance. I was pleased to be asked—indeed, flattered that she thought I could do something for which she knew I had absolutely no working credentials. I might have thought differently if I'd known what I was later to learn of Sommers' *modus operandi*. Being oriented more to issues than individuals, once her priorities are established, she drives hard to accomplish her goals. Rather than extending a search for talent, she reaches out for talent (or the show of promise) at hand. The chosen person can expect, and will get, Sommers' total cooperation and support, including financial support, if needed, and will have full rein in working toward an agreed-upon goal. Hers is the role of one who paints in broad strokes but who is willing to cut her losses if need be and strike out in new ways to gain her objective. On the whole, Sommers' judgment has been on the mark; and in most cases, chosen talent has developed as she had hoped.

Her approach to salaries paid to those working in nonprofit organizations is similarly unorthodox. To ask what a proposed job would pay is to be answered with the question "How much do you need to live on?" That is a totally different approach from one that seeks to find out what you think you're worth, and it makes one examine the importance of acquired tastes. Like others before me (and some after), I quickly discovered that working for a cause in a nonprofit organization doesn't put you on the road to riches; but I *was* surprised to find that just by changing to a simpler lifestyle, I could live adequately and happily on a fraction of what I might have expected in the "normal" business world.

Our political strategy for ADH was determined not so much by what we knew but by what we didn't and, in the case of Tish and Barbara, by what they didn't want to know! Neither was comfortable working within the political system, and I felt I didn't know enough about lobbying to be effective in Sacramento; but I did believe I could organize other women like myself to act in their own behalf. Our game plan was to lobby from the outside rather than inside the system.

Given our limited budget and the possibility of the bill quickly moving (or dying) in committee, my immediate task was to contact and organize other displaced homemakers living in the districts of legislators serving on those committees. Everything had to be done "immediately." Since we were starting from scratch, that meant drafting a newsletter, fact sheets, press releases, and lining up a schedule of visits throughout the state. Our goal was to organize a letter-writing campaign to encourage constituent advocates to visit their legislators' district offices. With the assistance of some NOW chapters, local YWCA staff, and church women's groups, a series of open meetings was set up in the targeted areas. I borrowed my daughter's yellow VW bug, and my days as a "footloose organizer" began.

For her part, Tish continued to organize activists within NOW and through other contacts began to build up an impressive list of organizations supportive of the legislation. Barbara remained the expert on the measure itself, drafting revisions to which we agreed when requested by the legislative offices. In a sense they were each doing something with which they were familiar. I, on the other hand, was off on a real tangent from anything I'd ever done. While I'd managed to do a cram course on the background, content, and promise of the bill, it simply hadn't dawned on me that I was going to have to do more than hand a roomful of strangers a fact sheet to study. I was going to have to show and tell!

Addressing an audience for the first time can be a harrowing experience. Unsure of myself, I'd painstakingly inked an outline of salient points on 3 x 5 cards, only to find when I arrived I'd left my reading glasses at home. It was just as well, because that night set the format for the informal meetings that followed. I told them my story and Tish's, explained the legislation, and invited their comments. The point, as I told them, was not to talk to them but with them. It was a style with which I was most comfortable; each meeting gave me a new high and created a warm glow of "togetherness" which I sensed those in the audience experienced, too. It was a physically demanding year but, for me, an extremely rewarding one; and it served to get me in shape for the tasks of the following year, when we concentrated our efforts on the federal legislation.

The number of supporters and the list of organizational endorsements multiplied, and ironically so did our troubles in Sacramento! Despite the fact that California's Displaced Homemakers Bill, SB 825, eventually passed in 121 working days of the legislature with near unanimous decisions in each of the bodies, it was not all clear sailing. All along the way opposition came—not as we had expected, from a handful of extremely conservative legislators (to whom any proposal of a new social program would be anathema), but from our newly elected Governor, Jerry Brown. Brown, the very candidate we had pinned our hopes on to liberate us from the fiscally frozen administration of the Reagan years. Not unlikely thinking for supporters of his father, former Governor Pat Brown.

But as Mary Ellen Leary, a longtime veteran political reporter in California, was to point out later in her brilliant critique of the 1974 election (*Phantom Politics*), our hopes were not only misplaced; the assumption on which we'd based them was false. Jerry Brown was related to Pat Brown familially but not politically. According to Leary, "When Californians went to the polls on November 5, 1974, and elected Democrat Edmund G. (Jerry) Brown as their governor, they knew remarkably little about him. . . . They knew little about the man as a person or about the politics he would promulgate as a governor."

Thus it was that along with most, if not all, of the members of the legislature, 1975 was a year of learning about Jerry Brown. For us, that knowledge was gained in bits and pieces, spawned by a series of ongoing crises-of-the-moment on the fate of the bill. For us, Brown ran a school of hard knocks.

Early on we had heard, through those unofficial channels that route rumors designed to rout hope, that the Governor "just doesn't like the bill." At first we discounted this unsought information; after all, the prime sponsor (newly elected Senator Jerry Smith) was, as he so often assured us, "a very close friend of Brown's." Innocently believing that "it's not what you know but who you know" in politics, we counted on that relationship to bring the Governor around. Still the rumors persisted. A number of reasons for his opposition were offered, none of which we were able to verify. As they were passed along by Senator Smith's staff, we did our best to counter them.

"He says it will encourage more women to leave their husbands." We pointed out that in California more marriages of fifteen years or longer were being dissolved on demand of the husband, and not the dependent wife.

"He says he's not seeing enough Hispanic names supporting the bill." We sighed and phoned Estelle and Philip Chacon, leaders in the Hispanic community in Southern California. They turned in literally hundreds of petitions signed by Hispanic men and women in support of the measure.

"He says if this bill for one pilot project is enacted, every legislator will want one in his or her district." Aha! This had more of the ring of real objection. The candidate who had, after all, campaigned on "small is beautiful" and who was by then openly aiming to out-Reagan Reagan on reducing state expenditures would hardly be anxious to encourage escalating costs, even if it did mean serving the needs of older women for the first time.

A bizarre incident happened one morning while I was waiting for Senator Smith to return to his office that gives us, perhaps, another insight into Brown's attitude toward older women. The Senator suddenly burst through the door calling out to his aide, "Get me a priest or a nun—fast." Obviously agitated, he explained he'd just left the Governor, who had asked a question Smith wasn't prepared to answer. Reportedly, Brown wanted to know why the legislation was needed at all, asking if it wasn't "religious institutions, friends, and relatives" such women should turn to in their need.

I was appalled! And quietly furious. How dare he make us into objects of charity! What we needed, what we wanted, was job training and *jobs*. Viewed through the prism of his narrow family experience, was it possible he seriously thought religious institutions were equipped to do more than lend moral support? Did this young man who had never personally experienced want in his childhood, whose choice of "poverty" as a seminarian was abstract at best (since all his material needs were furnished by the order he entered), really believe displaced homemakers should be shunted aside, quietly dismissed with a handout? Was one of Brown's unsuccessful opponents in the primary campaign correct when he charged that Brown lacked an understanding of the "real world of family life"?

I left Smith's office before he got an answer and don't know if he did; but later that day I was speaking to a group of obviously affluent women in one of the most conservative counties in the state. Having explained the purpose of the proposed legislation, and the problems with which it dealt, I decided to put the

Governor's question to them. "What do you think?" I asked them. An impeccably groomed gray-haired matron wearing basic black, complete with a string of cultured pearls, sprang to her feet. Her voice was cultured, but her language was strictly from her gut: "That," she spat out in fury, "is a bucket of shit!" I suggested she relay the message to the Governor. Other equally furious women took that advice and sent us copies of letters they wrote to Brown, couched, however, in less descriptive terms.

If the bill was not then a burr under Brown's blanket, it quickly became a gnat that eluded his not so subtle swatter. The first attempt to kill it came during the hearing before the Senate Finance Committee. We were told in advance an Administration representative would speak out against it. Our concerns were further heightened when we arrived for the hearing. The Senate was locked up in debate over the annual budget, and only a quorum of Senators was released for scheduled hearings. We needed the "Aye" vote of each of the seven men present that morning. We could count on only two for certain. Worse, sitting in for the Chairman who was supportive of the bill was the Vice-Chair, a known opponent of all women's issues.

Slumped down in his seat before the committee, the Administration's representative led off, as predicted, with a droned-out pastiche of negatives: "duplicates existing services, the need has not been definitively documented . . ." Joan Jensen, a registered Sacramento lobbyist who had been working with us, slipped into a seat beside me as the witness closed with "and for these reasons we feel this legislation has a very low priority." She patted my arm. "Not to worry," she whispered.

"Wally Steirn just might surprise you." Steirn, a veterinarian by profession, elected to the legislature in 1958, had a seemingly lifelong hold on the seat representing a largely agricultural district. His voting record reflected the conservative thinking of the majority of his constituents. It would, indeed, be a surprise if he rallied to the cause of a social program, especially a new one for women.

But as the Administration's witness concluded, Steirn rose to his feet. A large man, bearlike in build, he made an impressive figure as he shook a finger at the witness and roared, "Now, hold on there, young fella. I don't think you understand what this bill is all about." Seated to his right, a moderate Republican who *did* know what the bill was about shot a quick, bemused glance at Steirn as though he wondered how well Steirn understood the bill, or by what miracle he did. (At this point, Joan whispered the answer to me: "I spent the evening with Wally and his wife and really briefed him last night.")

Steirn's presentation, worthy of an Oscar, confirmed the hard lobbying efforts. Warming up to his subject, clearly enjoying himself, he made point after point, thundering at the injustice of a society that would neglect and "short-change these little ladies" and "desert them in their hour of need." His colleagues began to squirm. One defensively said he "yielded to no one in my concern for the little ladies." One hesitantly mentioned cost. Wally roared again. *"Cost?* It's peanuts, gentlemen." He thumped the table for emphasis. "This should be a ten-million-dollar program. These little ladies have *earned* it. Two hundred thousand dollars is a miserable sum to put up against all they've done for this state, for our country!" A wave of applause swept through the room and did not go unnoticed by the Chair. But he prefaced his call for the vote with his own version of why it should be "aye" instead of "no." "If we can get these women retrained, ex-husbands won't get socked with all that alimony." In the right action for at least one wrong reason, the roll call registered seven "aye," none opposed.

From then on there was never any question in our minds that Brown wanted the bill killed. We were equally determined to keep it alive. We kept a file of his statements to the press and used them in hard-hitting newsletters to our growing group of supporters. When the Associated Press reported that Brown was concerned "about ordinary citizens who have been taxed, harassed, and forgotten," we asked if he believed that, how could he oppose helping displaced homemakers who were indeed "ordinary citizens," neglected and forgotten. When he advocated conservation of our natural resources, we asked why he wasn't equally concerned about wasting human resources. When he spelled out for the *New York Times* some of his aims as Governor—"to reduce the sum of human misery a bit, to help people expand their lives a little bit, give them an awareness of their own potential"—we found it hard not to choke on the irony of his statement. In fewer than twenty-five words he had summed up the purpose and the promise of our bill.

We had gradually been building up supporters among legislators and their staffs, and it was good that we had. In a thinly disguised attempt to discredit the bill, the Administration suddenly called for an investigation of "existing services," including Jobs for Older

Women, since it was assumed (mistakenly) that it would be the agency to implement our legislation if enacted. JOW was then in no way able to compete with well-funded community-college programs; but these, in turn, were not geared then to address the needs of older women or to implement the innovative program proposed by the bill. In any comparison, without a track record, JOW was bound to come out on the short end of the stick. Assemblyman John Vasconcellos, a co-sponsor of the bill, intervened on our behalf and added staff person Joan Leahy to the investigative team to keep the probe more objective.

Brown's opposition to the bill was finally overcome—not by his friends or our "champions" but by his own aversion to group confrontation. It can now be admitted, for the first time, that it all came about through sheer luck and a bluff that didn't start out to be one at all.

In the final weeks before the last hearing, we had been trying unsuccessfully to get an appointment with Brown to clear up the misunderstandings we thought he had about the bill. Rather than going through Senator Smith, we wanted to put our case directly to him. About the same time, Tish and I were scheduled to attend a series of meetings throughout Southern California. The opening event was an important NOW state conference in San Diego. Geri Sherwood, NOW's lobbyist in Sacramento, had asked Tish to keynote the conference. Privately, we had discussed with her our frustrations with the Governor. She said she'd think of ways to help. Shortly before Tish was to speak, Geri sent a note to the dais: "The only way you're going to smoke him out of his office is to stage a big sit-in in it."

NOW had already endorsed passage of the bill, and Tish departed from her intended address to whip the audience into a frenzy, spelling out all of Brown's opposition. "Maybe," she challenged them, "maybe we'll just have to stage a big sit-in in his office until he agrees to come out and talk with us." Calls to action and demonstrations are, to NOW members, the meat and potatoes of their activism. The hall rang with shouts of support. Plans were hastily formed to make up caravans of cars or to hire buses for the trip. The press in attendance broke the story in the evening papers: "Older feminists pledge to sit-in in Brown's office."

Two days later and two hundred miles to the north in Ventura County, Tish fired up a more conservative audience. She urged her audience of supportive older women to let their Assemblyman know "We're going to mow Brown down!" The local paper dutifully reported that and added, "Governor Edmund G. Brown, Jr., got fair warning Monday that an army of little old ladies in tennis shoes is going to stage a sit-in Friday." The fat was in the fire and blazing nicely.

I returned to Oakland to organize local women for the demonstration while Tish continued to issue marching orders at two additional stops on her way home. My first order of business was to contact the Governor's office. It appeared that word of the demonstration had reached them, but I reminded the staffer that a sit-in would not be necessary if we could get an appointment with the Governor. She said she'd relay the message.

The following day she phoned to say the Governor's schedule was full but that he would arrange to have us meet with one of his advisory staff. I didn't recognize the name of the person designated, so I told her we'd take it under advisement. A quick check revealed the named representative was a holdover from Reagan's administration with no known influence in Brown's inner circle of advisors. We declined the offer and gave our reasons. "Does that mean," she asked, "That you are still going through with the sit-in?" "Every blessed mother and grandmother of us will be there," I cheerfully assured her.

Within hours there was another call from Sacramento. We were offered an appointment with Marc Poche, widely known at that time to be one of the Governor's close friends and one of his more influential advisors. I readily accepted the offer; but because the sit-in had been scheduled to coincide with the hearing the following day, I warned the staff person that we might not be able to reach everyone although we would make every effort to do so.

But when I began checking, I was chagrined to discover that our army of revolutionaries, for one reason or another—"can't get the time off," "trip costs too much"—had melted away to fewer than forty diehards from Oakland and Sacramento. I met Tish at the airport that night, and we discussed our dilemma. It seemed clear to both of us that if Brown or his staff got wind of the dissipated demonstration, plans to speak out against the bill would be reinstated. We had no Wally Steirn on this committee; and as I pointed out, even our supporters might think twice about voting for a measure which in no way benefited their districts if it meant going against the Administration. We lapsed into a glum silence as we waited for her luggage to tumble onto the carousel. Suddenly I had an idea.

"What if," I asked her, "we send the Oakland women directly to the hearing room and I sit in the Governor's reception room and catch the Sacramento women as they arrive?"

"How would that help?" asked Tish.

"Well, remember that I said we might not be able to reach everyone today. There are only going to be about ten women from Sacramento, but it could appear there would have been more; or at least I'd bet that's what they'd assume."

"A bluff, huh?"

"Well," I responded with a grin, "what have we got to lose? The bill is on the line. All they know is what they've been reading in the papers; and because they don't know our group—haven't bothered to get to know us—they're going to go with the percentages, that we *will* march an army of little old ladies in tennies into his office."

Tish's face broke into a broad smile. "The old thing about when you've got lemons, make lemonade, right?"

I agreed, and the two of us left the airport with lighter hearts. As planned, the next day I introduced myself to the receptionist in the Governor's office, told her why I was there, and seated myself close to her desk. It wasn't difficult to pick out the local NOW women. They were all wearing large NOW buttons. As each of them neared the desk, I explained we hadn't been able to reach them to tell them the sit-in had been called off because the Governor had met our request. I suggested they join the others already in the hearing room. I had no doubt all of this was reported to Poche, since the receptionist pointedly slipped away from her desk when the women left.

A runner from the hearing room, followed by Tish and Barbara, arrived to report the bill had passed unanimously, with no voiced opposition from the Administration. Almost at once, though well past our appointment time, we were ushered into Poche's office. He was polite but somewhat cool.

"You know why the vote went in your favor, don't you?" he asked and went on before we could reply. "Because you called off the demonstration." Out of sight of Poche, I couldn't resist nudging Tish's foot as I spread the two-finger victory sign on my knee. Otherwise, we displayed no outward sign of our inner emotions. Instead, we pressed an important question: Did this mean Brown would sign the measure? Poche said he didn't know, but he added with a stern shake of his finger at all three of us, "No more threats of demonstrations, or he'll veto it for sure."

Barbara couldn't resist needling authority. "Oh, I don't know," she said with a grin. "Why should we rule them out? It's hard to quarrel with success, isn't it? Or how come we're sitting here talking to you after a unanimous committee vote?"

Poche's smile was friendly as was his tone when he ruefully acknowledged, "O.K., you won this round." He then confessed his wife had lobbied him on the bill, causing me, at least, to think again that it was too bad Brown wasn't married.

But a woman did influence Brown's final act on the measure. As the midnight deadline approached on September 25, he vacillated between signing the bill or letting it go into law without his signature—a sign that he didn't like the bill but wasn't prepared to quarrel with the legislature over their vote. Nor was he apparently willing to veto it, probably because he wished to avoid unfavorable publicity that might follow refusing to help, even in a small way, former wives and mothers—all in the faithful-voter age range. Poche, because he knew of her interest in our cause, had alerted Vasconcellos' aide, Joan Leahy, that Brown was likely to consider the bill that evening, and she had driven up from San Jose to join other advisors in Brown's office. She watched him as he considered his options. In answer to his question as to "What's in it for these women—Sommers, Shields, and Dudley?" she snapped, "Personally? Nothing!" Still wavering because he obviously had reservations about the measure, he suddenly said he'd let it go through without his signature. "Don't bother," Leahy told him. "What the women want is your signature on the bill. If you can't sign it, veto it." She later confessed she held her breath, amazed at her own daring. But all's well that ends well. Brown took her advice and signed SB 825 into law.

That gave California the first displaced homemaker law. It called for establishing a two-year $200,000 pilot project Displaced Homemakers Center in Alameda County. In his written message to the legislature and the press release the following day, it was clear Brown had some deep reservations about the legislation:

> I am deeply concerned about the difficulties faced by widowed and divorced homemakers set adrift in our uncertain economy. The increasing breakup of the family and the separation of generations from each other

will not be wished away. But how government changes all this is an unanswered question in my mind.

As a society becomes further fragmented with more people isolated and unemployed and bereft of supportive relationships, we are facing big trouble.

This bill appropriates a modest sum for one project, in one county, in one state. Out of it, I expect we will all learn. But I don't want to delude anyone into thinking that mere money or government programs as presently constituted will get at the roots of the economic and moral dilemma facing this country."

In retrospect, I wish we'd had the sit-in.

It was only one project in one county, but not for long was it to be limited to one state. While the California bill was still moving through hearings, Helen Koss, member of the Maryland House of Delegates, had heard of it and wrote for particulars. Her bill quickly passed, making it possible for the Baltimore Center for Displaced Homemakers to open in October 1976, just six months after California's Displaced Homemakers Center began to operate on the campus of Mills College in Oakland. In that same year, Margaret Garvue, a displaced homemaker and a NOW member from Tallahassee, Florida, wrote, "Help! Now that I've got a legislator interested, how do we get a displaced homemaker bill drafted for our state?" Shortly before the Florida legislature adjourned, that bill was enacted. The victory was Pyrrhic. At the last moment, the legislature amended out the funding but gave the state's Department of Health Services and Rehabilitation "permission" to raise funds from any source to implement the provisions of the bill. No doubt many of the elected returned to their districts to assure displaced homemakers they had acceded to their wishes and passed a bill to help them. (Fortunately, the women pressing for the programs did not give up and, the following year, were able to get funds appropriated for the programs.)

In Oregon, Representative Nancie Fadeley was equally persistent in her championing of displaced homemakers in her state. She filed her bill with the co-sponsorship of every woman member of the legislature and was delighted to have several of her male colleagues reproach her later for not having asked them. Enacted, the measure called for expanding the services of a successful program in Eugene as a pilot project.

All of this action in other states, unsolicited by us, helped us to formulate our political strategy for moving the federal legislation. We reasoned that if we could incorporate the tactics used in California, concentrating on getting bills enacted, especially in the states of Congressional committee members, we might have a better chance of convincing Congress that the case of the displaced homemaker was a national issue.

In January 1976 we submitted a proposal to the women's divisions of some of the country's leading religious denominations, asking for modest funds to enable me to travel cross-country publicizing the legislation and organizing women to work for bills in their own states. The response was immediate and generous. As Ellen Kirby, Executive Secretary of the Women's Division, United Methodist Church, acknowledged, "In every one of our congregations there are women who are displaced homemakers." The grant from her organization made possible a swing through the Southeastern states. One from the Council on Women and the

Church of the United Presbyterian Church of the USA and Church Women United provided for an extensive tour through the Southwest. In an early merging of traditionalists and feminists, the national board of NOW added a special grant which funded an organizing effort in the Midwest and Northwest. Money from the United Church of Christ rounded out travel that year. By the end of 1976, I'd been able to hit the major cities of all but eleven states.

The payoff for the determined action of local women who had responded to that year of footloose organizing came in January 1977, when legislators from twenty-eight states filed displaced homemaker bills. Several of these improved on the earlier California measure. Minnesota's original bill, for example, drafted by the then four-term veteran member of the House of Representatives, Linda Berglin, was the first to call for pilot projects for women in rural areas. It became the model for other states with large rural populations and represented the first time any program had targeted such assistance to older women in rural areas.

One of those trips brought me to the city of a woman I'll call Polly who'd written earlier—a woman struggling to take over the breadwinner's role because of her husband's sudden and permanent disability. I phoned to tell her where and when I'd be meeting with women in her community and said I hoped she'd be able to attend. She said she'd try but that evenings out were difficult. She was still doing odd jobs—cleaning houses, part-time retail clerk—and came home very tired; and her husband's condition had worsened. She hated being away from him when they had so little time to share these days, but she said she'd come if it wasn't one of Bill's bad days.

That meeting was a large one. It wasn't possible to have people introduce themselves as I'd asked them to do in smaller groups. Because I wanted her to be there, I kept searching the audience, trying to match a face with a voice—a woman with a letter. It wasn't until after the meeting concluded that I found her. She had hung back, outwaiting others who came up to tell of their experiences or to offer to help with the legislation. As the janitor began to stack the chairs, it was evident we were expected to leave soon. It was also obvious that she wanted to get something off her mind. I asked if she'd like to stop someplace for a cup of coffee. She preferred to go home. Would I care to visit with her there for a bit? I said I'd be pleased to.

In the car she was quiet, but shared silence can be a powerful communicator. I sensed she was fighting for emotional control and was close to the end of her rope. The house, when we arrived, was at the end of the block. The only thing that distinguished it from its neighbors was its location. The small, white-painted, one-story frame building was well kept, and the lawn and bordering flower beds gave witness to a gardener's loving care. As we mounted the stairs to the front door, I suddenly remembered her sick husband. "Are you sure this won't disturb him?" I asked. There was a hint of bitterness in the tone of her answer, "No!" Just that. "No." Yet, like viewing a stop-action shot, I knew there was more to come. She held the door open as she finished her reply. "Bill's dead."

Dead! We stood for a moment in that doorway, looking at each other. "When?" I asked, knowing that he'd been alive when I phoned a week earlier. "Two days after you called," she replied. Steeling herself, she added, "He killed himself." I don't remember which of us made the first move, but suddenly I had my arms around her, and we both just stood there, weeping.

We made our way to the kitchen where we shared a box of Kleenex and a pot of coffee. Her earlier reticence disappeared in a flood of released pent-up feelings. "He couldn't take it. Not just the pain, but the frustration. All of our plans for the future were down the drain. Over and over he told me he was going down and dragging me down with him. It wasn't true, but he thought it was. He hated my having to go out looking for jobs, and I never did tell him about the house-cleaning jobs. It would have . . ." She stopped as she realized she was about to say "killed him." Nervously, she laughed and paused to blow her nose. She wadded the Kleenex into a ball in her hand, which she unconsciously clenched into a fist from time to time. "You must think I'm crazy, just spilling all of this; and we've never met before. When I wrote that letter, I was so desperate. I didn't know where to turn." I assured her I well knew how she felt, that I'd been drawn to follow up with her because of my own experience. I told her of how her letter and what she'd just been saying reminded me of how I'd felt when pain had driven my ill husband to wish he were dead and how hurt I'd been when he said it. She nodded and tears made fresh tracks down a face twisted in pain.

"Look," I said, "if you'd like, why don't I stay here tonight? We probably could talk half the night away anyway." As was true of all those overnight trips, I avoided using hotels, staying instead with whomever the local coordinator could find to have me. All it meant was phoning to explain a switch in plans. Since it was an old friend I'd planned to stay with, I knew she wouldn't mind.

Polly bit her lip and nodded unspoken agreement as though she couldn't trust herself to speak. I made my phone call and went back to the kitchen. She was a bit more controlled and politely asked if I'd like something to eat. "Good Lord, yes! I just realized I missed dinner tonight." She seemed pleased and rushed about whipping up eggs for an omelet.

"Bill and I always have an omelet late at night. He says it helps him get to sleep." From an old-fashioned breadbox came another of Bill's favorites—homemade wheat bread. "He hates store bread." From a shelf came a jar of apricot jam. "We have a number of fruit trees in the back, and every year I make enough jam and jelly to see us through till the next crop." Then: "His favorite is guava." She suddenly turned from the stove, her eyes wide with disbelief. "I'm talking just as though he's still alive."

Because I had been aware she was and because that had triggered painful memories of my own days as a new widow, I had to take a deep breath before saying, "You probably will for a while. I know I did; and there were so many times when, for no reason at all, I'd suddenly choke up. Some unexpected incident would remind me of our life together; and I'd literally ache, wanting him back to share the moment with me." She nodded as though it had already happened to her. "And," I continued, "for a long, long time I resented it when friends or relatives didn't write to me as Mrs. Arthur Shields. Not that I didn't want to be me, I think I just wanted people not to forget him, who had been so much a part of me."

We concentrated for a bit on the omelets she'd placed on the table. Picking at her own, she said, "I know what you mean. It kills me because people around here never mention Bill at all, as though they're afraid of talking about the dead." She paused and then with a little rush of breath added softly, "Or maybe it's knowing he killed himself that makes it different." I disagreed. "I think it's just that we're all afraid of dying and maybe a little ashamed that we're still alive. That makes it hard to find the right words to say when someone we know dies."

I leaned across the table and rested my hand on top of hers. "Bill's act, you know, could be considered a really courageous one. As you said, it wasn't just the pain that drove him to it. He may have been much more upset by what his illness was doing to you. Surely, the greatest act of love would be to give your life for someone else." She hadn't considered that possibility, and it seemed to comfort her.

We sat there in the big kitchen unaware of the night speeding toward daybreak. We exchanged stories of our lives, our families. She brought in pictures of their wedding and one of Bill standing in front of the first house he helped to build. They'd had no children, but there were pictures of lots of nieces and nephews. "They're all in Australia," she said, "and they're all his relatives. I was an only child, and my parents died the year after we were married. I was just eighteen. More than ever, Bill became my whole world."

We talked a little about her future. They'd borrowed on the insurance to meet the increasing costs of Bill's illness, so there wouldn't be much of that money coming to her. The house, though, was free and clear of any mortgage. All she had to do was figure out a way to keep it up and meet taxes. She was sure she didn't have anything to offer an employer—no training and no experience being high on the list. I urged her to take a look at the skills and talents she might not have even considered as a means to paid employment, and I told her I knew how hard this was to do on her own. "It's very important to have some help, some guidance at this point. But most important, you should try to find a support group with whom you can share your experiences, ideas, hopes."

It was four in the morning when the talk wound down. With a stream of apologies for the late hour, she led the way to the guest bedroom. The bed was covered with one of the most handsome quilts I'd ever seen. "Your work?" I asked. She rubbed a hand across it lovingly. "Yes, my grandmother taught me how to make them when I was just a child. I love making them."

"No talent, huh," I said teasingly. "Let's see . . . tne best homemade honey wheat bread I've ever tasted, superb homemade apricot jam, and now this—a quilt that anyone would gladly pay two hundred or three hundred dollars to own, assuming they have the money to spend. No talent?" She laughed as she left the room, but agreed, "More than I thought I had, I guess."

We embraced as I left the next morning, and I never saw her again; but there was a happy ending to her story. Invited by Bill's family, she paid a short visit to Australia. I had a letter from her much later. She'd returned to the States, sold the house, and moved to Australia. "I've thought so often," she wrote, "about all we talked about that evening and wanted you to know that with help from Bill's family, I've been able to do something with that seed you planted in my head that night. I've opened a small shop, and I sell 'homemade

American goodies' which, surprisingly enough, are moving well. I make quilts to special order and haven't felt so good about myself in a long, long time. I've been seeing a lot of one of Bill's old schoolmates, now a widower; but it's great to know I can be with him and like him for himself and not have to think of him just as someone nice who could take care of me. I might marry him if he asks me, but I'll be my own woman when I do." He did ask and she did say "yes." They both work in *her* shop.

Peer counseling was one of the major demands of the displaced homemaker legislation. Although it hadn't happened to me, many women had expressed their reluctance to "open up" to young professional counselors—even those they sensed were sympathetic. "How can a young woman, my daughter's age or younger, understand what I'm going through?" they'd ask me. I had sometimes gently chided them for what I thought was a reverse discrimination, old against the young; but after that experience with Polly, I had a better grasp of what peer counseling could provide. It wasn't a case of feeling sorry for a new widow; I knew how she felt. She didn't have to tell me. I *knew*!

Staff persons within programs for displaced homemakers who have "been there" are especially valuable, not simply because they are better able to empathize with program participants but because they provide role models for those in transition. In fact, in every aspect of the program, displaced homemakers can and should be made part of the team, with an emphasis on self-help and collective responsibility.

How that actually worked out in some of the early-state displaced homemakers programs will be discussed in the next chapter.

CHAPTER THREE

Laboratories of Hope

On July 22, 1975, scarcely three months after the California bill had been filed, twenty women gathered for an Alliance for Displaced Homemakers meeting which Dudley chaired and at which Sommers shared their thoughts on "the new center." My notes from the meeting are headed "Tish says . . ." and end with three large question marks.

She began by saying it was the first of many meetings needed to "prepare for an eventuality"; the bill would be passed, and a pilot project center would be opened in Oakland. "By us." Not because it was our idea in the first place but because we were "going to plan a model multiservice center—one without precedent. All the components of a program which will deal with the complex change from a displaced homemaker to a competent, self-sufficient worker would be right there in one center. No more pillar to post for the meager services that, even if available, are not geared to the specific needs of older women."

The Center, however, would "not just provide services; it will be an organizing center with the clout to really create jobs and make needed changes in existing job-training programs." The Center was to offer a chance to "be real innovators, working not only in our own interest but for the social good of many." She reminded us that "public job-training programs have too long been geared to providing manpower for business and industry. In our own small but gutsy way, we'll turn it around," she said, "and provide jobs for people, fitted to their needs but also geared toward filling other social needs not yet met."

If we could do that, she said, it would be "one of the most significant things we can do in our lifetime—something which will give courage and hope to women like us all over the country."

Even as I drew the question marks as she finished talking, I found myself deeply moved by what seemed an awesome challenge. Observing the excited and enthusiastic response of the group, I was reminded of Adlai Stevenson's reported observation that when Cicero spoke, people commented on his eloquence, but when Demosthenes spoke, people said, "Let's march!"— which is what everyone in the room seemed ready to do.

Even so, as we were closing up the office, I raised my chief reservation to the thrust of the presentation.

"Isn't it," I asked, "all pretty utopian? I mean, is it realistic to think we can really turn things around, create new jobs *and* be a force for change?"

Dudley's response was quick and sharp. "Listen, we're social activists; but that doesn't mean we're not pragmatists."

Sommers interrupted. "And we know we can't win the whole enchilada. The thing is, you have to have a long-range plan but also accomplishable short-range goals. Jobs *can* be created and we'll do that, but you always offer a step ahead with the clear understanding that you may have to compromise and accept lesser accomplishments. You build on every breakthrough.

In the weeks and few months that preceded passage of the bill, Sommers and Dudley, sometimes with members of Jobs for Older Women but more often as a team of two, hammered out the program to emerge from the specifics of the legislation. (A copy of SB 825 is included in the Appendix.) Working with a handful of newcomers who brought highly specialized and needed skills, the planners sought to flesh out the mandate of the law, yet retain the spirit of what was later called "Tish's dream."

With regard to job training and placement, the language of their proposal was unequivocal.

> Rather than merely preparing the displaced homemaker to compete for the too few existing jobs, our solution is the creation of new ones. One of the major tenets of our center project will be that job placement will not depend solely on the traditional avenues of employment, but will be the result of the *creation of jobs* [their emphasis] to meet public policy projection and to provide needed community services.

The Center was envisaged as a laboratory, flexible in structure, with the freedom to fail as well as succeed as they experimented with new methods, new approaches, and new ways to work—all aimed toward transforming participants into a force for social change.

It was an acceptable and easy concept to hang on to during the planning stages. When the Oakland Center opened its doors, it proved more difficult to implement, primarily, as one former staffer recalls, "because there was too little money, too few staff, too many clients. We just couldn't implement all the innovative ideas."

Under the best of circumstances, creating new jobs was never conceived by either Sommers or Dudley as being an easy task. They knew, however, it called for total commitment to the long-range need to do so. Although Sommers, who was elected president of the Center, served as a full-time volunteer staff member until April 1977, neither she nor Dudley had the responsibility of the day-to-day operations. Overwhelmed by the response to the Center's presence, staff opted by April 1977 for the more immediate and doable: to serve the needy in a wider community with the best they had to offer—empathetic counseling and mutual support. The idea of the Center as a laboratory for job creation was abandoned. Training of groups of selected participants was dropped. Workshops designed to build self-esteem and self-awareness and to develop job readiness became the major service.

Sommers resigned from her elected post as president of the Board of Directors in order to help me with the national legislation, which was beginning to move. Despite the Center's radical departure from the original plans, she was deeply concerned for its future. Funding for the program was due to run out in December. A bill to get additional money had been filed in Sacramento, but the Center had neither the time nor the staff to go out and find and talk to women, get them to sign petitions and volunteer their help—all of which was needed to get the bill enacted. Because of the mounting hostility of the state administering agency and the tension building between Center staff and administrators, it was doubtful the bill would pass without a concerted effort to rally support.

We agreed that what was needed was another California Alliance for Displaced Homemakers and someone to head it up. Neither of us had the time to take it on, and our ADH national budget couldn't cover the added expense of new personnel. We were barely getting by, plowing back honorariums from conferences and workshops to supplement the thin stream of private donations from ardent, but not overly rich, supporters.

We knew of one woman who had been through the Center program but had not latched onto a job. At one time she had mentioned being "mildly interested in politics." Although few knew it then or know it now, Sommers personally provided the money to hire Alice Melvin and covered the expenses incurred in setting up the new California Alliance. Melvin proved a quick study and, though she'd never done anything like it before, turned in a superb job over the next eight months, organizing individual and institutional support throughout the state, marshaling groups to attend hearings, and working with Sacramento-based feminist advocates to lobby legislators.

Despite the appearance of a report which stridently recommended the Alameda County Center's funding be cut off, the legislature approved Senator Smith's request for $100,000, an additional year of operation, and a change in administering agencies. Melvin modestly plays down her contribution, but there is no question that those who staffed and those who used the Alameda County Displaced Homemakers Center in 1978–79 are in her debt.

Just as California's center was beginning to operate in May, 1976, a second state, Maryland, passed Delegate Helen Koss' measure to establish a similar pilot project. The wheels of government in Maryland ground as slowly as they did in California; but when the Center for Displaced Homemakers opened in Baltimore in October of that year, there were some apparent differences that augured well for its success. Koss, who had contacted the Alliance, was able to restructure the language of her measure so that those things the Californians were finding difficult to do were no part of the mandate of the Maryland law. She eliminated some of the job descriptions and removed the requirement to set up a "well women's health clinic." Not, as one Baltimore NOW member angrily charged, because Koss yielded to colleagues who thought even the phrase itself constituted "inflammatory language," but because trial and error on the West Coast indicated it was too difficult to do with the money available and with limited staff then committed to job creation and employment as the bottom line of their program.

Funding and the length of operation was much better than Oakland's contract. It may have been due to a sharp legislative move on Koss' part. She first requested a statewide program which, it was estimated, would have cost $5 million. When her colleagues objected, she graciously yielded and amended her bill, limiting it to one pilot project. Then, with the assistance and support of the influential Chair of the Ways and Means Committee, Benjamin Cardin, she had it attached as an amendment to a tax reform bill which provided funding of $190,000 each year for a three-year program. It was assumed in one report that this amount, "$190,000, was similar to the amount in the California bill." Someone hadn't read the fine print. What Koss got for the Baltimore center was $200,000 more than Oakland had for a two-year program and an additional $190,000 for a mandated third year.

There were other differences; and the most significant involved the administering agency (the Department of Human Resources), which, while it had opposed the statewide idea, unlike its California counterpart, was cooperative and supportive of the pilot project. It was helpful, too, that the Secretary of the Department had had good experience with the nonprofit organization that would administer the Displaced Homemakers program, the Baltimore New Directions for Women. It was the administration of New Directions, under the leadership of Mandy Goetze, that provided, in Sommers' view today, two key elements missing from the West Coast experience: It had been operating as a job-referral and employment-assistance organization; and because of other grants, it had experience with the precise methods of reporting the state would require. Neither Sommers nor any of the others associated with the Oakland center "had any prior experience with the administering of publicly funded employment programs. We knew accountability was essential, but we believed the record-keeping we set up during the first five months of operating was accurate and sufficient." Actually, the data they collected didn't dovetail with California's processing system—a fact that worked against them when the program was evaluated.

In 1979, a more enlightened Sommers passed along the lessons of that experience in a section of an advocacy manual written for older women, *How to Tame the CETA Beast*. "You can do anything you want with statistics except ignore them. You can prove any point by proper selection of data which substantiate your position, but lack of required statistics leaves you at the mercy of the opposition. . . . The most constructive approach is to view collection, analysis, and use of data as skills to be learned according to your goals."

One change in the language of the law made the Baltimore center unique. Instead of recommending, as did the California law, "that displaced homemakers be used as supervisory staff" whenever possible, Koss' bill, perhaps because she was a woman legislator, mandated the state's pilot project be staffed *"primarily* with displaced homemakers." Had it insisted that all staff be displaced homemakers, Cynthia Marano would not have been hired as the center's director. Having been divorced, she was currently remarried. Had Sommers been doing the interviewing, she wouldn't have hired Marano. Marano, then in her thirties (despite prematurely gray hair) and not herself a displaced homemaker, would have had two strikes against her. Says Sommers, "You've got to remember my headset in 1976; I was adamant about older women directing these programs."

Fortunately for Baltimore, Mandy Goetze had a sharper eye. An excellent administrator herself, she was quick to spot the potential Marano offered. Clearly comfortable with the mandate to use displaced homemakers "primarily" as staff, Marano has found such staffing makes it possible "to demonstrate visibly that different kinds of displaced homemakers can succeed."

"In Maryland," she says, "we have learned the variety of displaced homemakers, battlegrounds and problems. Our staffing reflects this. We have employed former welfare mothers and former upper-class, country-club matrons; persons widowed, separated, divorced and no longer eligible for public assistance. We represent various racial, income, lifestyle, and age groupings. We have staff members who still support young children, some who have always been single parents, and some whose children have been out of the home for years. This eclectic mix generates the true picture of displaced homemakers to the program participants, the community, and the media. All kinds of women (and men) can be displaced, and all kinds of displaced homemakers can make the successful transition to self-sufficiency."

To assist displaced homemakers in altering our lives is the prime concern of all who direct these programs, but some centers are changing lives in a different way—shedding light on how age-old differences can be dissolved once the commonality of problems surfaces. Joan Suter, director of the Los Angeles Center for Displaced Homemakers, herself a black woman, spoke frankly of the misconceptions black women have of white women and the problems this can cause.

Black women feel white women have unlimited advantages, whereas the truth is the white displaced homemaker feels very vulnerable, more so than the black woman in this situation. She doesn't know the system that black women have dealt with all their lives. Black women have more of a handle on dealing with crises, and they've developed survival skills and methods for coping that are better than those of their white peers. White women are much more shocked; their first reaction is to ask, "Why is this happening to me?"

Suter and her assistant Marsha Rickler told of a situation that developed in one of their first groups of trainees which taught everyone an important lesson—tolerance evolves when it is demonstrated that intolerance commonly touches lives, regardless of color.

As Suter described it, "The group of about twenty was made up almost equally of black and white women. The oldest was sixty, six were in their fifties, and the youngest was thirty-five." There were "some strong middle-class black women who knew the whole ball game plus some low-income black women—bright and street smart . . ."

"Who," interrupted Marsha, the white former displaced homemaker then on staff as a counselor for the group, "challenged every word I said!"

All of the participants were on stipends, including one white woman, age fifty-four, whose clothes, speech, and manners spoke of better days than any of the black women had lived. She had a master's degree and a long record of involvement at a high level in many community activities.

"In short," said Suter, "she was the stereotype for the blacks of white women, who had every advantage."

To make matters worse, the woman "was an overachiever. Whatever the class assignment, she did extra research or work which, though she did it for the common good, tended to widen the gap between herself and the black women."

Marsha: "She was really adding to the problem."

But Suter quickly added, "She didn't know she was. She'd been dumped by her husband for a younger woman. It blew her away—totally. Her reaction was to look for love and approval by giving of herself the only way she knew how."

Tension began to mount, and in one stormy work-shop all of the black resentment broke out. Why did she deserve a stipend? Why was she in the program at all since she had a master's degree that ought to be her ticket to something most of them could never dream of getting? Why was she always putting them down by doing extra work? Marsha, who with Joan's concurrence had just the night before determined to take the issue head on and bring everything back to employment, stepped into the fray as the white woman fled the room.

"She gets a stipend," Marsha began, "because she needs it, just as you do. She has no income other than that she gets from some babysitting jobs." That rocked them. "As for her master's degree, it's over twenty-five years old; and she's never practiced in her field. She has no paid work record. That degree is just a piece of paper, not much better than your GED or high-school diploma. You know far more than she does right now about surviving in the work world at age fifty-four."

As far as the extra effort they saw as actions to "put them down," Marsha concluded, "Right now, she needs to be needed; and she needs to do things to keep her mind off what, to her, is the most shocking thing in the world—her husband dumped her for a younger woman. She's only trying to be helpful, but she's also reaching out for help."

The white woman involved later told Marsha and Joan the encounter had initially hurt her; but after she dried her tears, she was able to look at herself more ob-jectively than she had ever done in her life. Beginning with her parents and through her marriage, she had al-ways done what she "was expected to do," little of which was for herself. It was the start of a new awareness of what she wanted for herself. When the training was concluded, she "found she had a real sense of self and purpose."

At the conclusion of the program all of the stereotypes women, white and black, had brought with them, of themselves or each other, had been laid to rest. "It was," says Marsha, "one of the greatest group experiences I've ever had"; and it produced one of those intangible results letter-of-the-law evaluators discount if they even discover them.

The Los Angeles Displaced Homemakers center was another that developed under the aegis of an existing nonprofit service organization for women. The contract for the second pilot project in California was awarded to the Career Planning Center, whose founder and executive director, Eleanor Hoskins, had skillfully built it into a multiservice agency in less than ten years. She began as a consultant to women's groups on employment possibilities, "operating out of the trunk of my car," she adds with a smile.

Today, with an annual projected budget of $4 million, CPC offers a range of programs to train or retrain women of all ages; but the Displaced Homemakers center is operated for women thirty-five years of age and older. Suter and her staff have the added advantage of being able to refer women ineligible for their program to other services within the parent organization.

The Baltimore center's contract did not specify job creation, but Marano shared Sommers' and Dudley's conviction that specific skills of homemakers could be transferred to new types of salaried employment for women. Analyzing the intake data of the center participants, she was struck by the number who listed "crocheting" or "needlework" as hobbies. It was work that called for concentration on minute detail. So, too, did technical drafting, a white-collar nontraditional job held by very few women of any age. She discussed her findings with Joyce Keating, the center's job-training program director. Keating suggested approaching vocational educators. When she did, several laughed; but Jim Harding, who taught a pre-engineering college-prep course at Eastern Vocational Technical High, was intrigued and said he'd try "a candidate." Keating explained why she felt he should take on at least ten; in such a new venture, the women would need the support of one another during the training course. He agreed.

The ten women selected were concerned about their lack of math skills. One of the center's staff, Alice Quinlan, a former teacher, devised a quick and simple crash course in mathematics and instructed the group before they entered Harding's class. Most of the women chosen were over forty; most had no previous paid work experience; the balance had been underemployed in retail sales part-time jobs.

One of the women was Nancy Ulbinsky, a forty-seven-year-old widow with three grown children. Today, she concedes that "never" in her life would she have considered a career as an "electronic draftsperson" and admits that the first day on the job she felt "terrifically insecure." As she explains, "There were several of us brand new to the job, but all the others were young people. They had all had longer training through vocational education classes." Their age made her more conscious of her own. "They talked another language, like my kids; social conversations weren't easy." But if that first week left her "filled with nerves," support from Harding and her own determination to succeed made her take herself in hand. "I just told myself, 'Nancy, you're O.K. and you're going to make it.'" One of two women and nine men in the department a year later, Nancy has had two pay raises and is comfortably holding her own with her younger colleagues. Six of the other women placed in similar jobs are still employed and have also advanced from salaries that started at $5.79 an hour.

Understandably, Harding is a hero to the women at the center; but much credit should go to the women who made the breakthrough, demonstrating through work experience that gender and age have little to do with the presumed qualifications of those capable of doing advanced technical drafting.

Seizing opportunities, being alert to new possibilities, and then translating that to the benefit of displaced homemakers is probably best illustrated by a story out of a displaced homemaker program in Iowa. The Door Opener, a private, nonprofit organization, "multipurposed and multifunded," had been operating in a ninecounty, essentially rural area trying, through their work, to "open new and meaningful doors for women."

After Iowa's state displaced homemaker legislation was enacted, it came as no surprise when The Door Opener was awarded the contract to develop a pilot project. Its director, Shirley Sandage, a tall, friendly, outgoing woman in her fifties, was known throughout the state for her concern about the changing role of rural women in today's society.*

* Her work has not gone unnoticed nationally. As this book goes to press, she has been nominated by the Winthrop Rockefeller Foundation for the Distinguished Rural Service Award of the National Rural Center, to be given to two individuals in the nation who have made substantial contributions to rural life.

An environmentalist herself, aware of the fact that the Resource Conservation Recovery Act of 1976 and the Toxic Substances Control Act were going to place new demands on agriculture, Sandage recognized that "farmers, as a general rule, do not do what they should do on the day they should do it." She spotted an opening for self-employment for displaced homemakers. There would be a need to do things in the area of soil testing, pest management, and monitoring; and with 80 percent of the land in Iowa under cultivation, the need was not insignificant. She contacted Iowa State University and hired a recent graduate, an entomologist, to set up a course of studies and find and train women interested in setting up a business, selling their services on a contractual basis to do the required testing and monitoring.

Although the main office of The Door Opener is located in Mason City, a community of about 30,000, it was decided to develop the program through their satellite office in Algona, population 6,500. The entomologist, Fran McCarty, worked out a curriculum with staff of Iowa Lakes Community College. She taught the sections on insects, and college staff provided instruction on the technical knowledge needed. Seven women, most with farm background, and all but two from the immediate area, underwent an intensive month-long training. Courses on management and self-assertion were part of the daily six-hour study program. When that phase of training ended, all were given additional tutelage in accounting, salesmanship, advertising, and the legal ramifications of operating a small business.

Sandage wisely formed an advisory board, which included prominent farmers in the area who not only addressed the group of women but could, as Sandage frankly stated, "be the ones that open doors." The group formed a company, MAC (Mobile Ag Company) Services and began negotiating contracts with local farmers. The combination of the three services offered provided the women with a year-round job—soil testing in the fall and spring, insect monitoring in the summer, and grain moisture testing from winter to all through the year. Research proved that performing these services saved the farmer an estimated $8 per acre for the cost of herbicides and pesticides over what they had previously spent.

In less than a month, the newest business in Algona serviced 10,000 acres and had several contracts in hand. One of the women in the group, thirty-seven-year-old Liz Thompson, a divorced mother with one daughter at home, told a local reporter, "This has given us an incentive to go out and do more with our lives. It has given us independence." The Door Opener continues to provide back-up support and advice and remains the contact for others who might be interested in replicating the program.

Many things are impressive about this innovative job development. It provided a brand-new role for the women who were mainly AFDC recipients and high-school dropouts. It was a splendid example of community services cooperating, blending their fields of expertise to open new doors to employment. It tackled a problem that has national implications, and it is not surprising that Sandage has already been contacted by the Environmental Protection Agency in Washington, D.C., who are reported to be "extremely interested in the program."

It proved once again that good ideas can be generated at very low cost. Sandage reports that the cost of the program, which was funded through the use of the Governor's CETA discretionary monies, "including tuition, transportation, books, required clothing, and all of The Door Opener's administrative cost, was somewhere in the area of $18,000." (As a footnote to the MAC story, the group received further national attention in January 1980 when Rosalynn Carter, touring the state in support of her husband's re-election campaign, made a special stop at the Door Opener to meet with the MAC team and discuss their novel project.)

Self-employment offers opportunities to put skills frequently exploited in the broader job market to personal profit. Diana McLaughlin, a displaced homemaker who arrived at the Baltimore center with a dollar in her pocket and desperately in need of a job, was the stipended intern who, a year later, drafted one of the center's most successful small-business training programs.

She became interested in the rising demand for the services of domestics. Researching the subject, she discovered that in Maryland alone there had been a 31.6 percent increase in the call for domestic service and a correspondingly high decrease in the numbers of workers available in this category. Turning to the national scene, she learned that in 1977, 97 percent of those domestics then working were women, 74 percent worked in urban areas, and 53 percent were black women. The median age was fifty, and 65 percent of the total cash income of these women was less than $2,000; 47 percent made less than $1,000 annually. Furthermore, 55 percent of all domestics were single heads of households; and 60 percent of these women were forty-five years of age and older.

McLaughlin believed that the role of domestics was ripe for change. Domestics, in the past, had worked mainly for middle-class families, generally on a weekly basis or, less frequently, for older, more affluent couples living in smaller quarters that demanded less attention. Workers had their "regulars" and, in many cases, formed deep attachments to the families of their clients. The pay was far from grand; and often, while it legally should have been, Social Security wasn't part of the package. The resale of gifts of cast-off clothing supplemented poor pay, or, if the size was right, furnished a wardrobe the worker couldn't have afforded.

It was hard work; but when economic push came to shove, domestics tended not to ask for a raise but to add one or more new customers. They trained their daughters, nieces, and younger sisters to take their places when physical infirmities or encroaching old age forced them to quit. When they "retired," they moved in with a son or daughter, providing that family with the services of a built-in babysitter.

McLaughlin guessed that the women's movement and affirmative action had probably slowed the supply of domestics down to a trickle. She knew that inflation and the boom of two-worker families, with more and more couples opting not to have children until later than they had in the past, opened up the way to change the nature of domestic work. There was less of a demand for personal involvement in the lives of the families served and more of a need for professional services to satisy "clients." She believed older former homemakers had an excellent chance to become self-employed as professional independent cleaning contractors.

In August of 1977, the Baltimore center began an Independent Cleaning Contractor Training Program to place a limited number of displaced homemakers into their own small businesses contracting for home cleaning. Diana McLaughlin was hired as full-time staff to head it up and was the one who devised most of the training program.

She reports that "after revisions, the training program now consists of 75 hours of classroom and on-the-job training conducted over a three-week period. The aim of this phase is to teach participants professional cleaning skills and basic business management." The course, which is entitled "The Realities of Owning a Business," covers topics such as planning, marketing, publicity, record-keeping, bookkeeping, contracting, and, most important, "learning to relate to clients not as a domestic, but as a home cleaning contractor." This proved early on to be one of the largest stumbling blocks; and McLaughlin says that led the center to include "workshops in assertiveness training, stress management, and public relations."

During the first three months following completion of training, ongoing support groups are held biweekly. Of the first two groups that completed the training, seven of twelve participants became self-employed. One now has an annual income of $25,000. She hired a public-relations person to get better coverage and open up new business prospects. Another took on a partner, hired one employee, and as a team quickly built up weekly service to forty clients. Her own weekly income rose to $425. Their average charge per house is $37.50.

Not that it's all been easy. There are still problems, but some of them serve to throw light on areas of injustice that need to be corrected. For example, some of the self-employed have found it difficult to get business insurance coverage—not just because they are women venturing into what has largely been perceived to be a "man's world" but because many insurance companies feel there is too little money in small businesses to bother serving them.

Although male displaced homemakers are relatively rare, the Baltimore center has had twelve go through their program, one of whom took advantage of the self-employment program. A middle-aged man who opted early in his marriage to quit his job as a florist's messenger in order to care for his disabled wife found himself, when she died, without a source of income and no record of recent paid experience. They had lived on her allotment furnished under the SSI (Supplemental Security Income) portion of the Social Security program. He had one special talent: He liked working with flowers, making floral designs, wreaths, etc. With assistance from the center, he is now self-employed and earning his living from what had once been a creative hobby.

Another example of turning often exploited talents to self-profit is described in the Summer 1979 issue of the Oakland center's newsletter:

> Agnes Durand, a gray-haired woman 60 years old, came to the Center in January of 1978. She was in a deep depression, convinced she would never be able to find any kind of employment. The Center, through its staff and the assistance of Barbara Milhous (then a peer contact and now on staff), helped Agnes create her job.

Barbara discovered that Agnes is an accomplished seamstress who made all her family's clothes. Here was a skill Agnes never thought marketable, but Barbara recognized its value and remembered her young friend, Paula Tobin.

Paula, a graduate of San Jose College with a degree in Textile Art and Design, often spoke about her dream of opening a special kind of shop. She wanted to help women design a wardrobe suited to their personality and way of living. Barbara introduced Paula to Agnes, and their partnership was born.

The two women took advantage of an opportunity to rent a small shop that became available on the Mills College campus; and six weeks later, "In Stitches" was in business.

The newsletter concludes:

> For both women, the shop is a dream-come-true. It is a partnership with each one working on her own job, a job created from her own resources to meet her own need.

Without the intervention and assistance of Milhous, Agnes may well have concluded her only option for paid employment was work as a seamstress, a low-paid job in the garment industry.

There has been a growing push to open up opportunities for more women-owned businesses. The federal Small Business Administration, under attack for its seeming resistance to helping women establish themselves as entrepreneurs, took a new approach in 1979. In May, President Carter issued an Executive Order, the full import of which may not have reached women who have long thought of going into business for themselves.

It directed each department and agency "of the Executive Branch, in a manner consistent with the law, to take appropriate affirmative action to facilitate, preserve, and strengthen women's business enterprise." Translated into action in one instance, it meant the Small Business Administration agreed to "establish a goal of $50 million in fiscal year 1980 for direct loans to women business owners and initiate a new mini-loan program for women needing less than $20,000 to start or expand a business."

Further, it agreed to encourage full participation of women in procurement activities by instructing SBA's Procurement Center Representatives to locate and assist women-owned businesses. Finally, it set a target to "try to add 15,000 women-owned firms" to its new Procurement Automated Source System by the end of the fiscal year.

The SBA was but one of at least sixteen departments or agencies that have developed new approaches to opening up a new market for women. Rona Feit, Executive Director of the newly created Interagency Committee on Women's Business Enterprise, and her staff have developed packets of information on the implementation of that Executive Order. It may not be the path for every displaced homemaker, but the signs are pointed in the right direction for those of us creative enough to take the risk.

There are success stories coming out of every displaced homemaker program now in existence. Some are more dramatic than others, but each in its own way proves that our homemaker skills can be turned to useful paid employment.

Holly Alexander, director of the Omaha YWCA displaced homemaker program, tells of two women who "used their parenting skills to get into two of the better entry jobs our people have found. One started as an assistant in a group home for the retarded, training residents in self-care and home skills. She's received further training and is now enrolled by her employer in a two-year human services program. Her job has built-in promotion ladders, and she's very happy with the work she's doing. Another woman does outreach and administers lead level tests to children to check for possible toxicity." Neither woman had ever worked outside their homes.

For those who enjoy working with children, utilizing our parenting skills is a natural route to paid work experience. Two older women among the early participants of the Los Angeles Displaced Homemakers center not only found financial and personal satisfaction in their first paid employment; they also contributed to a more effective job program for black youth. Although neither had more than a high-school education, their rich experience gained as mothers of black children and their natural talents turned them, with minimal training by the center staff, into paid staff of an area Youth Project—one as a job developer, the other as a counselor. Neither of these women would have been considered for the jobs if they had gone through existing channels of employment training.

One reported "success" story left Holly Alexander wondering who gained what. An ad in the Omaha paper called for "a companion, no housekeeping, $1,000 per month." As she says, "Most of us were skeptical, thinking it was a come-on or cover." However, one woman in the program, a fifty-three-year-old divorcee, decided to apply. She found the advertiser was a widowed businessman/rancher who needed an "executive secretary." She was hired, and Alexander reports, "Four months later they were married. A year later the marriage is still working, but as a wife she's also still doing bookkeeping and personal affairs management."

From the beginning we said that "at heart, the purpose of a displaced homemaker program—anywhere— should be to start an epidemic of creative excitement, energy, enthusiasm, so that anyone who enters feels the glow and leaves the despair at the doorstep." Where the concept of providing displaced homemakers a place of our own has been followed, the "glow" exists. There is a tangible warmth that literally can be felt. It is not created by sumptuous furnishings but rather by the rapport between the participants themselves and the level of concern and caring emanating from staff. Each center or program is unique, and yet one stands out in my mind as embodying all of the hope and the promise for new futures for older women coming from penurious pasts.

WISH, Women in Self-Help, is one of New York's state programs for displaced homemakers. It is located in Brooklyn, in the heart of an integrated blue-collar worker neighborhood. On my first visit to the center I almost missed it. The entrance is off a busy street, and it is two flights of stairs up to what had formerly been a factory loft. Two-thirds of the large room houses the "Brooklyn Women's Center for the Martial Arts." The front third has been partitioned off for the displaced homemaker program into small but adequate quarters for a common meeting room and two small offices. The walls are tastefully covered with cheerful posters, encouraging slogans, and photographs of groups of participants.

The program is funded by the New York Department of Labor and sponsored by the Sisters of the Good Shepherd. The founder and co-directors of the program are pledged not only to counsel and make job-ready the women who come to the center and support them once they are working but also "to help them organize, mobilize around common concerns . . . to politicize women around the issues of their potential power to push for the programs and funding that are needed to bring about necessary services."

Having read that, I naturally *had* to visit the center. I wondered about the women in the program and the staff. How radical were they? How political was their program? How successful were their efforts?

The day I arrived a group of seven was completing the last few weeks of a seven-week cycle of workshops and training. The women reflected the ethnic mix of the neighborhood, including black, Hispanic, Italian, and German women. Two were widows, two separated from their husbands, and three were divorced. All had a work history of underemployment; most were on welfare. The youngest was thirty-eight, the oldest fifty-nine.

Some, like Carmen, who came to this country from Puerto Rico with a fifth-grade education, had by painful effort tried to better their circumstances before turning to the center. Carmen, for example, studied English and received her GED (General Educational Development Test) while raising her children. When the last was grown, she enrolled in a community college and earned an A.A. degree in community service. She got a job after graduation but wound up the victim of age discrimination when she was fired and replaced by a younger woman. Because she had come so far on her own, the disappointment was traumatic. She became very depressed, especially when she had to apply again for welfare.

Estel Fonseca, a co-director of the program, herself a Puerto Rican, explained the special circumstances in Carmen's case. "Hispanic women are strong, but you have to remember the culture calls for male dominance. Carmen's drive to improve herself was not supported by her family and was resented and ridiculed by her husband from whom she was separated. It took a great deal of courage for her to push herself through the educational process. It also called for a great deal of self-sacrifice. While she was going to school, she was also working twenty hours part time at a day-care center and held a second part-time job as an office aide. She was supporting her children as well. When she lost that job, it was a real blow to her self-confidence."

Carol McVicker, Estel's partner, continued, "I think the thing that helped Carmen the most was the support of the other women. They helped her to see how really strong and motivated she is, and they also urged her to take credit for what she is capable of accomplishing. The generosity of these women to one another is almost unbelievable."

Carmen is now forty-six; and with the assistance of the center, she has a well-paying job in the New York Department of Human Resources as a bilingual caseworker in the Department of Social Services. Her current plans are to attend Brooklyn College at night to get her B.A. At last report, she's "still nervous about her age, but she loves her job."

Carmen's success has had its impact on other women in the group less certain about what they could, or wanted, to do.

Aurelia, a statuesque, soft-spoken forty-six-year-old woman from "a beautiful little island, St. Martin, in the French West Indies," twice divorced, mother of two teen-age sons, was uncertain about her future. But she was emphatic about one thing: "My ambition in life is to get off welfare and be independent."

After her first divorce, left with two small children, awarded no alimony and minimal child support, she applied for welfare. The judge had awarded her the house purchased early in her marriage; but it was badly in need of repairs, and she had no money to fix it up for possible income-making property.

Getting on welfare wasn't easy. In a recent letter to me she spelled out the difficulties the poor experience at the hand of the system. She couldn't take a job because she felt her place was with her young sons.

> As a Catholic, I went to the priest and explain my situation. He told me I need a lawyer. He sent me to Catholic Charity, and they referred me to Legal Aid. Legal Aid told me "we cannot take your case for you have property." I remember bursting into tears and said to the lawyer, "In this big city of New York, must me and my two children die?" He look at me and said, "I think I can do something." He wrote a letter, seal it up, and sent me to Social Services. They accepted my case when I signed over half of my property to welfare for their supplement.

Today, Aurelia has a part-time job and is working to get her GED. She is aiming at self-employment as an independent cleaning contractor, and the center is helping her work toward that goal. Of her center experience, Aurelia writes, "It gave me a brand-new lease on life"; and she adds:

> I need not tell you about Carol and Estel for you met them and all the beautiful people in the program. It is thrilling to see how hard they work with us to help us achieve our goal in life. It makes me feel I have to keep on for I won't just be letting myself down, but all the people who worked so hard and had so much faith in me.

Meeting Carol and Estel helped to change my own attitude toward the desirable age of program directors. I'm not as certain as I once was that only older women who have experienced the problem should head up these programs.

Carol McVicker, the older of the two women, is thirty-five. Deceptively fragile in appearance and almost painfully thin, she is a former educator who spent many years teaching remedial writing to older women, "99 percent of whom were Third World women." A good listener, she thoughtfully considers advice before giving any. She is extremely successful with shy, uncertain, or fearful program participants. As a feminist, she sees her role as one in which she "helps people become independent and realize their full potential."

Estel Fonseca is twenty-nine and brought to the program nine years of social work "in the field" but has no degree. She gravitated to the program because she realized her mother, "an incredible role model," had been a displaced homemaker. Her parents separated when Estel was three. More than Carol, Estel is politically oriented and has become a leader in the Hispanic community. Carol's quiet determination to have the program succeed is matched by Estel's bubbling enthusiasm for every woman's success. Together they have made some choices normally not considered by service deliverers of publicly funded programs. They have carefully nurtured their grant of $80,000, choosing to furnish the office from cast-off city equipment, built and installed partitions, and painted the premises themselves. This brought their entire repair and maintenance costs to $507.46. They could have hired additional paid staff but sought out social-work interns from Hunter College and applied the savings to the pool of stipends available for program participants. They each earn the same minimum salary.

The political motivation of the women was not evident that first trip. But I later learned of a good example of their desire to act in their own behalf. When Governor Carey cut the funding for all state displaced homemaker programs from the budget, WISH participants rallied to a call for a one day-lobbying trip to Albany. They filled a chartered bus and after a brief enroute training session on lobbying, each woman was assigned to keep prearranged appointments with individual legislators. "In less than four hours," Carol and Estel told me, "we got the displaced homemaker story to every legislator." The concerted effort of the first time "lobbyists" bore fruit several months later when the legislature voted to refund the programs. WISH and three other New York programs also won new funds through the distribution of federal monies from the national displaced homemaker program in CETA.

WISH is neither typical nor atypical of displaced homemaker programs, but it and others prove conclusively that the displaced homemaker legislation was not a "white, middle-class woman's bill" and, perhaps more important, that the "older poor" need not be locked into the welfare system.

Two of the most difficult tasks that face us as displaced homemakers is how to gain a clearer, stronger sense of self with established short- and long-range goals and then how to plot training to make it possible to reach those goals. It might be useful to share descriptions of techniques which came out of the experience of the two earliest centers and worked exceptionally well.

The Life Focus was developed by Aliyah Stein (an educational psychologist, counselor, and one of the original Oakland Displaced Homemaker Center staff) and Tish Sommers. It is described by Stein* as being "of particular value in helping individuals gain a clearer recognition and overview of their strengths, personality resources, capacities, and potentialities" and, therefore, a stronger sense of self. It calls for a group setting and was first employed by Stein and Sommers, working as a team, with the initial groups of selected trainees in the Oakland program.

Before beginning, a large blackboard is divided into headings of the four steps of the Life Focus experience.

STEP 1: THINGS TO BUILD ON

All those wishing to participate are asked to write their names on a slip of paper, which is then placed in

* "Program for the Development of Self-Esteem in the Displaced Homemaker"—an unpublished manuscript by Aliyah Stein.

a box or hat from which the "focus person" is selected. The facilitator then asks the focus person to share with the group key experiences or incidents in her life to help the group know her, what is important to her, what interests her, how she likes to spend her time, the nature of any paid or volunteer work she has done. The key statements from her description are put on the blackboard under the heading of "Things to Build On." These statements should reveal personality strengths (e.g., coping skills) or abilities (e.g., loves reading and doing research). For each life focus, another member of the group is asked to copy down all of the data on the blackboard; and these notes are given to the focus person for her reference and later support.

The first step generally takes about fifteen or twenty minutes. Some women have to be urged to summarize; others feel so poorly about themselves they feel they have nothing to say. A good facilitator or team will then prompt her with questions—e.g., How many children do you have? What were your favorite activities when raising them? Did you help your husband with his business?

STEP 2: STRENGTH ACKNOWLEDGMENT

When the focus person concludes sharing her experiences, she then turns to the group and asks what strengths or potentials they see in what she has revealed.

Group members share their perceptions of the focus person; and as each strength is mentioned, it is written on the board under the proper heading. This serves a double function of building self-confidence in the focus person. She not only hears her strengths enumerated;

she sees them recorded on the board. Members are asked to address their comments directly to the focus person. It is important to encourage participants to point out any behavioral or other clues connected with a perception of strength. Instead of saying, "Maureen, you have a lot of courage," Stein believes it should be spelled out. "Maureen, you stood up for your rights when going through the divorce. That took a lot of courage. I feel this is one of your greatest strengths."

As Stein and Sommers discovered, each step of the Life Focus can be emotionally both exhilarating and draining for all involved. The strength step, in particular, elicits a great deal "of caring support from the group for the selected member. The individual is often overwhelmed and very moved." It is a most effective bonding tool for any group beginning to move through a new program. (More than half of the fourteen center trainees who began this way in 1976 are still close friends and meet periodically for social events and to exchange notes on their progress in their jobs.)

STEP 3: BLOCKS TO STRENGTH

This step was originally called "lemons" on the theory that lemons (weaknesses) can be squeezed to make lemonade. Here the focus person herself begins by identifying what she sees as her "blocks" or "lemons" because, as Stein discovered, use of those terms helped to keep the participants' reflections constructive. Facing the blocks to strength is an essential part of helping a person identify and develop strengths and potentialities.

When she finishes, the focus person again invites the group to participate, thereby encouraging a conscious decision to ask for help rather than being a passive recipient of their comments; and it teaches other members restraint—that one doesn't immediately leap in and take the responsibility for solving another's problem.

STEP 4: JOBS

As originally developed, this last step evolved from correlating strengths, interests, and personal traits which could be built upon for new careers in fields participants had expressed some desire to enter. For example, one of the first center trainees, a fifty-nine-year-old woman, Margaret Harralson, had a burning wish to "help older women like me so they won't have to get ripped off in a divorce as I was." She was too old to go through law school, and she thought nothing in her life experience (she had been a professional dancer) offered any hope to reach her goal. One of the group thoughtfully examined the first column of things to build on. She pointed out that dancing called for great discipline and concentration; and if Margaret had been able to do that so well, why couldn't she do the research and teach herself all she had to know to be a paralegal aide? With help from the center staff, Margaret did precisely that and today is employed not as a paralegal aide but as an attorney's assistant, specializing in divorce counseling.

The Life Focus takes one to two hours per person, and it is most effective if sensory awareness or relaxation exercises are done between presentations. Originally conceived as a tool to help identify skills that might be turned into marketable talents, Life Focus can also be used as a method to enhance self-awareness, which for most displaced homemakers is more than half the battle.

Risking the ire of the professionals who might see the need for a background of training, I think readers who are displaced homemakers might like to try out the method, using friends or family for your support group while you and they assess new ways to put your skills or natural talents to work.

Having found our focus, how do we get trained for the job of our dreams? Joyce Keating, who helped develop and refine the job-training program for the Baltimore Center for Displaced Homemakers, describes the process that evolved from their experience.

From the beginning, Keating established requirements for training: "emotional stability" as determined by the participant's counselor; "direction," meaning that some choice of career or job goals has been arrived at; and "completion of Career Path," a month-long series of workshops dealing with self-evaluation, coping skills, and job preparation.

HOW WE DO IT IN BALTIMORE

"Once a participant completes the Career Path and determines with her counselor that training is the next step in her Plan of Action, an appointment is made to meet with a member of the Training Department. These first training meetings are attended by the displaced homemaker, her counselor, and a training representative. It has been determined through trial and error that the counselor is needed to bring out particular facts about the participant's skills and work history that might not be mentioned by the participant herself.

"At the conclusion of the first training meeting, assignments are made for both the participant and the training representative in order to carry out the plan. About two or three weeks of assignments are set out on the plan at this meeting. Examples of these might be:

1. Ms. J. (the participant) will call the Community College to determine the cost and schedule of a Psychology of Aging or Recreation for Seniors course.

2. The training representative will make an appointment with the Physical Fitness Director at the Senior Citizens Center.

"A general plan of events is developed for the remaining weeks of the exploration period. The participant receives a copy of the entire plan. She is requested to call her training department representative weekly. This telephone contact will be their checkpoint to: determine whether the week's plan has been carried out, what feelings the participant has in response to new information or employer visits, confirm assignments, or establish a new plan for the following week.

"The purpose of training exploration is to:

1. Help the participant make an appropriate decision.

2. Have her explore more than one possibility for her own training.

"After the first training meeting the participant often feels overwhelmed by the number of options she actually has. We have found that displaced homemakers coming to our center have a very narrow view of the job world. They are trying to make a choice from among the set of jobs they knew were available to them twenty to twenty-five years ago. The training exploration period is an important tool in helping expose the displaced homemaker to her real options.

"We try to arrange at least two and no more than three employer visits with possible on-the-job training providers. The employer, the participant, and the training representative discuss the kind of training to be provided, what a trainee's duties might be, what kind of supervision there would be, and the possibilities for employment at the business or agency or elsewhere.

"We have found that after more than three employer visits, confusion sets in for the participant. After some weeks of training exploration and discussion with the training department representative, a decision is made about the type of training that will be undertaken. The decision seems to come about naturally once the participant is exposed to real places which provide on-the-job training. Other factors that hasten a decision might be a course starting date or the need for income that a stipend would provide.

"It is perfectly understandable for a displaced homemaker to take an internship because she needs recent work experience and an income right now. Even though she may acquire no new skills, she may brush up on old ones, gain a current reference and, perhaps most importantly, time to breathe easier without the panic about her lack of income. Often that is the first thing needed in order for a displaced homemaker to determine a long-range plan in which new skill training or the pursuit of a college degree might be included.

"Other displaced homemakers really desire training in a particular field or a particular skill. For example,

one person wanted to sell real estate. The center paid
for a real estate course for her. In addition, on-the-job
training was arranged at a community housing aid
center where she was a home-ownership counselor.
When she sold her first condominium, she knew that
her life had taken a turn for the better and that she
was in control of her life.

"Medical records has been an attractive field for
displaced homemakers at our center. It is one of the
few jobs for which training is still carried out at a
hospital. In addition, opportunities for advancement to
supervisor are available within a reasonable time
period. Almost as appealing is the fact that an
Accredited Records Technician certificate can be
obtained through a correspondence course. Finally, the
center has made an excellent contact with the
employment manager of one of the hospitals. Since our
first trainee was such an impressive success, the
Personnel Director has been very eager to work with us
and to provide training for displaced homemakers in
medical records.

"Perhaps explaining how that original trainee's
contract was negotiated will throw light on the
negotiation process. Prior to the meeting, the employer
was informed that a job description or a description of
the specific tasks the displaced homemaker would be
trained to do must be prepared. At the contract-writing
session the job description is read. The employer is
asked to recommend a time period in which the skills
recorded on the description can be obtained. The
employer has been informed that the maximum length
of training can be six months. Generally a trainee
works twenty-five hours per week. For the medical

records training, the supervisor who was present with
the personnel manager indicated that four months
would be sufficient time for a displaced homemaker to
become used to the routine of work and learn some
new skills. The trainee wanted to work only three days
a week. She planned also to take a brush-up typing
course at night, and she wanted some mornings to rest.
This was acceptable to the employer and training
supervisor. The dates of training and the hours of work
were recorded in the contract. The job description was
attached. The trainee, the employer representative, and
the training director signed the contract; and the
training began within a few days.

"Contract negotiation is normally a very simple
matter. It is understood from the first contact with an
employer that the training will be arranged with the
utmost flexibility to suit the needs of both parties. Most
employers agree with the time schedule suggested by
the trainee. In some cases employers have indicated
they preferred a certain number of hours be worked
hard each week, but have been flexible about starting
and leaving times. The framework is usually described
before the negotiation. The employer understands the
maximum hours and duration. Sometimes because of
limited funds, we must negotiate contracts for shorter
periods than employers suggest. Other times we suggest
longer training periods to allow a particular displaced
homemaker enough time to adjust to a new schedule,
become accustomed to the electric typewriter or the
multiline telephone, and learn to be assertive and ask
for more challenging assignments. If job descriptions
are not detailed, we ask that they be rewritten; but the
trainee starts work as soon as possible. The job

description is used for evaluating the training and performance.

"Evaluation conference dates are also recorded on the training contract at the time of negotiation. The evaluation conference is attended by the trainee, the supervisor, and the training department representative. The first conference is held usually one month after training has begun at the training site. At this time, if there is some dissatisfaction or problem it can probably be redressed without much disturbance to the trainee or employer. If the first evaluation occurs later than one month, and there has been a problem, the trainee's self-confidence is undermined and the employer develops a distaste for the entire program! It has been our experience that if a negative relationship exists between the trainee and the supervisor, the training should end with that employer and another training situation should be developed.

"Two conferences are usually held at the site during a training period and a final written evaluation is requested. At the conference, if there are no problems, the job duties are discussed. The center representative determines whether in fact the trainee is learning all the skills recorded in the description. The supervisor gives the trainee a progress report, or evaluation of her work and work habits so far. The trainee also shares a written evaluation she has prepared. She comments on which duties she enjoys most and least, what she'd like to learn to do next or better, and what her supervisor and the center can do to help her. The exchange is usually very honest, supportive, and rewarding. Although the trainee undoubtedly faces the meeting with trepidation, she comes away with a feeling that she can indeed learn something new and get complimented for doing well. She also learns where she needs to devote her attention during the next month or so until the next evaluation. During a training period all interns and trainees return to the center on Fridays for the Intern Lunch.

"At this time they share their feelings about returning to a work setting and learning new skills. They also pick up their stipend check. Usually discussion revolves around predetermined issues such as: co-worker–supervisor relations; the value of evaluations; how to get a good reference; the effects of the trainee's changes on her family; and the job hunt.

"During a training period, the trainee is encouraged to seek permanent employment. The employer-training provider understands that the trainee can be allowed up to five hours per week away from the training site for job interviews or résumé-writing workshops or other workshops that would be helpful in the job search. The trainee receives a stipend for these hours as well. She is also advised to clear it with her supervisor before arranging to attend a workshop or to provide the supervisor with a few days' notice before a job interview appointment.

"In many cases, the trainee is hired by the employer with whom she is training. This occurs even at times when an employer has never indicated that a job might become available. We believe the displaced homemaker has become such a necessary part of the work force that she will be missed if she is not hired. At other times the employer may have known that an opening was coming up but did not want to promise anything. From the outset there is no pressure to guarantee employment of the displaced homemaker trainee. The employer is asked to provide a reference. For the displaced homemaker, she has her work experience in 1978. Of course, we prefer to develop training positions where the possibility of employment exists."

The Baltimore center did a follow-up project after their training plan had been in operation for a year. The study revealed that eighty-five displaced homemakers had been under contract for training between December 1976–January 1977. Keating reports:

> Because some of the participants received on-the-job training as well as courses of one kind or another (GED, driver's training, etc.) 117 training contracts were written up in that first year. Of those, 61 were for on-the-job training and 56 were for courses. The rate of placement was over 60%; but if the students who are included in that rate are excluded, the placement rate jumps to 70%.

How about cost if participants are eligible for stipends during training? Keating says:

> The amount of money that we can spend on a particular participant is determined by the use of a family-size income scale. This makes an individual (that is, a family of one) eligible for the maximum ($1,625) if her income is less than $6,999. Most displaced homemakers coming to the Baltimore Center have dependents and incomes far lower than $6,999, so most participants are eligible for the maximum grant. However, because the training needs vary, our average cost of training per participant works out to $600 or less.

All of this action on the state level encouraged us to press enactment of the national legislation. Not just to open up federally funded job-training programs for middle-aged and older former homemakers but to focus attention on our special needs. To make Congress and federal agencies more aware of those of us who fall through the cracks of all social programs. To bring older former homemakers out of the shadows of a youth-oriented society. To force recognition of the contribution homemakers make and have made to society.

We didn't think it would be easy, but neither were we prepared for the level of age discrimination and rampant sexism that compounded the rough-and-tumble game of politics as it's played in our nation's capital.

CHAPTER FOUR

Where There's a Bill There's a Way

By anyone's yardstick, the measure that became known in Washington as the Displaced Homemakers Act should have languished and died in committee. It was not considered "major" legislation by anyone, except perhaps by those of us who knew the need. It was immediately tagged as a bill to aid "a categorical group," bad news to penny-pinching Congressional converts to the politics of austerity; and it was a "woman's issue." The best guarantee of any bill's success lies with its sponsor. The most promising sponsor is one who sits on the committee that will consider the measure. Neither of the prime sponsors of the House and Senate displaced homemaker bills sat on the committees to which they were assigned.

The intent of the bills, establishing federally funded pilot projects that would experiment with creating paid jobs in the public and private sectors which would utilize our skills as older former homemakers, was never understood or deliberately rejected. The same Congress that had approved an $82.2 million, five-year job-training experiment for high-school dropouts, drug addicts, ex-offenders, and mothers on Aid to Families with Dependent Children questioned the social need to help women whose age alone made the transition to decent self-sufficiency difficult, if not impossible. One long-time observer of the Washington scene waggishly suggested that it wasn't just the absence of any statistics on our numbers that made Congress blind to our needs.

"You little old ladies just don't figure in the crime statistics. Congress isn't here to change society, just to protect it; and, of course, to get re-elected."

But he also predicted that if we kept up the push from "home," we "just might pull it off. You won't get everything you want, but you'll get something."

For many of us older women, brought up to believe participatory democracy turns the wheels of government, "politics" is a dirty word. In our minds, it's a game played by ward heelers in smoke-filled back rooms. We know there are times when the odd "rascal" will be voted into office; but on the whole, we faithfully go to the polls, trusting that the man—seldom the woman—we give our vote to can be depended on to represent and serve us, his constituents, honorably and well. The dependency role we accepted in our homes is extended through the ballot box to the House, Senate, and Oval office.

Despite Vietnam, Watergate, and Koreagate, we have, for the most part, clung to our battered beliefs; we are not among those who are voting today with their feet as they turn from the voting booths. As older women, though, whose votes will be increasingly wooed with ardor, we must now learn to cut through campaign hyperbole, examine candidates' records, and vote as men have long voted—in our own best interests.

We also need to understand that Senators may be no less wise and members of the House no less representative of their constituencies than their counterparts were when our civics books were written but that the arena in which they all operate is vastly different from what it was thirty or forty years ago.

Columnist Jack Anderson has written extensively about the increased power of "special-interest moneymen," lobbyists, "who traffic in favors and in return provide political donations and re-election campaign workers." No doubt they were present in earlier years but not in the numbers today. According to Anderson, "An estimated 15,000 lobbyists prowl the Capitol's corridors and lobbies in behalf of their clients."

Within Congressional offices on the Hill, "players" of the political game are no longer confined to those persons we vote into office. Staff no longer sit on the bench or serve as "go-fers"; they're part of the team, and in many cases they call the signals.

Part of this arises from the growing complexity of governing. The burgeoning of issues translates into calls for legislative action. It is next to impossible to demand that every member of Congress today be totally knowledgeable on every measure when some 25,000 bills are introduced in each session. Most never make it beyond being recorded in the *Congressional Record;* but the 95th Congress, for example, when it adjourned October 15, 1978, had recorded 2,691 votes as it considered 23,942 bills and resolutions. What can't be mastered by one elected member of Congress can be maneuvered by powerful lobbies or directed by knowledgeable staff.

Energetic, ambitious, and hard-working staff who take the time to bone up on complicated subjects develop a reputation for expertise in given areas and provide invaluable assistance to those they serve. Such attention to detail and specialization is also self-serving. In election upsets it is not uncommon for staff of the defeated member to turn up working for the newly elected, often without regard for party affiliation.

Our elected officials have always been served by staff, but never by so many nor have they been so well paid. In fiscal 1978 the Senate, for example, employed 7,000 aides and/or consultants at a cost of $51.3 million. Senators, who hiked their own pay from $44,600 in 1977 to $57,500 today, have 64 aides earning $50,000 or more and another 331 who make more than $40,000. Members of the House of Representatives are alotted 18 staffers each and have $228,000 a year for salaries. The size of a member's staff and the salary level is up to the member, hence there is a variance in pay for presumably the same job description on the House side. It employs 11,000 people, but in general Senate staff are better paid.

Besides developing special areas of expertise, what are the duties of staff? They act as buffers, often determining who gets to talk to the legislator and for how long. They often answer mail which may or may not be seen by the member to whom it is addressed. They draft form-letter replies which are fed into computers and signed with an automatic pen that duplicates the member's signature. For legislators assigned to multiple committees, subcommittees, or joint committees, staff provide detailed knowledge. Staff organize all hearings and frequently select witnesses. They supply committee members with a list of questions to be asked of witnesses; and they write up the final committee reports, including those that resolve differences between Senate and House versions of any bill.

In short, staff are people with power. Is this bad? A former Senate legislative aide, Michael Andrew Scully, in an article written for the *Washington Post,* said of the growth of the Senate staff:

> ... the real significance of the growth of staff is probably unrelated to any particular staff function, healthy or abusive. The real question is not "who runs the Senate" but rather which group, the elected or the unelected, dominates the operations—Senators by being elected or staff by being so numerous. If the authority were to shift, ever so slowly, from the elected to the unelected, from the principals to their seconds, that would be the most newsworthy event of all—and the most difficult to discern.

A chilling prospect, perhaps even more so than the rise in the power of lobbyists, who are at least visible. Without assuming the worst will happen (or has happened), it can be said that the system that prevails on the Hill in Washington today is not the system we studied nor is it as taught even in today's political science and American government courses.

It can also be said that our Displaced Homemakers Act wound its way through the meat grinder of Congressional committees with and without the aid of staff and, in some cases, in spite of staff; but it took a push from "home" to get it started.

Letters had been streaming in to Representative Augustus Hawkins, Chair of the House subcommittee to which the bill had been assigned, urging that he set dates for hearings. How many of the letters he actually saw is unknown; that they found their way to the staff of the subcommittee *is* known. There they sat, mounting evidence of increasing interest in the issue; but they prompted no move to set hearing dates.

Late in 1976 Hawkins heard from a constituent with a great deal of political savvy. The late Hallie Tenner (a staunch advocate of women's rights who died at far too young an age) was then a member of the Los Angeles Commission on the Status of Women. When a state bill that would have set up a second California pilot program failed to pass that year (it did in 1977), Tenner moved on the national measure. Shrewdly, she pulled together a Los Angeles Ad Hoc Committee, made up of women's business and professional organizations, women from community groups, and voluntary organizations—all from Southern California, most from Hawkins' own district.

In response to Tenner's request, Hawkins agreed to interrupt his cross-country hearings on the Full Employment Act, a measure he had been fighting to get enacted long before it became known as the Humphrey-Hawkins bill, HR 50, and hold a half-day field hearing in Los Angeles on Burke's bill, HR 10272. Tish and I were among eleven invited to prepare a statement and testify. We asked to bring along two women from the new Oakland center, assuming that the committee would be very interested in how that first pilot project was faring.

Our decision to take an early-morning flight down on the day of the hearing was prompted by the frugality a lean purse dictates. It saved a hotel bill. Months later when the printed report of the hearing was available, we found our frugality had been costly.

We had been scheduled to testify immediately after Mrs. Burke. As the report indicates, we would have been in a position to deal firmly with two charges that came up in the committee members' opening exchange with Mrs. Burke—charges that dogged the life of the bill from that day forward: that it was "a white middle-class woman's bill" and that "the older woman would *probably* need the assistance of the bill but that the bill obviously covers a substantial number of women." We had earlier heard the latter charge in exactly those words from senior staff. This time it was Chairman Hawkins who made staff thinking part of the official record. How little he knew of the actual intent of the bill seemed implicit in his comment to Mrs. Burke, "I know that one of the first attempts will be made to narrow the bill so that a much smaller group would be included."

His colleague, William "Bill" Clay, a black Representative from St. Louis, raised the color and class issue questioning Mrs. Burke, prefacing his remarks by saying he was a supporter and a co-sponsor of the bill. "How do you answer the critics of the bill who say it is primarily a white middle-class woman's bill?"

Burke's answer was adequate but abstract. Willy James, the black woman trainee from the Oakland center who was to testify later, provided a better response drawn from personal experience:

> My name is Willy James, and I am forty-nine years old. I have been single for a few years, and three of my four children are grown. My youngest is nineteen and

no longer eligible for support. I hadn't worked in eighteen years, and I had no recent job experience that would qualify me for a job.

Neither the Chair nor Mr. Clay asked any questions of either of the two participants from the Oakland center, the only ones in the room with "hands on" experience on the subject of the hearing. Perhaps they would have if we'd arrived on time. Unfortunately, our flight from Oakland was delayed by fog for three hours. We skidded into the hearing room just before the last scheduled witness was to speak. Although the report indicates age had been discussed at length with earlier witnesses, it was not pursued by either man during the brief questioning that followed our testimony.

The year 1977 was chaotic. As we pushed toward our goals to get Burke to file a better bill, to get hearings in the House in D.C., to get the first hearing in the Senate, to continue to build grassroots support, to try to hang onto the age focus, and to broaden awareness of the issue and win over other committee members by helping other states enact bills, there were times when I felt it was like pegging down a beach blanket with toothpicks in a bad windstorm. No sooner was one "corner" considered secured when a fresh blast blew it loose again.

The good news was that we were growing in numbers; members of Congress other than those on the committee were beginning to learn of the term and the issue with letters from back "home." The list of cosponsors of Burke's bill in the House began to lengthen. In October of the year before, Tish and I were invited to appear on the Phil Donahue TV show. The response within the first month added another 3,000 supporters to the cause.

Staff on the House side seemed to be mellowing, especially so when we later took their suggestion to change the legislation and offer the basics of the Burke bill as an amendment to existing legislation on federal job programs.

The Comprehensive Employment Training Act, more commonly known as CETA, was due to be reauthorized. One section of that act contained provisions for serving those considered "economically disadvantaged" for special reasons. Migratory workers and Native Americans were among the groups targeted. It seemed the right place for pilot project programs for displaced homemakers.

Jimmy Carter's election to the Presidency gave us reason to hope we'd have the new Administration's support. We had polled all the Presidential candidates during their campaigns and asked each if they would support the displaced homemaker legislation if elected. Gerald Ford's answer was flat and final: "No." Carter not only said he would support us, but his added remarks suggested he understood the issue. "Displaced homemakers are among the most vulnerable members of our society. A compassionate government would give attention to their needs."

We printed and distributed thousands of those statements as a political consciousness raiser. Since we viewed the issue as being nonpartisan, we were equally quick to acknowledge the wholehearted support later given the bill by Mary Crisp, co-Chair of the Republican National Committee, and by the members of the minority in both the Senate and the House who favored it as co-sponsors.

We took it as a good omen when we received a call from Midge Costanza's office in the White House. Costanza, then President Carter's "assistant for public liaison," had begun her daily series of meetings with groups from all over the country. The Alliance for Displaced Homemakers was invited to have a session with her in the White House. We said we'd think it over. On the one hand, the trip would be at our expense; and there was no point in going simply to add another name to Costanza's guest list. On the other hand, as I pointed out to Tish, "It might well be worth it if we can request and ask through Costanza for the Administration's support. Especially with the Senate."

We checked with other displaced homemaker activists and found they, too, thought it worth doing if we had some input in the agenda. Several of them said they'd borrow the money to go and tell their own stories for Costanza to pass along.

In the end we all went, assured by Costanza's staff that not only would the displaced homemakers' stories be heard, but Tish and I would have time on the agenda to put our case for the legislation to Costanza. We arrived with prepared press packets. Along with copies of the bill and fact sheets, we included the flyer we had distributed on Carter's pre-election statement of support. We gave them to the gathered press as we awaited Costanza's delayed arrival.

Following a warm welcome, Costanza invited the women to share their experiences with her. When they finished, we thought we were to follow with our prepared statements. It didn't quite work out that way. After the women spoke, Costanza rose to say a few words. What she offered was some advice to make use of all the programs available, "especially centers that already exist." She cited as an example a center one of her assistants had helped to found in Brooklyn. We waited for her to conclude so that we could reiterate what the women themselves had just told her—there were no programs or centers, other than the few created by state bills, that dealt realistically with job training and placement of older women.

We never got the chance. She announced she would conclude her remarks with a special message from the President. Then, as though hot off the typewriter, she read, word for word, the statement Carter made at Sea Island, Georgia, July 12, 1976. Our twenty-minute meeting was over. She was, she explained, "running behind schedule," which, of course, was the reason her assistant offered for the fouled-up agenda. It may even have been true.

The year 1977 started off to be promising. Largely because of the efforts of Yvonne Burke's capable and supportive staff, an amended measure was ready for her to file opening day of the first session of the 95th Congress. A few weeks later Indiana Senator Birch Bayh filed an identical bill, and for the first time the legislation came close to meeting our requests. The bills called for the establishment of a minimum of fifty multipurpose service centers for displaced homemakers to provide job counseling, training, and placement; health education and counseling; financial management services; educational services; legal counsel and/or referral. The services were not to duplicate existing services;

the centers, instead, were to coordinate community resources available to displaced homemakers. The bills called for appropriations of $10 million for fiscal 1978 and $15 million for 1979.

Burke added a twist to funding that later had some unfavorable impact on new state bills. Within the appropriations section, she called for the centers to receive 90 percent of their funds from federal money and 10 percent matching funds from the state. In 1977, some twenty-eight states filed displaced homemaker legislation; sixteen were enacted, but of that number few offered state funding other than the percentage due should the national bill be enacted. Montana's legislature, for example, was even more specifically restrictive. It enacted a bill calling for the establishment of an urban and a rural pilot project, funded for $300,000. The amount of state money they approved was $30,000 and mandated that it be advanced only if the federal monies were obtained.

We felt better about the definition of a displaced homemaker over which we had sweat blood working for agreement with House staff. A displaced homemaker was defined as an individual who:

1. has worked in the home for a substantial number of years providing unpaid household service for family members;

2. is not gainfully employed;

3. has had, or would have, difficulty in securing employment; and

4. has been dependent on the income of another family member but is no longer eligible for such assistance, or is supported as the parent of minor children by gov-

ernment assistance or spousal support but whose children are within two years of reaching their maturity.

We would have preferred specifying an age (most
state bills said "35 years of age or older"), but we were
assured the phrase "substantial number of years" would
cover our desire to help older former homemakers. Ambiguous language, we were told, would be worked out
when the administering agency developed the regulations and guidelines for implementing Congressional
intention when the measure was enacted. The outlook
in the House began to look much brighter. There were
hints we could expect dates to be set for a Washington
hearing, especially if agreement could be reached for
Burke to resubmit the provisions of her bill as an
amendment to CETA.

From time to time during our experience in Washington we received unsigned typed notes or copies of
memoranda pertinent to the legislation. We never knew
the source and jokingly referred to whomever our obviously friendly supporter was as "Brown Throat" since
all the communications arrived in plain brown enve-
lopes. That is how we learned that, among other things,
the use of the term "centers" was sending cost-con-
scious legislators up the wall. To them that meant the
construction or purchase of buildings. To us it simply
meant a place of our own—a room within a YWCA, an
available cottage on the grounds of a college in
Oakland, an old townhouse in Baltimore.

Shortly after getting Representative Burke's promise
to change her bill, we heard again from Brown Throat.
We were warned to keep a sharp eye on the age focus—
told it was still not popular with senior staff, especially

on the Senate side. The effort in the Senate would be to "mainstream," provide a program that would throw older women into competition with younger women. That report was confirmed when the stern-faced chief of the Senate subcommittee chaired by Senator Gaylord Nelson personally told me, "There is no way you are going to exclude younger women *if* you ever get the bill passed."

Why were staffers, mostly young men, continuing to miss the point? It was *not* our desire to "exclude younger women"; the point was to design a program that would meet our special needs as women who had been out of the job market for perhaps twenty or thirty years or who had for the same time been continually underemployed older women who had been excluded from job-training programs in the past.

However, it wasn't only Congressional staff who failed to see the purpose of the legislation. At least one leading feminist refused to endorse the measure "because it discriminates against younger women." Another advocate of women's issues argued that white older women didn't need the bill as much as young minority women, thereby helping to promote the misconception that the bill was "a white middle-class woman's" bill. *"Age,"* we screamed back, "not race, creed or color or class!" and we were heartened by the thousands of our "honorary older women," young women who did understand and who fully supported our position.

Brown Throat reminded us that we couldn't count on Congress to add displaced homemakers as a category of "economically disadvantaged" to the new CETA legislation if the Administration failed to do so when it sent its version of the reauthorized measure to the Hill. We immediately began a letter-writing campaign to the President and Mrs. Carter and to the new Secretary of Labor, Ray Marshall, and Ernest Green, the head of the Employment Training Agency.

The Administration's bill did add displaced homemakers for the first time to the "laundry list" of those to be served by the public jobs bill, but it stopped short of recommending service under any one title of the Act. That, we were told by a high-level source in the White House, was "considered the prerogative of Congress." All it did, as a senior Senate subcommittee staffer pointedly reminded us, was "give the Secretary an authorization to serve displaced homemakers; it doesn't say he has to if other groups have priority on existing funds." We were back at the foot of the mountain feeling more and more of a Sisyphean despair of ever being able to push our bill of stone up and over the Hill!

Then we got word that Representative Hawkins was setting the date for a half-day hearing in D.C. It was to be July 14. I thought it was fitting for us to bring our quiet little "revolution" to the nation's capital on Bastille Day, though I was certain the coincidence had eluded the scheduler's mind. We were asked to supply names of likely witnesses and firmly advised not to include our own.

"There should be new voices heard; the committee doesn't like to keep seeing the same old faces."

I was surprised that the five minutes each of Tish's and my testimony at a field hearing a year ago, involving just two members of the committee, constituted overexposure, and argued the point. We were, after all, the only people at that point who knew the overall national picture; the committee was interested in learning about that, weren't they?

We worked out a compromise. I would be invited by Hawkins to join the first panel and "serve as a resource person."

In point of fact, as it proceeded it was clear that all the hearing was supposed to put on record was the author's intent to switch the program, with committee approval, to the CETA program under the Department of Labor.

The witnesses we recommended were accepted and invited. The first panel included two state legislators, Nancie Fadeley and Steve Waldron, prime sponsors of displaced homemaker bills in Oregon and Montana. I had been particularly anxious to have Steve on the panel, reasoning that an all-male committee needed to know the issue was one men endorsed. The second panel, Cynthia Marano (the director of the Baltimore center) and two displaced homemaker trainees (one from Baltimore and one from Oakland), put testimony on record from women who were displaced homemakers and, at long last, from someone with "hands on" experience in implementing these new programs.

That hearing taught us many things. We learned it is not unusual but rather par for the course to have hearings conducted by just the Chair and one other member of the committee. Nor was it unusual for other members to come in late, ask a question for the record, and leave early. That whether the bill being considered is thought of as major or minor legislation dictates who and how many members will make an effort to attend. Two suggestions were offered by friendly staff "guaranteed to fill those empty chairs up there: have a witness from the district of each member or get the TV networks to cover the event." We found out that staff and legal counsel nearly always attended hearings, suggesting that absent members frequently vote a measure up or down on advice of staff who may or may not always view the issue dispassionately or objectively.

With the House formally committed to considering programs for displaced homemakers under Title III of CETA, we had a breather and could turn our full attention to the Senate, where no action had taken place since the filing of the first bill. The House action had strengthened our case for pleading for a hearing. The impression we had gotten in our earlier contacts was that neither the issue nor the bill counted for much in the Senate.

Outside the hallowed halls of the elected, there had been no voiced opposition to our legislation. The only so-called enemies we, as displaced homemakers, had were apathy, indifference, and ignorance. True, there had been small flurries of opposition to some state bills raised by right-wing, anti-feminist factions. That had surprised me because I felt displaced homemakers by definition would be those of us whose cause conservatives would understand and support. Who were we but the believers in the traditional role of women? Wasn't it better to provide an assist to get us back on the roll of taxpayers rather than have us by default wind up on welfare? The strong and conservatively oriented National Council of Catholic Women appeared to understand as they voted support of the Displaced Homemaker legislation even though at the same convention they voted to oppose passage of the ERA. In fact, I sincerely believed that if ever there was an opportunity to share a platform, or even a cup of coffee, with Phyllis Schlafly herself, the two of us could find common ground and merge our efforts on this issue.

But in August of 1977 Mrs. Schlafly dashed any hope of that. In her newsletter *Eagle Forum,* she fired her blunderbuss of bile at what she perceived to be yet another feminist conspiracy. She spelled out to her followers four reasons why the national displaced homemaker legislation should not be enacted. Three of them reflected an ultraconservative position against any government-funded programs of social service—opinions she was entitled to hold although we did not share them. But her fourth reason could only make sense to those who slip from the periphery of paranoia into the depths of senseless hatred.

"Such centers," she wrote, "which are already in existence, are nothing but indoctrination and training centers for women's lib. The feminists who run such centers use them to push ERA, abortion, federal child care, lesbian privileges, etc. Now they want to do this at the taxpayer's expense."

At first I ignored it. "Consider the source," my mother always said. Nor was I overly concerned by the fact that she had ordered her followers to write letters of protest to the members of Hawkins' subcommittee. The hearing, after all, had been concluded. But the campaign resulted in subcommittee staff including fourteen letters in the hearing report even though they arrived well past the deadline for acceptance. That changed the scene.

We were concerned similar letters might affect the anticipated Senate hearing. We doubled our efforts to generate support mail. Once again, churchwomen came to our aid. Two of the service groups within the United Methodist Women's Division and Church Women United's national office provided modest grants to cover the cost of reproducing materials and mailings to a roster that had by then grown to 14,000 displaced homemakers and our supporters.

It was a time when I was on the road again. Plans were under way in all the states and territories to elect delegates to the first national conference on women, sponsored by the U.S. Commission on the Observance of International Women's Year (IWY). Invited by state conveners, I was holding workshops on displaced homemakers at as many of the conferences as I could cover. Since I was going for "travel expenses only," piggybacking three, or sometimes four, meetings within the same region and on the same weekends meant a saving of each state's travel funds. Cutting corners by going stand-by or flying the "red-eye specials" expanded the travel schedule. I was amused when I heard that one of the male House committee staff was suspicious of that schedule.

"ADH must have a lot of money behind them to go flying around the country all the time."

Poor unenlightened young man! Little did he know we were operating on the first technique a homemaker must learn—how to stretch a buck.

My name and that of the Alliance began to turn up at these state IWY meetings in leaflets disparaging the legislation along the lines of Schlafly's opposition. Except for the Kentucky meeting where one woman spat at me as I left the workshop, the only expression of overt hostility was a silent one. Women would attend, many of them with tape recorders in hand, and sit silently glaring at me throughout the presentation. On the other hand, in Idaho a pleasant-faced young woman, wearing a large "STOP ERA" button and pushing a youngster in a stroller, seemed to go out of her way to thank me.

"You've made me feel very proud of being a homemaker with what you said today, and God will bless you for what you're doing for older women like my mom."

Some hear, some don't.

In the end, the Schlafly forces made no impact on the final outcome of the national legislation, although they proved bothersome in a few states. The epilogue to the *Eagle Forum* story came months later. After learning from the press that Mrs. Schlafly planned to be in Houston and was calling her own convention during the time of the IWY meeting, I asked a reporter friend, if she got the chance, to put three questions to the lady. She did; and the answers, which were taped, are curious and revealing.

REPORTER : "Why do you object to the displaced homemaker bill?"

SCHLAFLY : "I object to a new federal bureaucracy. Just because women have husbands who die or leave them, I don't think this calls for having a new federal bureaucracy and more money. I think maybe the purpose for it is to give jobs to all the people who are working for the IWY. I don't see that it would solve any problems. What those women need are jobs—and jobs are created by private industry. If you put more people on the federal payroll, you simply are taking money out of somebody else's pocket."

REPORTER : "Do you know how many centers there are?"

SCHLAFLY : "I don't know how many. I know there's
    some."
REPORTER : "Have you visited any?"
SCHLAFLY : "No, I haven't; but I have been told by
    people that they use them to pass out feminist propa-
    ganda."

It seemed pretty slim evidence on which to build the
specific charges of reason number four. Worse, it indicated a callous attitude toward women she purportedly
championed—at least until our "husbands die or leave"
us.

Mrs. Schlafly is an aggressive, capable woman of
means—some earned, some gained through marriage—
and it would seem the best she could offer us was, in a
sense, to tell us to pull up our socks. What a force she
could have been if she had turned around and hectored
private industry into creating the jobs she admitted we,
as displaced homemakers, needed.

Apart from the excitement the first national women's
conference created and the feeling of being part of
something historically important, it provided a personal
experience I'm not likely to forget.

I was not a delegate but had been invited by the national committee to present workshops on the displaced
homemaker movement for invited guests from overseas
and for any of the alternate delegates released from the
floor to attend issue-oriented sessions. There were perhaps fifty at my first session. Except for one man, all
were middle-aged or older women. I began by asking at
random why some of them had chosen to come to this
particular workshop. I really wanted to know why the
tall, distinguished-looking black man, who carried himself so proudly, had decided to attend; but I didn't

want to appear to be singling him out. When I did ask he replied, "I am an ordained minister, but I am also an Air Force counselor at a base nearby. Many women come to me with these problems. I want to help, but I don't know how. I thought I might find out here."

The workshop went well. Everyone participated; there was a good crossflow of ideas; questions were pertinent. Just before the sound of the closing buzzer, a young woman rushed into the room. She paused directly behind the aisle seat of the minister. Waving her hand for attention, she said with a rush, "I'm sorry I'm so late, but I know you've been talking about this displaced homemaker stuff; and what I want to know is, why should the government spend our good tax dollars on programs for women who are just too lazy to help themselves?"

Before I could answer, the minister swung around until he faced her directly; and in a voice that carried the length and breadth of the room, for all that the tone was soft, said, "Because *we* are the government; and those of us who can, help those of us who can't help themselves."

The room was deadly silent. It seemed she threw me a look of panic. She's lost, I thought. No one programmed her for that answer. Aloud, I asked, "Are you married?" I'd used the technique before. If the answer was "yes," I'd ask if they didn't have to sign a joint income tax return and didn't that suggest the government claims taxes from even dependent wives; ergo, what's wrong with older women getting some delayed benefits from our taxpaying years through a program to help us find jobs? Even if the answer was "no," it served to open the door to spelling out the problems of

older former homemakers. Generally, it at least gave
complainers pause to think.

Not this time. Her answer was dynamite.

"No, I *work!*"

The women in the room exploded in rage. Did she
think they didn't? Didn't she realize homemaking was
work? The buzzer put an end to the heated reaction
through all of which the girl had stood speechless. As
she edged past me toward the door, I urged her to
come back for the afternoon session. "I really think
you'd feel differently about the bill if you knew the
whole picture."

She shook her head and said, "I really can't, ma'am.
We were all bused up here for Mrs. Schlafly's convention today, and I can't miss that."

Behind her the minister caught my eye and slowly
shook his head from side to side. "No way," he seemed
to be saying, "are you going to reach her." He was
probably right, but she was very young; and to this
day, I wish I'd had the chance to try.

Back in Washington, when the time came for
the Senate to act, notice of the hearing date was short.
It was left to a junior staffer to arrange, a young
woman newly arrived in Washington from Sacramento.
We were again asked for assistance in putting together
the list of witnesses. This time we decided to apply
some of the lessons we'd learned from the House
experience.

Since Senator Gaylord Nelson chaired the subcommittee, we recommended the lead-off witness be one of
his constituents. Marian Thompson was worthy of the
invitation in her own right as an associate professor and
specialist in women's education at the University of

Wisconsin. Further, her husband, a state Senator, authored and filed a displaced homemaker bill; and the Thompsons were longtime friends of the Nelsons, socially and politically. (It was not an unprecedented move, but it reportedly infuriated the senior staff member. Unfortunately, for whatever his reason, he could do nothing about it. The junior staffer had already extended telephone invitations to all we had suggested.) Learning that it was likely Nelson would not chair the whole hearing but would, instead, turn it over to Senator Don Riegle of Michigan, we added Michigan State Senator William Fitzgerald to the list. He had filed a bill then moving through the state legislature.

Richard Batterton, Secretary of Maryland's Department of Human Resources (the administering agency for the Maryland center), and a panel with Mandy Goetze (the coordinator of the Baltimore organization, New Directions for Women) and two program participants (both older women, one black and one white) made the list. So, too, did two carefully chosen prime sponsors of state bills in Illinois and Nebraska—Susan Catania, a Republican member of Illinois' heavily Democratic legislature and Chair of that state's Commission on the Status of Women, and State Senator Jo Ann Maxey, a young black woman appointed by Nebraska Governor J. James Exon to fill a vacancy, who had nevertheless succeeded in getting her colleagues to overturn the Governor's veto of her displaced homemaker bill.

At the end I added my own name because I was certain there would be no other opportunity in the Senate to get our views on the record.

Senator Nelson, as expected, opened the hearing with a brief statement and an even shorter message which acknowledged Marian Thompson's presence and their longtime family friendship. He then turned the hearing over to Senator Riegle. Senator Orin Hatch (Republican, Utah) represented the minority members; but when he left after the second witness testified, Riegle remained the only member present. Perhaps because he was, he followed all the testimony intently.

As the testimony began, a member of the subcommittee staff came over to advise me that the hearing would conclude with the testimony of the sixth witness, State Senator Jo Ann Maxey. The remaining witnesses, Michigan State Senator Fitzgerald, the panel of Mandy Goetze and the displaced homemaker participants, and I would not be heard. Staff was adamant; a second half-day hearing was "out of the question." Senator Riegle did not agree. He rearranged his own schedule for the following morning and resumed the hearing for the record. He was not joined by any other member of the subcommittee.

Riegle's questions indicated his support of the legislation, but it was also evident that the witnesses were strengthening his position. That was later to prove important, even though his convictions brought him in sharp conflict with senior members of the subcommittee.

On our return to Oakland we found a lengthy letter from Brown Throat. In it he or she warned us not to assume that, since the age question had not been raised at the House hearing, it was no longer a threat to older women. A program for older women was still violently opposed by senior staff and by prominent committee members. Although the writer reaffirmed the desirability of going for coverage under Title III of CETA, we were told the chairman of the full committees in the Senate and the House were against the CETA approach. They believed there was adequate job training available through the education acts, especially the Vocational Education Amendments of 1976. The letter ended with the gloomy prediction that unless we succeeded in getting "an influential" member of the Senate subcommittee to cary the CETA amendment, we'd lose the whole thing. The writer saw it as a "lost cause" in the House. Burke not only wasn't a member of the subcommittee; she had recently declared her intention of running for office in California and would be absent a great deal from Washington as she campaigned during the session when CETA would be under consideration.

Once again we were puzzled by the resistance to a program to aid older women. Was it age bias? A deliberate blindness to the special needs of older women? Was it an attempt to split us off as older women from younger women, playing one age group off against another or because other programs earlier designed to help younger women, such as WIN, were failing? Was this a way to bail out legislators who designed that program? Was it a means to quiet the women's movement whose bills that year on domestic violence and welfare rights were doomed to be bottled up?

"Okay," said Tish, "let's make them show their colors on age. Let's draft the amendement to help displaced homemakers forty years of age and older."

We drafted the amendment and sent it on to Senator Birch Bayh's staff. We had discussed with his aide the possibility of getting California Senator Alan Cranston to submit it formally to the subcommittee. Cranston, a senior member of the subcommittee, was the Senate majority whip and had a reputation of being the "best nose counter" in the Senate. We didn't think he'd take it on if he couldn't get it through, and we thought there was a good chance he'd agree to carrying the amendment. Naturally, the request had to come from Senator Bayh; but his aide made it clear any help we could give would be welcomed.

With an assist from some of our friends on Cranston's staff and the added support of Senator Bayh, Don Riegle, William Hathaway, Wendell Anderson, and George McGovern, Cranston did take on the assignment. There were differences of opinion among staff assigned to work on the amendment as to the definition; but surprisingly, the age focus of forty held—at least up to the subcommittee meeting at "markup," the session at which members resolve any differences before presenting the bill for the full committee's consideration.

All hearings are, by law, open to the public. The trick is to be in D.C. and to know the exact day and hour of the meeting. That's not always easy for people who work on Capitol Hill; it was impossible for advocates living 3,000 miles away. Thanks again to Brown Throat, we know what happened; and though it was a small comfort, even if we'd been there, we would have been powerless to change the outcome.

The report of the recorded exchange between committee members confirmed earlier reports and our own suspicions. Any attempt to limit the program to women "forty years of age and older" was out. So, too, was the alternate position of a separate provision in the amendment: "priority for participation in projects shall be given to displaced homemakers who have attained 40 years of age." Even an ambiguous back-up line within the definition, "an individual who has attained an age in which discrimination on account of age is likely or entry or re-entry to or advancement in the labor market is difficult," was challenged.

Riegle, in defense of those sections, pointed out "that the problem increases for displaced homemakers as they become older, that, based on the hearings we have had and discussions we have had with the groups that are most directly involved, it appears from age forty on it becomes substantially more difficult."

Senator Nelson disagreed: "I really think that's very arbitrary, and what you're saying isn't necessarily so. As a matter of fact, a younger woman with four or five children, who didn't finish high school, has no skill whatsoever; and then she's thirty or twenty-eight, and she's in a disastrous situation. There are all kinds of people—young, with no education—who are much worse off than those who are forty who have some educational background and who can adapt much more quickly to the opportunity than people who are younger."

As I read that, it seemed to me impossible that he could arrive at that latter conclusion even if all he read was his own Senate subcommittee hearing report.

Cranston intervened with a suggestion. "The reason the age is in there was Senator Bayh's insistence on it and desire for it. It was supposed to read: 'Priority for participation in projects supported under this paragraph shall be given to displaced homemakers who, as prescribed in the regulations, are most in need of services by virtue of age, education, and training.'"

New York Senator Jacob Javits, the ranking minority committee member, liked that; but not Senator Nelson.

> NELSON : "I don't know what that means. I just repeat, a sixteen- or seventeen-year-old who never finished more than grade school, and now has four or five children, is twenty-seven years old and . . ."
> RIEGLE : "That's not a displaced homemaker."
> NELSON : "Yes, it is. They're displaced if they have lost their husbands."

Riegle tried once more: "You see, in our definition . . . it says, 'has not worked in the labor force for a substantial number of years but has, during those years, worked in the home providing unpaid services for family members.' "

> NELSON : "That's exactly what I'm talking about."
> RIEGLE : "How does a seventeen-year-old qualify?"
> NELSON : I'm saying somebody who got married at sixteen or seventeen, never finished high school—maybe not grade school—and is now twenty-eight and has four or five children. They're much worse off trying to get into the labor market than a forty-five-year-old woman who has a college education."

Oddly enough, it was presumed incorrectly that women forty-five years of age had a college education; but the reality of what could happen to the forty-five-year-old without a college education or with a degree twenty years or more out of date, or to the older woman whose four or five children have grown past the age of being eligible for the assistance Nelson's "twenty-eight-year-old woman" would have was totally overlooked.

It was all very depressing. Some Senators, no less than other men, apparently miss the point, perhaps precisely because they are men and have never experienced our problems or our needs as older women.

There was one recorded action at the end of the discussion that is interesting in light of later developments. Scott Ginsburg, the subcommittee chief of staff, raised a question about the definition.

"In definition (B) (1) and (B) (2), it says this individual 'has been dependent on the income of another family member but is no longer supported by that income or (2) is receiving public assistance on account of dependent children in the home but is within six months of no longer being eligible for such assistance.' I would presume (2) goes to the question of a person who is losing public assistance because they no longer have any children at all. Does that go to an age question as well?"

In their haste to conclude the session, the record indicates he was never answered directly by any member. Riegle suggested and the others concurred that it was an item "staff could resolve."

The meeting to "mark up" the House amendment went much the same way. Ted Weiss from New York was carrying the amendment for Burke. The opening criticism came from the ranking Republican, Albert Quie of Minnesota. He proposed the forty years of age be removed. When Weiss offered the explanation that actual experience at the two centers suggested this was the group to serve and without "some reasonable age limitation, there may be a certain amount of skimming and creaming," meaning only accepting younger, more placeable trainees, Quie disagreed.

"Take, for instance, a person who was married at nineteen years of age or eighteen or any of the young

age. They have not learned skills, and they have not
had job experience. Then you take another person married at twenty-five or twenty-six and could easily qualify on the forty-year age. They had a number of years
of work experience to develop skills . . . ."

It might be recalled that Mr. Quie was not at either
House hearing, which is fairly evident from his comments about older displaced homemakers having "years
of work experience." Weiss tried for a compromise, to
have the report language indicate a concern for those
over forty. The Chair, Mr. Hawkins, agreed with them
both; he was for removing the age from the amendment but kindly disposed to a priority of "some kind"
in the report language. His follow-up comments indicate how closely senior committee staff work between
the two Congressional bodies.

"My understanding is that the Senate has already
knocked it [age 40] out."

Staff may also have had the final word on the age
question. After the law was enacted and the Department of Labor's Women's Bureau and others began the
hard work of drafting regulations, we learned that the
language of the conference report that presumably contained provisions jointly agreed upon by Senators and
members of the House was not what had been signed
into law. The one section of the definition questioned
by Ginsburg during the Senate subcommittee discussion on age appeared in the *report* with the language in-
tact: "is receiving public assistance on account of
dependent children in the home but is within six
months of no longer being eligible for such assistance."
What was sent over to the President as the *law*, which
staff drafted as reflecting Congressional wishes, cut that

section short by omitting the phrase on the six-months requirement.

In essence, as the law which Carter signed reads, any and everyone, regardless of age, who is on public assistance is eligible for the services.

The language of the conference report was restructured to indicate Congressional "intent" with regard to program participants: "Priority . . . shall be given to displaced homemakers who, as provided in regulations which the Secretary shall prescribe, are most in need of services by virtue of age, education, training, household support obligations, and employability."

The House amendment had called for reserving "not more than 2 percent of the funds available for Title III for Displaced Homemakers programs." The Senate, in their deliberations of all sections of the CETA measure, preferred not to recommend specific "set-aside" funds. Instead, prior to the full committee hearing on the Senate CETA recommendations, Senator Nelson requested a commitment in writing from Secretary of Labor Ray Marshall as to the funds the Department would make available for the Title III programs for Displaced Homemakers. In an appearance before the committee, Ernest Green, responding for Marshall, committed the Department to an expenditure of $5 million for fiscal 1979–80.

With the limited funds made available for the pilot projects and the age broadened, it opened the doors to Ted Weiss' claim—"creaming" would be a temptation; and in this case it would be covered by law. There was agitation on the part of some members of Congress who felt it totally subverted Congressional intent and subsumed their responsibilities. Investigations were threatened; none that we know of took place.

Eventually another brown envelope arrived giving several explanations then current on the Hill as to how the omission occurred.

"It was done at a high-level joint staff committee meeting at which, among others, a member of the Department of Labor, a former Senate staffer, was present."

It was being said that it happened because "the section was inadvertently dropped with the rush of last-minute business before adjournment made writing up the law a hasty assignment"; or a second reason reportedly being bruited about was that "it was a deliberate staff choice based on abolishing the age focus but that the move was covered by sending a memo on the deletion to other committee members," whose staff, many of whom were supportive of the age priority, also were involved in the rush to button up business and easily missed it until it was too late to protest. The letter from Brown Throat concluded with a suggestion to read Michael Scully's article on the power of the unelected.

Senator Riegle, in general comments during the Senate hearing, indicated that since members of Congress were largely male, "one of the difficulties, particularly in the Senate, is the task of trying to understand women's problems and issues through the eyes of individuals who have not experienced first hand the matters that arise."

As older women, indeed as women of any age, we need to keep that in mind as we consider candidates for office. We all learned some valuable lessons in Washington as we experienced the truth of the late Richard Daley's pithy comment: "Politics ain't beanbag." We know a great deal more than we did when we started. Politics may be a game, but it's one in which we don't always have to be on the receiving end of "curves." With enough practice we just might learn to throw back a few. As older women we have more to gain than lose by learning to play the game. Together with younger women, we may even clean it up a little.

CHAPTER FIVE

Organizing for a New Life

Organizing our lives after a husband dies or leaves us alone through divorce or desertion is more a matter of reorganizing for the future. Widows and divorced or deserted older women share more than we sometimes think, and yet there are differences. Society is more considerate of the woman who loses her husband to eternity. There is still a lingering notion among our peers that the older woman who loses her husband to a younger woman brought about her own misfortune. Whether she says it aloud or not, frequently even the divorced woman asks herself, "What did I do wrong?"

Self-recrimination won't change the picture; neither will shaking an angry fist at the inevitability of death. It's more than O.K. to cry and therapeutic to mourn our loss, but there must come a time (sociologists call it "closure") when we firmly shut the door on the past and move forward with the rest of the living. The length of our anguish will vary with individuals, and there will always be fleeting moments that stir up past memories. I can now listen to a special recording of Handel's *Messiah,* which Arthur and I made a point to play during Christmas and Easter of all the years we were married; but it took me two years after his death before I could put those records on for the pleasure of hearing the music.

Anniversaries can be another source of pain or joy. The dates of our weddings seem to stick more firmly in the minds of older women. Most widows may not be as lucky as I think I am. When we were married Arthur was a widower with a seven-year-old daughter. I wanted us to start off as a new family, so we took Christine with us on our honeymoon. Since his death the two of us do something special on each anniversary—not to mourn a loss but to celebrate a new beginning of our relationship as women who each, in our own way, loved a good man.

Most divorced older women have special problems widows seldom encounter. Where death usually unites a family in their grief, divorce too often splits more than husband and wife; it sometimes leaves children with divided loyalties. This is difficult for a mother to accept at any age; but the older we are, the deeper the hurt. Curiously, the divorced women I've met who seem most happily adjusted to their new sought or unsought independence are those who have not reached out to their children for support—emotional or economical. The most unhappy divorced women I've known are those who cannot shake what they view as unjust rejection and whose inability to channel their anger in constructive ways has turned them into bitter, morose individuals.

Admittedly, it is not easy and strains tolerance almost beyond endurance to suffer the rejection of someone you loved and thought loved you, particularly if your former spouse remarries and perhaps begins a new family. It's humanly natural then to look back over a long-term marriage and view it bitterly as years of lost opportunities to develop your own talents. Just as with widows, it's more than O.K. to cry even if all we mourn for is ourselves.

Divorced and deserted wives, like widows, need to shut out the past and look to the future with as much hope as we can muster. Instead of scaring ourselves to death by saying, "I'm all alone!" we might stop and reflect on the fact that perhaps for the first time we're free to be whatever we want to be. Instead of thinking we gave our families "the best years of our lives," we might consider our best could well lie ahead. Whether we nursed a well-loved husband through a final illness; suffered, for the sake of keeping a family together, the physical brutalities of an alcoholic mate; or were "dumped" for another woman—we as women become stronger for the experience, and it is that courage we must draw on as we face the future.

The first stage in going it alone is to learn how to cope. You need some quiet time to think about what you have and where you're going. Start with the premise that you have inner strengths because each of us has capabilities we may never have tested. What older former homemaker, wife, and mother hasn't had to deal with crises and emergencies throughout her marriage? Review those and be honest with the evaluation of your own contribution to the resolution of the situation. Too often as wives we tended to underestimate ourselves and, even when we were strong, preferred to credit "John," "Bill," and, yes, even Arthur for bringing out the best in us.

List those things you know you've always done well. If there's an immediate need for an income, consider the example set by a woman I met here in California. An excellent cook whose specialties are homemade breads, cakes, and cookies, she supports herself and two small children by whipping up batches of her best products and selling them over the weekend from a stall in a large local flea market. That, plus a part-time job during the rest of the week, has eased her concerns for instant income. She takes the kids with her and, by example, is teaching them how to be self-sufficient. It may not be the way Julia Child started, but it is nice to know that the First Lady of French Cooking "seldom set her foot in a kitchen till she was thirty-five and didn't start her TV career that made her famous until she was past fifty."

After you've compiled your list of marketable talents, ask yourself these questions: What kind of a job would I like to do? What kind would I be able to do? What would I settle for? Can I handle a full-time job, or should I try to find a part-time one?

Part-time work is booming as never before, though I suspect for the wrong reasons. Always the anchor for the unskilled to cling to earning subsistence wages, some employers are now using part-time help as a means of lowering operating costs. In a report to the Department of Labor, Professor Stanley Nollen of George Washington University found that employers using part-time help reduced overtime costs, absenteeism, wage rates, and fringe benefits. Correspondingly, part-time workers are deprived of those benefits.

But part-time work can be used creatively to brush up on old skills, to build toward a new career. Some innovative part-time work experiments seem to offer incentives to both employer and employee. For example, the First National Bank of Chicago has developed a Temporary Work Force providing opportunities for temporary help to receive on-the-job training in specialized banking functions. After 500 hours of temporary work and a satisfactory work record, workers are eligible to apply for part-time permanent positions at the bank.

One widow, a longtime personal friend whom I deeply admire and respect, has cleverly used a part-time job not just to supplement her income but to rout the inevitable loneliness of weekends. She applied for and got part-time work as an admissions clerk at a large local hospital, offering to cover the shifts most other workers preferred to be off. The hospital was delighted to hire her, and she worked some holidays that might have been desperate times for her. She has the real joy of knowing she's helping others while she helps herself.

When listing your "credits," don't overlook your volunteer work. Many a community effort was kept alive by our volunteered hours. The good news is that business is beginning to acknowledge the experience we gained through our voluntary efforts and accepting it as "work experience" for salaried jobs of a similar nature. Also, according to a survey by the International Personnel Management Association, some "38 state governments have revised job application forms to include volunteer experience."

Volunteerism today also offers another way to build a new career. The whole outlook on volunteerism has changed since 1973 when Tish Sommers helped to draft NOW's stand on it which distinguished between that which seeks to create needed social change and volunteerism, which serves to maintain women's status quo. In 1976, along with another woman, Caroline Voorsanger, she applied a new twist to volunteerism to make it work to the benefit of the Oakland center displaced homemakers.

Caroline Voorsanger was one of many volunteers to serve in an unpaid position at the center. A widow, she brought to the program a wealth of skills developed over years of paid employment, twenty-five of them as the training director of a leading department store in northern California. She had directed personnel and training for the San Francisco Poverty Program and served as a supervisor of the San Francisco Volunteer Bureau.

She agreed with Sommers that unpaid work could be an effective means of on-the-job training; and together they drafted a proposal that was submitted to ACTION for a grant to fund a model volunteer program, develop a volunteer contract, and design the methods to use it as a means to secure paid employment. The money, $5,000, was used to pay the volunteers' out-of-pocket expenses.

The contract subsequently developed formally recognized that volunteer work is employment like any other, with mutual obligations and expectations from the volunteer and employer.

The contract calls for a description of the job, the amount of salary it would provide if it were paid work, a job title, and in general calls for the treatment of the nonpaid employee in the same manner as the paid. The employer is expected to keep personnel records and provide the training if necessary. Volunteers can expect letters of reference when the contract expires if employment hasn't opened up before that time. Each volunteer contract worker is supervised by center staff, who maintain contact with the employer as well on the trainee's progress.

One early center trainee with a great deal of interest in antiques but no experience in the field was able to negotiate a contract with a local dealer who agreed to train her for three months. Within two months a job opened up with another dealer, and she got the position on the recommendation of her last "boss."

Aliyah Stein recalls another volunteer contract story—one which also involved a woman who had no experience in her chosen field of interest. The trainee wanted to work in a travel agency but hadn't the money to go through any formal training for the position of agent. She drafted her own contract and took it in to a travel agency in her neighborhood. She offered to work for free the first month, on 10 percent commission the second, and 50 percent the third month. After the fourth month, there would be a review of her work. If she liked working there and they were willing, she would become paid staff or be given references for openings at other agencies. Her plan worked. She was hired before her contract expired and is still happily employed in her dream job.

(A sample of the volunteer contract and instructions for using it are included in the Appendix.)

On the East Coast, Herta Loeser, founder and co-director of the Civic Center and Clearing House in Boston, organized Project Re-Entry in 1976 to give women opportunities to explore career options by working in volunteer intern positions and apprenticeships of their choice. Loeser reports that "75 percent to 80 percent of the women who enrolled in the nine-month unsalaried work experience and career counseling found jobs."

If you have the time to invest, carving out a career niche through volunteer work is a good way to start; but you can also use the volunteer contract yourself if you know what you want to do and can find an employer willing to cooperate.

The difficulty is that as displaced homemakers, we don't always know what we want to do. Often economic insecurity or the fear of it causes us to snap up the first paid job that comes along. Sometimes that works, sometimes it doesn't. Nor do we always know what we *can* do. Skills tests are nearly always available at vocational technical schools and some community colleges. Keep in mind, though, that most of these are designed to measure male skills; you may have to interpret the results as they apply to you, a woman.

Not long ago a woman stopped by our office to present us with a beautiful hand-lettered poster of our motto, "Don't Agonize, Organize!" She told us she had been a displaced homemaker, divorced after twenty-seven years of marriage, with no record of paid work experience. She went to a local community college that specializes in vocational training. Her tests revealed an interest in art, but the field recommended was taxidermy! The thought repulsed her. "I can't even *look* at a dead bird!" she told us.

She reasoned that what the tests really revealed was that she had high development of hand motor skills as well as an interest in art. She chose to study calligraphy and moved from that to hand-designed greeting cards. She is about to mass-market her first product—a handsome Jewish New Year's card; and she concluded with a grin, "My ex is helping me finance it."

Education is considered by many to be the key to better paying jobs, but I think we have to examine that premise carefully in light of our job prospects as older women. Many of us are caught between conflicting views of the work world for women. We are told, for example, that jobs long considered to be "women's work," often seen as our only re-entry opportunities, are underpaid and undervalued precisely because women dominate in those fields. Conversely, jobs held to be male fields of endeavor are valued and paid accordingly. The question currently causing considerable debate among those who champion women's issues, particularly in the field of vocational education and among those who represent women now in the labor force, is whether efforts should be made to open up so-called male-dominated jobs to women or to upgrade and raise the wages of jobs women traditionally perform.

Joan Goodin, Executive Director of the National Commission on Working Women, supports the latter premise and wholeheartedly endorses the concept of "equal pay for work of comparable value," which she says will be the "hottest issue of the '80s." She believes upgrading and raising the wages of "women's jobs" will inevitably result in an integrated work force.

Eleanor Holmes Norton, Chair of the Equal Opportunity Commission, agrees. In a well-researched article on comparable worth for the *Washington Post*, Carol Krucoff quotes Norton as saying:

> ... it's important to come to grips with the hard reality that women's jobs will remain a pattern of work for

women in years to come, despite all of us going to law
school, medical school, and getting our MBA's [Masters
of Business Administration].

According to Krucoff, Norton believes the key to
achieving equal pay for work of comparable worth is to
establish

... valid job evaluations that take into account all
relevant job factors and are free from bias.

Dr. Barbara Bergmann, Professor of Economics at
the University of Maryland, disagrees. She contends
that no evaluation system can be expected to increase
the value of "women's" jobs up to the value of traditionally male jobs which have provided their holders
with varied experiences and autonomy. She told a 1979
audience at the Women's Work Force Network Conference the most desirable recourse is to move women into
the higher paying nontraditional jobs and thus abolish
men's "turf rights over jobs."

Neither approach offers an easy path to success.
Equal pay for work of comparable worth is bitterly opposed by management because, of course, it will impact
on the profit system. (No doubt plantation owners felt
the same about freeing slaves!) Integrating women into
previously all-male jobs is far from being uniformly
supported by contractors, unions, or industrial employers. Despite a concerted effort by the Department of
Education to increase the number of women in nontraditional jobs, and backed up by the Department of
Labor's guidelines and compliance regulations, the success has been more apparent in press coverage of the
few women who made it than in the number of those
employed.

Majorie Moore, Assistant Director of the Women's Affairs, Labor, Education Advancement Program of the National Urban League, says:

> If progress were based on publicity, it would appear that an overwhelming number of women across the nation have broken through the sexist and racist barriers that they face and are handling all of their on-the-job adjustments fairly well.

But, as Moore points out:

> Ten years ago women represented only 1% of the skilled workers in the trades. Today, women hold a mere 2% of the jobs in skilled trades.

She concludes:

> "It can be argued without question that a 1% increase over a decade does not indicate meaningful success."

Women's rights to jobs for which they qualify in every way except gender must and should be supported. I think that in new technological fields where gender dominance hasn't had a chance to develop, women, including older women, will get a fair share of work, providing age and sex discrimination haven't infected the employer. But in the push to open up "nontraditional" work, too much emphasis seems to be placed on getting women into "construction, welding, bricklaying." Not only will our age work against us, the physical demands of such labor are often beyond those of us in our middle years. (Women of any age also need to take into consideration the practical prospects of obtaining work in fields whose ranks of present male workers are being decimated by our current economic situation, construction being a prime example.)

To undertake one or two years of technical training without the assurance of job availability forces us, once again, to sacrifice the one thing we can least afford to lose—time! One is reminded of the former axiom that "a degree is the key to a career." A lot of older women took that as gospel and wound up, four years later, well educated and highly unemployable.

I suspect vocational education will open up jobs for women in the future. I concur with Judy Murphy, the director of a two-year program which attempted to break the gender barrier.

"I can see the value," she said, "of reaching young women at the high school and college level who are forming career goals and having them consider nontraditional careers, but it is the unusual woman over forty who can make it in what is today considered a nontraditional job."

One fifty-year-old Midwestern woman who did break the gender barrier in heavy industry was returning to an old love; she had been a lathe operator before her marriage. After a brush-up course at a local vocational technical school, she was hired at a base pay of $5.21 an hour for ten weeks, the rate at which her piece work was figured. It's clear when talking to her that she really loves her work.

"When I walked back into that shop and smelled all the things I'd been familiar with years ago, it was, well, like coming home."

She's proud of her work, though she admits "it's hard work and it's dirty." She credits the director of the women's center at the technical school with providing "a lot of encouragement and support." Her gross salary for 1979, which included cost-of-living raises, was

$18,700, and she thinks that is "very good for just being back in the work force a year and a half." Her male supervisor, with whom she believes she has a good working relationship, admitted that when she came into the shop, he deliberately put her on a large and complicated lathe "to test her." She finds nothing discriminating about the fact that four or five months ago he assigned her "to another category of lathe," which meant she had to take a cut in her base pay to $4.79 an hour, but a cost-of-living hike raised that to $6.83. Shortly after we spoke, I had a letter from her indicating that she would soon be receiving another cost-of-living raise which would put her pay over $7.00 an hour if she remains assigned to the same machine. As she explains, "Whenever I go on another machine that pays more, they must pay me the base rate for that machine. The foreman is supposed to take care of that on our time slips."

She'll be eligible for a pension if she remains employed for ten years, and the job does provide "good health insurance." She works from 7:30 A.M. to 3:30 P.M., five days a week, and an additional five hours on Saturday. Except for assembly-line workers, her colleagues are male. She says she gets on well with them all but asked that her identity and the city in which she lives not be revealed. She told me as she made the request, "There's been a lot of resentment to the publicity I've gotten; it's even brought prowlers around the house."

As for reaction in the community to her choice of work, she told of trying to buy a pair of work shoes. The smallest of the men's shoes were too large, and she asked the salesman why the company didn't manufacture them in women's sizes. His answer: "You should be in the kitchen!"

I admire her ability to laugh off criticism and share her delight, knowing she is doing work she enjoys; but she and a very few other older women across the country are exceptions. It is an illusion, if not a cruel hoax, to claim that we as older women can expect to move into men's jobs simply because a few older women have done so. As the National Urban League's year-long study confirms, blue-collar employment, despite high wages, is generally perceived negatively by young as well as older women.

There is hope for the future. Currently two studies are being pursued which may make vocational educators more responsive to our needs as displaced homemakers and take the guesswork out of curriculum planning. Under a grant from the U.S. Office of Education, Occupational and Adult Education Branch, a "displaced homemaker project" is the joint responsibility of the Education Development Center in collaboration with the Wellesley Center for Research on Women and the American Vocational Association. A two-year effort begun in 1980, it is charged with developing ways to help the displaced homemaker use vocational education to move from the home to a job; and it also will produce a manual and resource guide for vocational educators to help them better serve displaced homemakers "over thirty-five."

Perhaps even more important, given our long-range goal of recognizing the value of homemaking, is the work being done under the guidance of Dr. Ruth B. Ekstrom of Princeton University. Since 1977 she and her colleagues have been conducting research on the academically accreditable competencies which we acquire from our volunteer and homemaking experiences. That early research led to the development of materials and techniques to help re-entry women and colleges identify and assess these competencies for college credit. What she and her staff are now in the process of completing is a way to determine the transferability of our life-experience competencies to employment and to vocational education. The goal of Project ACCESS is to design, test, and implement a system for recognizing the job-related skills acquired by adult women—former homemakers.

The results of both studies will be eagerly awaited by those of us who have long asserted that "homemakers are an unrecognized and unpaid part of the national work force whose skills *are* transferrable to the traditional labor market."

As the year 1977 drew to a close, I found myself thinking more and more about what I would do when this "job" ended. Barbara Dudley had much earlier moved to Salinas and was continuing her work as a legal-rights advocate for a new constituency: migrant farm workers and their families. Although I enjoyed working with Tish and we had by then evolved into a good working team, I had made no commitment to continue with the free-lance agitator as a footloose organizer when the work of the Alliance was phased out. Like other displaced homemakers in center programs, I had developed a greater sense of self-confidence and had been pleasantly surprised to find I could tackle work I'd never done before. The question was, what kind of job did I want? There was no longer a great desire to get back into advertising or merchandising.

Writing? That seemed attractive; but then again, it was a lonely job, and if I'd discovered anything about myself, it was that I was a "people person," happiest in group work. Maybe something in radio or television.

I'd made no decision but was still pondering options the morning Tish casually asked what I thought about the idea of calling a national training conference on displaced homemakers. I was stunned! What did we know about putting on a conference?

"We've been to enough of them," replied Tish, "to know what works and what doesn't. Besides," she added, "think about it. Who else has all the contacts to the best resources on this issue? All those state programs, the community-college projects. Every one of those fledgling outfits is building up information no one ever had before. I think it's time to pull it all together and share ideas, pool and trade information on what works and what doesn't."

My resistance was weakening; but remembering that I kept the books, I asked, "What do we use for money?"

The answer was typical. "Money's no problem. The time is ripe; the issue is a hot one, and I can think of a number of ways to get it funded. All we need to do is get it organized. That, I grant you, will take time and lots of effort. We'll need someone to take over the bookkeeping. I think we can do it on fifty-thousand dollars, but we'll have to watch every penny."

That ruled me out. My only experience handling the Alliance funds had been limited to "nickel and dime" donations, simple journal entries. Martha Gresham joined us and listened quietly as Tish went on to explain her ideas of how the conference should be structured.

"The way I see it, it should be made up of selected participants from various types of service deliverers: those who want to start displaced homemaker centers; representatives from state and federal administering agencies; professionals from fields related to displaced homemakers; but most of all, displaced homemakers themselves, especially those now in centers or who have gone through center programs."

Martha broke her silence. "Sounds great."

"Sounds like we're about to form a new organization," I said; but it was more a question than a statement.

Tish nodded and added with a grin, "How would you like to be the executive director? You better than any of us know the people across the country we'd want to attend."

She and Martha seemed to be waiting for my answer.

I threw up my hands. "O.K., I guess you can count me in."

Tish's comment was unexpectedly laconic: "I'm glad!"

She extended her hand; and though I felt a little foolish, we shook hands as though to seal an agreement. What I'd done, of course, postponed immediate action on any other job; I'd just re-enlisted for another cruise on the good ship Social Change.

I became more enthusiastic as we worked out the details for the conference. It would be held in Baltimore, where the volunteer services of the center staff could be utilized to handle most of the detail work. The center and New Directions would "co-host" the occasion. Cynthia Marano, given a leave of absence from the center, was to chair the conference and would be responsible for gathering together all the "how-to" materials from the existing programs for a manual which every participant would receive as part of the fee charged. Fees would be levied to meet costs; no profit would be built into the budget. It would be a working conference of 300 selected participants; and for those not selected, the how-to materials would be made available at cost after the conference.

There was an incredible amount of work to be done. With rare exceptions, it was on-the-job training for everyone; but we were not without resources. Jan Mowry, for example, a former displaced homemaker, then between jobs as a part-time community-college counselor, co-authored the grant proposal to ACTION, which provided funding of $50,000 and signed on to manage all the financial end of the project. With no experience in formal bookkeeping beyond the usual budget experience a homemaker acquires, she sought and got "pro bono" advice—assistance from business or other nonprofit organizations provided at no cost. One contact led to another, and she soon had the free services of a woman professionally engaged in setting up conventions.

As expected, I wound up on the selection committee. We sent out 2,000 conference calls to persons hand-picked from our files who would reflect the desired balance. To our surprise, nearly 1,000 replied. We had originally thought a top figure of 300 would insure the most effective dialogue, but the demand forced us to raise that figure to the maximum the hotel could handle—475. Seventy-five of those women would be displaced homemakers from across the country, and the entire expense of their participation was to be covered by a funding assist from the Women's Bureau of the Department of Labor.

As the dates drew near, Jan, Tish, and Martha left for the East Coast. The last task to be done was to assemble lists of the participants, broken down into regions of the country, 500 copies of each. I said I'd bring them along as baggage. I would be the last to arrive in Baltimore, the day before the conference began. I warned the skycap the bags were heavy.

"I had a problem getting them in the car," I said.

He heaved them out, one at a time. "*You* put these in here?" he asked. He wheeled them to the counter and put them on the scale. One weighed ninety-six pounds, the other seventy-five. I paid the excess baggage charge; and back home five days later I paid the doctor's bill for treating a sprained back.

Sprained back and all, the conference had an enormous uplifting effect on me. I was excited about seeing many of the displaced homemakers for the first time in two years. I looked forward to meeting others I knew only through an exchange of letters, but they weren't the only people I wanted to see. It was fair to say I knew, one way or another, everyone on those lists. I wanted to see everybody! The thought of working together, sharing, yes, and caring for one another was something I eagerly looked forward to. Even so, I could not have guessed the conference would end the "buzz" processing of my development as a feminist and my search for another job, or that in just one workshop, the "click," the positive turn-on to both feminists and a career of social activism, would happen!

It was billed as the "Displaced Homemaker Speak-Out." Several displaced homemakers, former participants of various state-funded programs, were to tell their own stories so that, as the moderator Charlotte Stewart said, "all of you can understand who the displaced homemaker is and how she became one." Originally scheduled for a smaller room, advance sign-up made it necessary to transfer the session to the hotel ballroom. People in the room settled down, seated around the luncheon tables that would have to be hastily set up when the session ended. There was a hushed silence as though the curtain was about to go up on the first night of a long-awaited play. It was drama, the real thing.

Stewart opened the session, speaking briefly of her own "credentials."

> I was a displaced homemaker, divorced after twenty-four years of marriage, and am now supervising and coordinating five programs for displaced homemakers through the YWCA in Dallas. I was a consultant on the film *Who Remembers Mama?* and that work helped me channel my destructive anger into a constructive force. [The film, which deals with the agony and grief an older woman suffers when she's divorced, had just won the American Bar Association's Silver Gavel Award.]

All of the women's stories were unique, yet alike. The past was painful for some, poignantly so, but all were on the road to reorganizing their lives—some still a little shaky, others resolute in their determination not to let anything or anyone hold them back. Thelma Knight from the Los Angeles center said:

> If somebody had told me at this time last year that I'd be at a national convention in Baltimore, I would have probably had a stroke because last year at this time I was very frightened and a worn-out person. I was going in several directions and very fast, getting

nowhere. I'm a mother of four, single parent and raised them all my life alone, it seems. The center teaches you who you are, where you need to go, and how to get there. I'm equipped now; I'm armed with everything, and I want to go out and tell everybody how to get what they deserve. Not just a job, but a job that *you* want. How to go out and hire yourself an employer!

Knight went from trainee to staff, and the pride in her work and herself was evident, pointing out that reaching the unskilled and underemployed wasn't easy.

Now, most of the women I serve are women too tired. They're worn out, and they cannot do these jobs any more. I changed the curriculum to meet their needs. We have this mobile mini workshop, and I take it right out to the community—go find them and get to them. I tell them, "We're going to make you first feel good about yourself. Then we go through the problems that are keeping you from getting what you want. After you are in love with yourself, then we'll teach you how to get a job—how to hire an employer." There's absolutely no reason why they won't get a job, and I see that they get it. I don't just drop them either. I stay with them; I follow them up to see how they're doing and what they're doing.

June, who followed, was totally different. She told her story in a measured monotone without a hint of an inflection to score or underscore her experience. It was as though she was using her voice to control the feelings her trembling hands revealed. She had been widowed in 1975.

Prior to that time, the twelve years preceding my husband's death, I lost seven significant people: my sis-

ter, my aunt, my best friend, my mother, my father's
second wife, my son, and then my husband.

A murmur rose from the crowded room; tears slid
down the face of the woman to my left. With her eyes
fastened on the podium stand, June continued:

> It seemed as though the road, the tunnel, was so dark
> and I was never going to see the light that I knew must
> be somewhere there.

She went on to say that on the day after her hus-
band's death she saw the notice of the Displaced
Homemakers' center opening up in Eugene, Oregon.
She tore it out and put it into a drawer.

> . . . hoping I might get the courage to walk in there
> some day. It was about a month later that I parked my
> car and walked about a hundred feet to this little hut
> on the campus where the center had opened. I walked
> up the steps wishing that it was closed; it was open. I
> received counseling; they were very beautiful to me. It's
> wonderful to find people who have gone through some-
> thing like my experience. Two women that I met had
> both lost their husbands. One with cancer as my hus-
> band had died, the other in an abrupt accident. The
> support I received and the offer to help was really the
> reason why I didn't choose to join my husband 'cause
> believe me, it had occurred to me.

Suddenly her head lifted up, and her eyes swept the
room.

> There's nothing like talking with a person who has
> experienced a loss.

For the first time her voice wavered; her delivery became even slower.

> I had thought I hurt when my best friend died; I hurt when my mother died. I *know* I hurt terribly when our son died, but there was nothing to compare with the hurt when my husband died.

Turning back to her prepared statement, she told of the difficulty of trying to find a new direction. She kept going back to the center trying to find a focus. Like so many older women suddenly cast on their own after years of never exercising any personal options, she tried many things. She worked briefly in an ice-cream store, as a cashier for a jeweler. The center kept gently pushing. She understood why.

> I really didn't want to get out where a lot of people would demand things of me. It's really a very scary feeling when you've been married to a very, very strong person who has made all the big decisions.

Her husband wasn't the only one who had made big decisions for her.

As she gradually discovered more of herself as a person, she realized that she'd been an elementary school teacher not because she wanted to be, but

> ... because I always felt it was what my mother and my sister wanted me to be. It was their choice. So I decided not to go back into that field where I wasn't the happiest.

She finally took on a Vista job, stayed almost a year, and discovered she had talent counseling other women. A week before our conference, there was a staff opening at the Eugene Displaced Homemaker Center. She ended by saying she got the job; and

... because the center was such a tremendous help to me, I want to help other women like me.

As she finished there was a burst of applause, a genuine salute to courage. "A regular two-Kleenex experience," whispered the woman on my left as she pounded the palms of her hands together.

Stewart took over the microphone and in a few seconds cleverly released the crowd from its pent-up emotions. I was the only person who didn't laugh at the end of her story. Though she threw away her opening lines in a self-deprecating, humorous manner, I had caught her eye and knew she meant every word. Never once in three years had I guessed the secret she was to reveal.

Laurie told me, about three years ago, when I called her—very suicidal myself—"Don't agonize, organize." She doesn't know that she saved my life that day because I had read about displaced homemakers in the *National Observer*, and rather than write a letter, because I was going to do it pretty quick, I decided to call them; and I was really agonizing. She said, "Hey, I've got a WATS line; I'll call you back." She did, and for the first time in probably two years I heard someone say after I told my story, "That *is* a dirty deal, and we can do something about it." After about twenty minutes—on her nickel—telling me about the bill, I said, "Laurie, I really want to help. What is it that I can do? Who is it in Texas that I can help?" and she said, "We don't have anyone; but, Charlotte, you're now it," and so I very quickly became the organizer for the state of Texas for the Alliance for Displaced Homemakers.

Stewart paused and shot a grin in my direction.

And you know, you just can't commit suicide when you have such an important job.

The crowd loved it.

Some of the most impressive speakers from the floor had given me a hint of what they'd say during a "displaced homemaker only" rally the night before. I wondered what the crowd would make of it all.

Feisty, white-haired Florence Griffin, with her cheeks aglow and her remarkably blue, blue eyes blazing, took the opening shot.

> We *are* going to start a network, and we *are* going to be united. One thing that has come out of the conference is that the Displaced Homemaker Program has only just begun. We have a long way to go, but it's going to be *our* ball game now. We're going to work with all the agencies, but we're going to tell them our needs.

As the cheers of the audience died down, Stewart called on a woman at the microphone nearest our table. Most in the room had not been able to see how agonizingly difficult it had been for her to negotiate the few steps from her seat to the mike. With her hands firmly clasped on the two metal supports that extended up to her elbows and served her as legs, she dragged useless limbs from side to side with the thrust of powerful shoulder muscles. It took her a few minutes to get steadily positioned in front of the mike.

> This conference has reaffirmed my faith in the sisterhood and has also given me the incentive to go back home and try a little harder. I am a displaced homemaker; I became one at the age of fifty, three years ago, one month after I was told I was going blind. At fifty-

two I got crippling arthritis; and I said, "It's not worth it." I felt like I just wanted to find a corner, sit down, and quit. I didn't quite go suicidal, but I just wanted to quit!

She paused, shifted her position, and continued:

But I had a woman counselor who told me, "No, you won't." She said to me, "You're black, you're blind, you're a woman, and there's nobody that can tell you no about anything unless you let them."

She waited until the hearty applause died down.

In the last two days I've discovered something about all of us here that are displaced homemakers. Every displaced homemaker is as handicapped as I am physically handicapped—handicapped by society, by the law, sometimes by ourselves, but mostly . . . [And she pounded the floor with her crutch to emphasize her next words] . . . mostly by the people that are supposed to be out there to help us. I want to challenge everybody here that's giving services to displaced homemakers. When you get back home, you look around. You're going to find sitting in a corner someplace where I almost wound up, a handicapped woman, a displaced homemaker who needs to be told not to quit because you believe she shouldn't.

"But," warned Terri Jackson as she concluded her remarks, "you just better believe it!"

From the far side of the room, a tall black older woman, Opal LaVerne, from a small town in Texas, took over the microphone. The resonance of her deep-pitched voice filled the room. There was something about her precise diction, the ebb and flow of her delivery that reminded me of Barbara Jordan, also from Texas, the member of the House Judiciary Committee who brought TV viewers to churchgoing attention during the Watergate hearings. The room quieted with her opening sentence.

> The fact that we've come together here is not only historic, but evidences the changes happening in our society. I believe that regardless of the goals and ideas coming out of this conference, even more and better changes will result for us as women, as displaced homemakers, and for the country as a whole. My efforts shall be to help form a network of common people for strength and advocacy of our cause. The commission to Christians was to go into the world and preach the good news of the Gospel.
>
> Mine shall be to tell women that we are either displaced homemakers because of our status and place in society or we have the potential of becoming so.

Her next words hit like a trip hammer.

> And so, for our survival, we must identify, organize, make aware, become *dissatisfied* as displaced homemakers. We must monitor existing avenues which may be used to help our cause; select means to further our cause and use our own creativeness, hobbies, likes, and even dislikes to maintain and hold jobs.

I glanced around the room. I wasn't the only one sitting on the edge of my chair, half holding my breath through her ringing words. She continued:

> I think we must redefine our values, look realistically at jobs as our society defines them, and begin—begin to understand that full employment as such will never be. Therefore, it is necessary that we start to make our own jobs, using our hobbies, our ingenuity. The Baltimore and Oakland centers have opened doors for us. They are leaders because they didn't stop in their own envi-

ronment and communities. Their ideas, experience, and expertise have been shared and are being shared to extend a movement of displaced homemakers. Their caring has developed a network, and now ... [slightest of pauses] ... and now, a *revolution* ... [furious applause muffled the last words] ". . . of displaced homemakers." When everyone sat down, if not calmed down, she went on.

> It is necessary for our survival. We may be a single head of the family as a displaced homemaker, but a family is still the basic unit of this society. As a "family" of displaced homemakers, in our homes, in our communities, and in this society, we have it in us to lead the nation to survival.

The room exploded. Women reached across the aisle trying to shake Opal's hand; others threw their arms around her. Despite the thin film of perspiration that bathed her face, she was serenely calm. If the earlier statements from displaced homemakers had jarred the consciences of others more well off, Opal had awakened the pride of the displaced homemakers in themselves—as women, "as leaders."

More than a few of the evaluations received after the conference were signed "A PROUD D.H." Others, in commenting on the session, called it,

"Beautiful."

"Very inspiring."

"This was the motivating session; we all sat at the 'learning tree.'"

"Fantastic! Consciousness raising par excellence!"

"The most significant part of the conference. Any attempt to keep service deliverers and DHs close as this did is laudable."

"Personal testimony keeps service deliverers on the track; it's always useful to reiterate the tremendous importance of support and caring."

"It really brought it all home and increased my awareness and sensitivity."

There were, of course, those who found it overlong for such a hot day; and in fairness, the hotel hadn't been able to cope with raising the air conditioning to counter the muggy weather, let alone cool down a room made steamy by multiple cases of raised adrenaline. At least one found it "a bit emotional" and warned, "We, as women, have to be aware of this tendency; we must fight from our heads, not just our hearts."

Displaced homemakers themselves took another view. Wrote one, "TERRIFIC! How energizing to hear DH's who are or were exactly where I was. The feeling was overwhelming. I love my sisters and admire *our* guts!"

Another summed it up neatly: "If all the courage in that room could have been bottled, nothing could stop us!"

That session was a turning point in my life. Up to then I had found it awkward to deal with the "sisterhood" of feminism even though I'd witnessed and experienced the close bonds of cooperation that can develop between many nonrelated women engaged in a common cause. The Speak-Out verbalized the spirit and the promise of the whole conference: the real power of "sisterhood," love and concern for one another as women. Women who arrived at the conference total strangers to one another left it bound together though our paths may never cross again. For two hot, muggy days in a hotel that had seen better days and offered few of the amenities of more expensive hostelries, some

500 of us experienced feminism at its best—women working with women in order to help others as well as themselves.

All the "buzzes" ended for me that late afternoon. The turn-on "click" was really two, not one. I not only finally was a "late-blooming feminist," I knew there was no other work I wanted to do but to continue as an advocate for older women. I recalled Tish's long-range plans for OWLEF: "digging into all the problems that affect us as older women; exploring, debating, and researching issues for action—pensions, Social Security, health." I realized how much I wanted to be part of that action, fighting with "my head as well as my heart."

Having made my decision, I couldn't wait to tell Tish. She'd gone up to her room to change for dinner. I reached her on the house phone and anticipated her surprise when I told her I had changed my mind about looking for another job. Instead she surprised me.

"Great! But actually I knew you were hooked the day you agreed to work on the conference."

In the early planning stage of the conference we asked Cynthia Marano if she thought there was a way new leadership on our issue could be developed.

"If the conference is successful in generating a sharing of techniques, experiences, and resources," said Tish, "there should be some means of ongoing communication."

"And," I added, "there will definitely be a need for continued organizational pressure on the Hill and in the Department of Labor. With the Alliance out of business and OWLEF seeking to broaden its scope of advocacy, this may be the time to pass on leadership to a new group."

Marano immediately saw possibilities for establishing a national clearinghouse, preferably in D.C., "which would provide all programs and prospective program developers data and resources, staff training, information on funding, legislative issues, further conferences or regional meetings, and, of course, a regular newsletter."

She thought there was a way to create an initial network with the participation of conference attendees interested in the idea.

"I even think," she added, "that we just could get some free office space in D.C.—for a limited time."

She proposed putting the request to her friend Jenrose Felmley, then executive director of the Business and Professional Women's Clubs.

Marano's plan worked well, and at the closing session candidates were nominated and elections held to select "network consultants" in each of the ten federal regions. The body voted to create the Displaced Homemakers Network with Marano as its acting coordinator. Felmley rose to offer free office space for six months, and the fledgling Network was on its way. Several attendees offered to seek funding. One raised nominal grants, OWLEF donated $500 and gave the Network distribution rights of the how-to manual; but for the first year of its operation the Displaced Homemakers Network ran on the "sweat equity" of a handful of women—women who, like Marano, Alice Quinlan, and others, held down paying jobs while they kept the Network afloat.

Solidly backed by OWLEF, the Network, especially through Marano's efforts, quickly established its credibility as being expert on the issue of service to displaced homemakers, nationally and at the regional level. Conferences were held in all but one region that first year, and organizing spread to new areas. The national office produced timely newsletters that dealt in depth with the rapidly changing status of state programs and the agonizingly slow development of federal regulations and guidelines for the new CETA monies pledged to programs for displaced homemakers. Fed information by grassroots representatives, the Network collated and issued the first national directory of existing programs.

The following year, the Network was on more solid ground but still dependent on dedicated volunteers. In 1980 it was awarded a sole source contract by the Department of Labor to provide technical assistance for the new CETA-funded displaced homemakers programs. The January issue of *Network News* announced the hiring of its first Executive Director, Sandra Burton, formerly project manager at the California Career Planning Center. Alice Quinlan was named Associate Director, and three field specialists (Charlotte Stewart, Priscilla Scanlon, and Gloria Bernheim) were added to the team. All brought more than academic credentials to the job; they either had been displaced homemakers or had developed "hands-on" experience in early state programs. (A list of all Displaced Homemaker Centers/Programs appears in the Appendix.)

The Network and those of us who support it should never lose sight of some good advice Senator Riegle passed along during the subcommittee hearing on S 418.

"I would hope," he said, "that the political organizing is going on, and the effort to organize to get concerted strength and a concerted voice continues."

Translation: The squeaky wheel gets the oil! But the work is not that of the Network alone.

In February of 1980 most CBS stations carried a program, "The Trouble with Women," hosted by Harry Reasoner. It was produced by Jane Roach, who had attended the Baltimore conference. She had an idea for a documentary film that would show the effects of the women's movement on women today. She was especially interested in finding an older woman who had lost her husband's support and was facing "going it alone." With the help of the Baltimore center staff, she found Irene Agee. She was the oldest of the three women whose lives were probed on camera by Reasoner.

Irene was then fifty-two, widowed two years earlier. It was obvious to viewers from her remarks that hers hadn't been the greatest of marriages.

"I knew what I should do; I knew what I could do, but I couldn't do it. Daddy made all the noise he wanted to, but I couldn't."

Making the best of a poor deal, she raised her children and kept in her place—quietly.

Agee explained to Reasoner that after the death of her husband, she went to the Baltimore center for help. She said the center "opened up whole new worlds" and taught her "I can do what I want to do." What she was doing then was cleaning offices to earn a living but also going to school to advance her education beyond the eighth-grade level. Unmistakably, her manner as well as her words indicated to viewing audiences that there were better things in her future. No more would she be silent. No more would she accept "peace at any price." Looking straight past Reasoner and into the eye of the camera, she sent a message into the living rooms of all of us: "We need to be heard—out loud!"

Speaking up is difficult for those of us warned, "Don't talk back!" But there are times when we must do both—speak up *and* talk back. We must learn to ask questions, to challenge the system, and dare to do even that which initially seems "undoable." We must stop confusing assertion with aggression. As Ruth Jacobs advises in her book *Life After Youth:*

> In contrast to aggression, assertion is not directed against another person, but rather is an effort to obtain what one rightfully deserves in domestic, vocational, political, and other situations.

And she quite correctly points out that

> In all these areas women have been taught to subordinate their needs to those of others. . . .

Can you challenge the system and win? Fewer times than you'll lose, but remember Sommers' advice: "Build on every breakthrough." Can one person take on the whole establishment? Yes, even though collective action is more often successful, raising one voice can turn things around. Patience is a "must"; one deals with the labyrinth of government with the understanding that its ways are Byzantine. A sense of humor helps, and often all it takes is a series of phone calls.

While gathering data for this book, I ran across a copy of a "Title III CETA Displaced Homemaker Program Summary." It briefly described a nine-month project in which 100 participants would be served and which had been funded for $39,120. What caught my eye was the breakdown of the participants to be served:

forty-four men; and of the women proposed to be served, twenty-one would be under nineteen, fourteen aged twenty through twenty-one, fifty-one aged twenty-two through forty-four, nine aged forty-five through fifty-four, and five aged fifty-five plus.

The contact person for the program was a member of the Governor's Office of Employment and Training Administration. A phone number was listed, so I decided to call and see what rationale had produced the required breakdown of participants. After all, even though we knew some men qualified as "displaced homemakers," forty-four sounded like a high figure. (For charity's sake, in the story that follows, all the names are changed.)

My call to John Dietrick found him out of the office; but an assistant, Manuel Charles, agreed it sounded pretty peculiar and offered to see if he could locate any file in the office which would explain the breakdown. Within thirty minutes he phoned back.

CHARLES : "I really can't explain this. It definitely says the breakdown you read me is the way it should be. . . ."

ME : "Does it indicate any needs assessment which dictated the percentages?"

CHARLES : "Well, that's what's funny. It says it was based on a 'splendid needs assessment' done a year or so ago; and I've got a copy of that, and all it refers to is women. Men aren't even mentioned."

There was a brief pause while we both thought about that. Suddenly he had an idea. "You know who you should talk to? Paul Tinkers. He's the director of that area; and if anyone knows about it, he does. He knows the answers to everything."

I took the phone number and asked if I could say Charles had suggested I call.

"Sure, and say hello for me."

After I identified myself, Tinkers's secretary pressed for the specifics of my call. I was happy to oblige. "I'm in the process of writing a book on displaced homemakers which will be published in the fall. I've run across some figures dealing with one of your state CETA programs that I'd like to verify. I've talked to Manuel Charles, and he suggested I phone Mr. Tinkers."

Mr. Tinkers was cordial and friendly. We joked about Charles's assertion that Tinkers had the answer for everything.

"You might like to repay him some day," I said.

"I will," he promised, "twice a day every day," because, it seemed, Mr. Tinkers did not have the answer to my question. "It was one of my planners who did that work, and I'm sure it was correctly done; but everyone's out to lunch now."

Then he cleared his throat and asked cautiously, "Er—what outfit did you say you were with?"

I told him but added it was immaterial. The information I wanted to verify was for the book.

"I would hate to have something come out in print that may have been an error. Even the best of us can make mistakes; and that figure, forty-four men, sounds pretty high to me."

His next question had no connection to my previous comment.

"How did you happen to talk to Manuel Charles?"

"Because John Dietrick's name is shown as the contact person for the program; but he wasn't in, and Charles took the call. He was most helpful; but neither of us was satisfied with the answer he came up with, which is why he suggested I phone you."

Tinkers sounded absolutely relieved.

"Well, Mr. Dietrick is right here. Let me put him on the phone."

There was a brief moment before Dietrick came on the line. He sounded wary and somewhat defensive.

"Precisely what is it you are challenging about the program?"

"Challenge seems a bit strong," I said and repeated the bit about wanting things correct in the book.

"Is there some reason to believe the figures are incorrect and why would you want to put this program in your book?"

That called for a longer explanation of the work of the Alliance and the fact that this was one of the thirty-six grants distributed from the monies won through the legislation. For that reason alone it belonged in the book.

I added, "We know men qualify as displaced homemakers—but forty-four? Either you've got many more eligible men than any other state or there's been a mistake, and either way," I said laughingly, "that's news!"

"Well," he replied, "I see your point."

After a slight hesitation he continued the conversation.

"That was done by a planner in this office. I haven't followed it closely and am not familiar with the details; but . . ."

He broke off and resumed. "Mr. Tinkers has just gone to see if the planner—his name is Ben Evers—is in his office. It's lunch hour, you know."

Well did I know! He suggested that if I didn't connect with Evers on this call, I might want to try him later. Then: "Wait. I believe Tinkers has found Evers in his office. Yes. We'll transfer your call. Just a moment."

There apparently hadn't been time for Tinkers to brief Evers. I went through the whole spiel, winding it up with "and apparently you are the one who drew up the requirements for program participants."

Wrong guess!

"Noooo, not really. I'm responsible for it, of course; but one of my staffers put it together. I really can't answer the question, and the staffer isn't here at the moment."

"I know," I said. "It's lunchtime."

He said he'd have the person phone back and inquired how long I'd be at the number. I assured him I'd be there the rest of the day.

"Well, fine. We'll be sure to get back to you before the office closes."

At exactly 5:00 P.M., their time, the phone rang. Timidly, the caller identified himself as "Dick Chance, and I guess, well, I guess I'm the one you want."

"You're it, huh?"

He sighed. "Yes, and I have to tell you there's been a big mistake. You're right, those figures are incorrect; but I can explain how it happened."

I told him I appreciated his forthright admission.

"Yeah," he said somewhat less than enthusiastically. "You see, we originally put in a proposal for a hundred-thousand-dollar program. That would have served two hundred and thirty-seven women and thirteen men. But we got turned down on that; and suddenly DOL said we could have forty thousand dollars, but we'd have to come up fast with a proposal. It was all done too fast, and I made mistakes."

I asked what he'd used as a yardstick.

"Well, they have to be CETA-eligible, so I used the Title Two-B requirements. . . ."

"How about the displaced homemaker requirements for Title Three?"

"Yes, well, that too, I guess."

"If you did that, how come there are provisions for only fourteen women forty-five and older for a program that specifically says planners should give special consideration to the needs of women forty years of age and older? How about those twenty-one participants under nineteen? How could they meet the definition that says a displaced homemaker 'is a person who, for a substantial number of years, has given unpaid service in the home to members of the family'? ["Substantial," by Department of Labor regulations, meant "five years."] "Had all twenty-one married at age fourteen?"

"Yeah, well—" his voice brightened up—"you'll be glad to know there's time to correct this. We've put this out to a subcontractor, and I've just finished talking to them. They are going to revise their proposal, and it will now serve ninety-nine women and one man."

"How about the age bit?" I asked.

"Yeah, well, I'll tell them they'd better correct that, too."

He said he was glad someone had caught the mistake but added, "DOL didn't. We sent it to them some time ago. Funny, huh?"

Not really, but it was good to end on a cheerful note; and he promised to send me a copy of the revised proposal. (He never did.)

It was curious, I thought, that in closing he added, "Of course, these are just plans. I guess anyone who walks in there and is eligible will be helped."

Why, then, have the figures? Why guidelines and regulations? How do you evaluate the program?

Those phone calls left me with other questions. Was it because the amount of funding was far from the millions they usually deal with that upper-echelon staff, who "hadn't followed that one so closely," had to bounce me from Tinkers to Evers to Chance to find they were in error? And what of the Employment Training Agency—regionally and nationally—how "closely" do they look at these "small" grants? Whether or not this one did, how many, if any, of them serve only, for whatever reason—politically or otherwise—to keep a subcontractor afloat? I don't have those answers, but I think they're valid questions for us to ask.

A good question we also might raise is what percentage of a state's CETA funds goes to provide job-training programs for women of any age, let alone women over forty. For the fiscal year 1979–80 California, for example, received $732,201,923 under CETA just for job-training programs. Additionally, the Governor had $4,682,524 in CETA funds. As for cities and counties, Los Angeles is a good example, with $111,916,509 available to the city and another $75,694,821 to the county. No answers are available yet on the percentage that went to women's programs.

According to Department of Labor regulations, CETA prime sponsors are required to give special emphasis to groups facing particular labor disadvantages, including displaced homemakers, in filling all Public Service Employment positions funded under Titles II and VI. They are also mandated to make special efforts to acquaint displaced homemakers with programs and services available under the Act.

However, as displaced homemakers, we are included in these titles as one "significant segment" among many. Since the decision-making on which segments will be served rests primarily at the local level, there will be considerable competition, especially from already entrenched groups. Who gets what, again, depends on how loud we squeak. For example, one ETA field memo to regional administrators states: "Prime sponsors will be expected to place appropriate emphasis on the provision of such services to displaced homemakers in the filling of all new PSE positions under the Act." How the word "appropriate" is interpreted will hinge on how well advocacy for displaced homemakers works at the local level. As Irene said, "We need to be heard—out loud!"

For Christmas in 1976 I received an unusual gift from Barbara Dudley. With tongue in cheek, she handed it to me, saying, "It's because you believe in fairy tales." It was one of those made-up front pages of a newspaper reproduced with the headline of the buyer's choice. In the size of type usually reserved for the declaration of war, my gift read: "DISPLACED HOMEMAKERS TAKE THE COUNTRY BY STORM." I immediately hung it on my office wall and reminded Dudley that mine was the generation that grew up singing "Fairy tales will come true/They can happen to you . . ."

Looking at that headline now, as my part of this book draws to a close, I know the "fairy tale" came true—not because, as the next line of the old song went, we "were young at heart" but because so many women, old and young, believed it could and would happen. We turned around the old saw that maintains that "if you like either the law or sausage, you should never watch it being made." We refused to be "watchers" of the process; we rolled up our sleeves, stirred up the ingredients, and delivered our own law.

There are, of course, critics who feel the win was insignificant. Depends on your yardstick; some people see bottles as half empty, others as half full. Without question, the door for displaced homemakers has been opened only a crack; but it is open! If some of the male members of Congress were blind to the needs of middle-aged and older women, more of them are more aware than ever before. In 1978 the House Select Committee on Aging compiled the first compendium of papers dealing with a wide range of socioeconomic problems of women in "mid-life." Bills to correct inequities in the pension systems that devastatingly affect us as older women have been filed; measures offering tax incentives to employers of displaced homemakers are under consideration in both the Senate and the House.

In the process of making legislators more aware of displaced homemakers, all of us as newly politicized women had our faith in participatory democracy bolstered and, by our stubborn refusal to be shunted aside, may even have reduced the cynicism of those who have abandoned any hope in the process of government. There will always be much to be done to change the social system to fit human needs—to chip away, if not blast, all of the "-isms" out of our lives and to recognize the value of homemaking with more than a collection of Mother's Day cards. During the whole campaign we frequently referred to the words of Francis Bacon: "All rising to a great place is by a winding stair." The challenge to all of us as women, as social activists, is clear. We wound our way up several flights of stairs, but there is a long way to go before we reach the "great place." A homemakers bill of rights may not come in our lifetime, but it will come.

In 1898 Alice Blackwell reminded a handful of that early band of feminists, "Every improvement thus far made has been secured, not by a general demand from the majority, but by the arguments and entreaties of a persistent few." At the Baltimore Displaced Homemaker Conference, the keynote speaker, Sarah Weddington, read a personal note from Rosalynn Carter to all in attendance:

Dear Friends,

You represent what I believe is an exciting new movement in our country, a movement of individuals who know that small, personal efforts to change things do count. . . .

If we really believe we can change things, we will. We know we can change things, because we have.

Epilogue

by TISH SOMMERS

Endings are always beginnings, but never more so than for this story. Recognizing that nothing in life is really completed but that every successful (or not so successful) closure is the springboard for the next enterprise is something many women are just learning. In our earlier romantic view of life, the wedding march brought down the curtain, followed only by happily-ever-after. Our futures were subsumed under the designation "Mrs.," complete with retirement income, health insurance, and disability benefits—all built in and not to be worried about.

It didn't work out that way for many of us. For older women, those romantic illusions came crashing down; but it took recognition of the social ramifications of older women caught in the middle before the first step could be taken to turn sad endings into new beginnings. This book has described that process. It took a name—often criticized as too negative but, nevertheless, apt and catchy—to bring to light the invisible older woman who had fallen into society's cracks and make her into a new category of "disadvantaged," recognized at last in public policy. It took a piece of legislation, Barbara Dudley's model displaced homemaker bill, to provide the organizing "handle" for building a movement; and it took a dedicated and talented person like Laurie Shields to spearhead that movement to a successful conclusion.

But how far have we come, and where are we going? Measured in terms of money allocated, displaced homemaker programs are hardly a drop in the bucket. Probably not too many of the proliferating programs will really make any lasting breakthroughs but will use the new popular label to continue business as usual.

Recognizing the political and governmental shift away from "categorical programs," "throwing money at problems," and "proliferating social programs which belong in the private domain," as they are described by critics, how long can even these sparse and pitifully underfunded programs survive before they are phased out altogether in an economy move? Programs, like people, are likely to be "last hired, first fired" in hard times.

This story has no happy ending, in the romantic sense; but it certainly does provide a sizable step forward and some lessons in political activism. Fortunately, the impetus started and remained with the grassroots. The Alliance for Displaced Homemakers was not beholden to community colleges, the Department of Labor, the Administration on Aging, or any other bureaucracy. It rallied support from women's organizations of all stripes and those in the aging field, but its basic workers were women who had experienced the problems themselves. From the beginning, the model legislation was put forward as the opening crack in a closed door, to be widened by continued pushing until homemakers are at last recognized in public policy as the workers they really are, with appropriate benefits as earned rights.

Having worked on the issue for seven years now, I confess to being older and wiser. I have not lost my optimist stance, but the scales have fallen from my eyes. If Laurie Shields learned the difference between politics and civics while working for passage of displaced homemaker legislation, I have learned to distinguish between my earlier amateur community activism and a career of "freelance agitator." Now we both prepare for an extended struggle and plot a strategy several jumps ahead.

The movement brought together the personal trauma and the societal problem: social policy failing to keep up with realities of life. The personal stories were no longer individual tales of woe but a flood of case histories which in congregate proved that something had gone awry in the social fabric and that many institutions needed reassessment. It all was a quieter echo of earlier movements in the past two decades—against racist exclusion, for equality of women, and, more recently, for independent living by the handicapped. It stated, in effect, "We have played the game according to the rules you set down. Now the rules are changed, and we're called out; but we have one-half to one-third of our lives still to go, and *we will not be shelved.*"

First there was consciousness of the commonality of experience ("I thought I was all alone"), then anger at the injustice of existing laws, and at last coalescence into political action toward a concrete reform. Not "the answer" but a beginning and proof positive that once aroused and mobilized, older women have political clout too.

But looking ahead, there are plenty of storm clouds. The 1980s are not promising for the orderly process of moving forward one step at a time. On the contrary, even untouchable benefit programs like Social Security are under attack. The mood change in Congress and in the statehouses is geared to cuts wherever they are politically feasible and to preventing new programs from sending down roots. We joined the scene a bit late.

But as a longtime activist, I am anything but discouraged. The '80s are likely to be turbulent with many crises, domestic and foreign; and crises are the mother's milk of social action. They produce misery and stench, but they are the only times when people rouse themselves enough to rearrange their thinking. For those of us who lived through it, who can forget the impact on the public consciousness of the Great Depression? The '80s should produce a shift away from purely personal solutions to group offensives. The age of Me-first is running its course and will be followed by We-need-each-other before the end of the new decade. Those of us who are dedicated to battling social injustice will be in the forefront, supporting the new doctrine.

The movement is not without resources. The Displaced Homemakers Network, founded in Baltimore the same week the CETA Act was signed by President Carter, promises to provide a strong nongovernmental advocacy base to keep programs moving forward while rallying support for using the full CETA funding allowable under that Act. This will succeed to the degree that persons using those programs are motivated to become their champions. No one can say it like the one who has personally experienced the problem and worked toward the solution. The trick will be to move from the displaced homemaker legislative victory of 1978 through the "austerity" mine fields of the next few years.

Despite the difficulties of implementing "the dream" and despite the 1980 storm clouds, job creation is still the crux of the problem. We look beyond the present gloomy job prospects for older women to bluer skies ahead. Rather than follow the pack down dead-end pathways, we will make more headway in the long run if we brainstorm imaginative new jobs and/or training ideas. Innovative programs have several advantages. They are likely to have media value and so can catch public attention, which in turn means good politics. Moreover, pioneering projects often generate enthusiasm and deep commitment by the participants which help ensure success; but most important, they can lay the groundwork for broader changes up ahead because they are banners which proclaim, "Look, it can be done; and with a little help, we'll make it happen." Pioneering is not without its hazards; but if older women are to make some breakthroughs, they must take risks and, like every other disadvantaged group, be willing to fight through to success.

Here are the major job-creation lessons we've learned so far and samples of projects that flow from them:

1. *The government can't do it all; design bootstraps for self-reliance and mutual help.* As public funding shrinks for service projects in the community (especially for the poor and elderly), local residents will become more in-

terested in mutual-aid projects. Out of necessity, self-reliance potential will grow and can be fostered by trained *community organizers.* Older women with extensive volunteer experience in community work are excellent prospects for such job creation. Trained and paid staff will be needed to mobilize neighborhood resources and volunteer leadership, to lick the inevitable problems of red tape and funding. Some typical mutual-aid projects crying to be organized are services to the homebound, consumer education projects, food-buying and distribution clubs, community vegetable gardens, minor-repair co-ops, etc.

Such projects are a middle ground between pioneer day roof-raising and more recent reliance on paid government services for everything. On the plus side, such community organizer jobs suggest an adjustment to limited service budgets while also building community clout. Women involved would learn varied skills, and politicians could be convinced of the cost-effectiveness of the mutual-aid approach. But risk-taking is involved because jobs at the end of the line are uncertain, and these projects could be used as an excuse to further reduce services.

2. *Catch the headlines and devise a constructive response.* Suppose you are painfully aware of the energy crunch. You think of the contribution that older women could make to promote conservation—women who learned at first hand to stretch almost everything during the Depression and World War II. You conceive of a corps of *home conservation specialists* (probably paid from oil profits) to visit traditional women's organizations, senior centers, churches, etc., to collect ideas from the American people on how to reduce energy waste. Realizing

that direct involvement, rather than relying solely on media, helped make the rationing plans of World War II effective, you see these persons as information gatherers as well as promoters of conservation, for when people contribute to a plan of action, they are far more committed to its success. Media would love it. Local politicians could see its advantages from their own interests. In itself, it could make an important social contribution. The persons involved would develop new skills and gain confidence. It just might be a forerunner of a national program with a grassroots base; and, most important, it could help defuse the OPEC situation.

3. *For best results with revolutionary ideas, tie in with established systems.* Home health care is a coming field, if only to reduce costs of nursing homes; but Congress and the Administration have been slow to provide Medicare coverage for "custodial" care. To date, most reimbursable home health services are low paid and the workers ill-trained. Yet in the long run, as documented by the General Accounting Office, in-home services for all but the severely impaired are less costly than institutional care. We should anticipate this shift by creating viable jobs with potential for advancement in home health care. For example, one breakthrough in this field is a proposed project designed to train selected displaced homemakers as *geriatric specialists* with a pay scale comparable to an LVN (Licensed Vocational Nurse). They will be trained in multidisciplinary skills which will allow them to work effectively in a team with doctor and nurse to provide a variety of home services to disabled elderly patients. The agency sponsoring research for this innovative project was the National Science Foundation in conjunction with the Veterans Administration.

4. *Wherever possible, link jobs with services.* There is a vast array of services for elders, but few older persons work in them for pay. The value of "paid peers" (that is, of providing jobs for the "young-old" to assist more fragile elders) is not yet recognized. A variety of projects could be designed to accomplish this purpose within existing Older Americans Act programs; for example, outreach to isolated persons not served in current programs. Training for such work (under CETA or the Older Americans Act) would also develop skills transferable to many other occupations but, most important, would provide a source of trained older persons for programs in aging.

5. *Develop a consciousness-raising industry.* Styles in clothing, hairdressing, and cosmetics are all geared to the youth cult, especially for women; but the time is ripe for a breakthrough. With the help of donated talent of a leading designer, a "Prime Life Styles" line might be developed by a nonprofit agency to raise consciousness on the beauty of aging ("designed especially for women who have lived long enough to wear them"). Media would love it (man bites dog), thereby providing quantities of free advertising. A training program could be incorporated into the production and merchandising of the products and/or a sheltered workshop for disabled persons. Plan fashion shows, train models, and move out into the community, selling pro-aging ideas along with style. For technical assistance, draw leading merchandisers into the project. This could be a big-time project!

6. *The paraprofessional is at the cutting edge of job creation.* Highly paid professionals such as lawyers are jealous of their domain and usually don't welcome paralegals except as assistants. However, there are strong pressures

for new ways to provide "dispute resolution" outside of crowded courts. Perhaps, with the assistance of a public interest law advocacy group, a small project could be designed to develop informal mechanisms for this purpose, as well as training of advocates to help old and poor people through the bureaucratic maze of their entitlements. One of the priority areas for service under the Older Americans Act as amended in 1978 is legal services, which will not be fully realized without paralegals.

7. *Use each project as a steppingstone to longer-range goals.* Nobody actually knows how many "early retirees" are really unemployed older persons forced out of the labor market. Middle-aged women, especially those with partial disabilities, are marginal workers, particularly in periods of high unemployment. Women "early retirees" are usually without pensions and forced to take Social Security at sixty-two and very often end on SSI welfare after reaching sixty-five. Since "assessment of need" is a ritual highly regarded by bureaucracy, and the lack of which is a common excuse for turning down even an excellent proposal, develop a project to "find out how many there are" who need a particular service or fit a category. For example, the Women's Equity Action League in Los Angeles was funded to hold town meetings for the purpose of finding out how many displaced homemakers would respond to the call. Or an "age audit" to determine the degree of hidden unemployment. The long-range goal is to move a step closer to an adequate national employment program.

8. *Build upon a technological advance by pointing out a new use.* Closed-circuit TV is a new technology with great potential. Since the capital investment is high, persons

connected with such a project are often looking for new uses to bring in more money. Special programming for isolated elders and disabled persons is one such possible use. One educational TV center in California has already received a sizable grant for such a project. Other emerging closed-circuit TV stations may be interested in similar projects and might be interested in one that would combine training and jobs for displaced homemakers with programming for homebound persons.

9. *When the system breaks down, devise an alternative.* When things are at a point of crisis, remember the "ill wind" adage. Some people are profiting from energy shortages and inflation. The high cost of living, especially for low-income persons, will revive variations of the barter system, some of which flourished during the Depression. "Barter is a system whose time has come and gone and come again," says one proponent. While used now primarily as tax evasion for and by large companies, on a local level it helps to build community.

Be the first to create a nonprofit barter center in your area, to provide work exchange, product exchange, learning exchange, or whatever. Whether it's an older woman who cooks a meal for a bachelor who does her shopping, or a trade of zucchini for tomatoes, the ramifications go beyond the immediate transaction. The role of the center would be to develop the system, encourage participation, maintain records, and keep it growing, creating jobs in the process. Barter for the technical assistance to get it started.

10. *Define a crying need, then develop a constructive step toward a solution.* The housing pinch is bad now and rapidly growing worse. No question but that home sharing

will increase out of necessity. Many displaced home-makers find themselves "house poor" when widowed or divorced but need a great deal of assistance and support to turn this liability into an asset. *Home-sharing expeditors* is a new job title for our times and appropriate work for a trained older woman with long experience in family management.

The Gray Panthers of Seattle, in conjunction with the Department of Human Resources, Area Agency on Aging, and a neighborhood housing improvement program, developed a proposal for Community Block Grant (HUD) money to make home sharing work. In this plan CETA-funded staff will interview prospective sharers, "matchmake" housemates, provide technical and financial information, negotiate home-sharing agreements, mediate problems, and provide information on related community resources.

I've learned the hard way how difficult it is to get even one project organized and properly funded, and the present political climate is anything but promising for new social planning; yet, I'm convinced that all of these are realistic goals. Actually, each one saves taxpayers dollars because the common denominator is self-help. All would reduce more expensive traditional social services and welfare benefits by substituting more appropriate ways of responding to society's ills.

PUBLIC POLICY AND THE OLDER WOMAN

If the needs of women in the middle years continue to be neglected in public policy, especially that concerned with employment, education, and health programs, and no effort is made to assist these women in becoming self-supporting, healthy, and independent, the government will pay the costs of that neglect in ballooning expenditures for aging women a few years later. As we worked on the displaced homemaker issue, we became painfully aware of how many of our institutions need re-examination from this point of view. A growing number of aging women are becoming dependent on government for economic survival, requiring an ever-increasing array of health and welfare services which will never catch up to their increasing needs. Yet the gender which is running into difficulties has not really been taken into account. The major issues of old age—poverty, isolation, poor physical and mental health, crime against the elderly, lack of affordable housing and transportation, and especially institutionalization—are disproportionately those of aging women.

In the past, aging women usually remained in a family setting. Now, both generations desire independence and separation, economically and personally—an option made possible by Social Security. Even though the price of such independence is poverty, the trend is in this direction, reinforced by the growing number of women moving into the labor force. There is rarely a daughter available at home to take care of an elderly mother these days, and wives usually outlive their husbands.

Customary modes of thought change slowly, sometimes long after the realities of life have altered; and institutions are brought into accord more slowly still. From the point of view of many of our laws regarding Social Security, pensions, inheritance, etc., man is the breadwinner, woman the homemaker, with marriage a lifelong commitment. But in real life, the "typical family" is the exception, not the rule. Even when laws appear to treat women and men exactly the same, the impact can be devastatingly unequal because the circumstances of women's lives are so different.

SOCIAL SECURITY

Even before the displaced homemakers bill was introduced, some of us were acutely aware of inequities in Social Security law affecting older women; and I had testified before Congress to this effect. But since Social Security, for better and for worse, is the mainstay of most elderly women and changes in the system will have a profound effect upon future beneficiaries, we approach it with caution. Social Security has withstood the test of time better than most institutions and, until recently, seemed solid as a rock; but in recent years the system has come under attack with the major pressure in the direction of containment or reduction of benefits. In the present politics of austerity, any changes are likely to reduce benefits rather than liberalize them, no matter how they are presented.

Apologists of the system argue that Social Security is neither the cause of poverty of older women, nor can it provide the cure. But in fact, it is very much a part of the cause because it extends into old age all the sins of the past in regard to inequity for women and justifies them at every turn. Here are some of the specifics:

First, sex discrimination in employment results in sex discrimination in retirement. Exclusion from "man-paying" jobs continues to haunt us into our old age because in an earnings replacement system it is on earnings that the benefit formula is based. Since women typically earn low wages, they also receive low benefits as retirees or disabled workers. So after a lifetime of hard work at low-paying, often exploitative jobs, a woman can retire at sixty-five to receive the minimum payment. The fact that benefits are weighted in favor of low-income workers does not compensate for a lifetime age differential.

Second, women are punished by Social Security for motherhood, which compounds the effect of low pay. The benefit formula averages out earnings, eliminating only the five lowest years so that every additional year out for child raising reduces average earnings. Given the child-care situation in this country and the presumed responsibility of mothers for young children, this method of computing benefits has a decidedly negative impact for mothers. As long as women have more years of zero earning than men, even the full elimination of job discrimination would leave benefits lower for women.

Third is actuarial reduction. If you are entitled to benefits, you can elect to take them at sixty-two; but the monthly payment will be reduced by actuarial tables to the equivalent on a lifetime basis of what you would receive if you waited until sixty-five. In 1970, half the women workers and only a third of the men claimed benefits at age sixty-two. Seventy percent of women did not hold out until they were sixty-five. Although some had other sources of income, the many who did not condemned themselves to a smaller benefit for life.

Fourth is the widow's gap. When the youngest child reaches eighteen, the widow's benefits cease until she is sixty or is totally disabled. Yet the homemaker-widow at fifty faces severe job handicaps, as we have seen. If her children are over eighteen, she is ineligible for Aid to Families with Dependent Children (AFDC), medical benefits, and, in some states, even general assistance. Her plight is exploited by those seeking cheap labor.

Fifth, the dependency status of homemakers under Social Security makes many older women vulnerable, especially in case of divorce. While a divorced wife (now after a marriage of ten years' duration) is eligible for benefits, these follow the breadwinner; so that if he is young or elects to continue working, the ex-wife is ineligible, even though her labor at home made possible her husband's labor at work. Also, a homemaker has no coverage for disability, although the home is a dangerous place, we are told by insurance companies.

For all these reasons, our present Social Security system contributes to the poverty of elderly women. Since 63 percent of aged Social Security beneficiaries are female, there is every good reason to examine the system from the viewpoint of this constituency—in other words, to consider the effects of our key retirement plan on the economic welfare of a majority of our citizens.

At the present time there is broad debate in Social Security circles on what changes are needed. Should the age of eligibility be raised? Should dependents benefits be phased out, and if so, how? Should employee and employer contributions be augmented by general funds? How should the changing roles of men and women be reflected in Social Security law? The debate is a healthy one; but it needs more input from older women, especially homemakers. For example, some organizations of career women are supporting the idea that dependents' benefits should be reduced to equalize benefits for the two-earner family. It is quite understandable that women who pay into Social Security should resent the fact that they may receive no more benefits than homemaker dependents, but reduction of benefits for dependents without significantly raising those for employed women provides only a psychological gain for the employed women while leaving the homemaker poorer. Sex equity should be posed as equality between males and females, not between single and married women or between women workers at home and those in the marketplace. Cuts should be resisted in any form, even in the name of women's rights. Grandmother may be a wolf in disguise.

PENSIONS

Other retirement income (government pensions, Railroad Retirement, and private-sector pensions) are even more stacked against women. Homemakers are the largest group of workers in the country; but in this country, unlike Canada, France, Germany, England, and Sweden, homemaking is not a pensionable activity. Homemakers are covered only as dependents, which makes them vulnerable in case of divorce or widowhood. Most women lose their pension rights if they lose the breadwinner.

Under most pension plans, public and private, the retiring worker can opt for a larger pension instead of a joint-life annuity which would provide for the survivor. The spouse need not even be informed of this decision. As of February 1979, more than 64 percent of federal civil service retirees, 31 percent of foreign service, and 95 percent of military retirees opted out of survivor's benefits; and the private sector is not much better. So much for taking care of the little woman! Since federal civil service and some local government retirees are not covered by Social Security, their survivors are left with no retirement income at all.

In case of divorce, none of these retirement plans provide for the divorced wife, no matter how long they were married. In the most progressive state in regard to domestic law (California) even unvested pension rights are viewed as marital property, subject to division on dissolution of the marriage. Unfortunately, the U.S. Supreme Court ruled (in *Hisquierdo*) that Railroad Retirement benefits are not community property. While the decision has been applied narrowly in California courts, other cases involving divorced persons' pension rights are coming down the pike in federal courts.

This puts the ball back in the Congressional lap, to bring these retirement laws (railroad, civil service, military, foreign service) at least into accord with Social Security in regard to divorced spouses and to return property rights in pensions back to the states. Bills have been introduced in all these areas but are not likely to pass until there is more organized pressure behind them.

HEALTH CARE

Meanwhile, there are other fronts to probe. When I was divorced at age fifty-seven and was turned down for group medical insurance because of a history of cancer, I learned that a person has access to such insurance either by virtue of employment or as a dependent of an eligible worker. Who are excluded? Primarily they are former homemakers cut adrift from a breadwinner's coverage by widowhood or divorce. Also left out are many part-time workers, lower income self-employed, such as babysitters and home health aides, domestic workers, and unemployed people and their dependents. All these groups include a large percentage of older women. At least 1.5 million women aged forty-five to sixty-four have *no* insurance coverage and are not eligible for Medicare or Medicaid, and the number is probably much higher.

Access to health care for displaced homemakers may seem like a small issue in the whole spectrum of people's problems; but to the women affected, it is a vital one. Being small, it is manageable from an organizing point of view; and like the original displaced homemaker legislation, it can raise consciousness on a larger injustice—nonrecognition of homemaking as work. We are now exploring ways to tackle this issue. Should we draft a model federal bill which would mandate continued coverage for the spouse at time of divorce? Since states regulate private insurance carriers, should we draft a model "conversion privilege" bill for state legislators? Fourteen states currently have some form of conversion provision which enables a divorced spouse to continue health insurance if she was covered under her husband's group policy, without proof of insurability (i.e., no physical), but none is really adequate. Perhaps a class-action lawsuit would be the most effective way to go. At the present time we are collecting information and case histories and studying the relevant laws to chart a plan of action.

Again, access to health insurance is just a starter when looking at the larger hurdle of staying alive and well in today's medical morass. Just as displaced homemaker programs introduced other employment-related issues, the right to insurance will open up broader questions for discussion. Certain threads will surely emerge: that the special health problems of older women have been neglected, even been invisible; that we need to fight for "fair share" of what is now available while we also work to widen the base of health-care delivery, especially for chronic illness; and if we want to stay well, we will have to do a lot more for ourselves.

In the process we will combat the myths that plague us and stimulate research to disprove them. Without solid information as a counterbalance, women internalize these myths and help keep them going. It will not be the medical profession but women themselves who break the cycle by demanding adequate research and, by their own example, put a lie to the myths.

MYTH I: MENOPAUSE IS A DISEASE

Since medical theorists are disease-oriented to start with and largely sexist to boot, it is not surprising that they should consider menstruation a pathological condition and menopause the final, incurable ill—the "death of the woman in the woman," as one writer described it. As long as the "change of life" is seen as a deficiency disease or an endocrinological disorder, surgery (hysterectomy) or drugs (estrogens or tranquilizers) are reasonable remedies; but if seen as a turning point and as a *beginning* of a new stage in life rather than as an *end*, alternative therapies (exercise, diet, stress reduction, etc.) seem more appropriate.

Middle age has been called the adolescence of aging, and the two transition periods indeed have much in common: hormonal changes, new beginnings, and new status. Young women experience stress from commencement of menses, acne, and search for self; older women have to contend with hot flashes, onset of age, and new roles. That new status may in fact be a lesser one in society's judgment, but that too can be changed when women redefine their new roles and enlighten their doctors.

The menopausal woman, caricatured as unstable, cranky, and difficult to live with, presently has good reason to be cranky. But even considering the very real problems and legitimate fears that menopausal women face today, only about 10 percent experience severe symptoms, 50 percent suffer mild symptoms, and the remainder have no symptoms at all except for the ending of menses. Apparently not every woman mourns her nonfunctional uterus, nor does she need medical intervention.

MYTH II: OLDER WOMEN ARE SEXLESS

If women are defined in terms of their reproductive function primarily, it follows that when this function ceases, sex and sexuality will fade away. Older women are seen as dried up physically and emotionally, without interest in sex and not of interest to potential partners. The research literature on sex and older persons is sparse, and most of it pertains to men; but *The Hite Report,* a nationwide study of female sexuality, smashes the cliché of the sexless older woman. Since sex is a popular subject for research, other studies will undoubtedly follow. *The Hite Report* found that: most women felt that their sexual pleasure had increased with age; other older women were interested in sex but were having difficulty finding partners they liked; some had lovers, others had begun to relate sexually to other women, and still others enjoyed sex with younger men or were content with autoeroticism.

The basic problem does not appear to lie in a lack of sexuality of older women but in a paucity of agreeable partners. In other words, if society's view of older women were enhanced, sexuality would fall into line.

MYTH III: OLDER WOMEN ARE UNATTRACTIVE

One reason so many older women lack mates is an ageist conception of beauty. Media reinforces childhood images of older women as hags, crones, witches, and mean stepmothers in more subtle forms. Madison Avenue usually pictures older women as comic characters or leaves them out entirely. The oft-noted sex differential in aging ("attractive" men with graying hair and wrinkled faces versus women clutching Oil of Olay) is not inherently part of the sex chromosomes but is created by society and can be combatted like other myths. New standards of the future will recognize the beauty of each stage of life resulting in improved mental health for all women—for those who are mid-years and older, a new joy of living; for those coming on, reduced fear of loss of youth.

MYTH IV: GOOD HEALTH BELONGS TO THE YOUNG

"What do you expect at your age?" is a refrain shared by too many medical personnel to the detriment of older persons. The expectation of ill health in later years encourages the practitioner to ignore symptoms which would be tended to in someone younger and often prevents older persons from seeking help. There is a corollary which assumes that health care is less important for older people. For example, the U.S. Commission on Civil Rights *Age Discrimination Study* reported that community health centers programs authorized under the Public Health Service Act are primarily geared to youth and women of child-bearing age.

Good health is the profound desire of most persons as they grow old. Neither age nor death is feared as much as the loss of health. This provides strong motivation for a turnaround in lifestyle, diet, and health habits and deserves the attention of medical personnel without age bias.

MYTH V: AGE AND SENILITY ARE SYNONYMOUS

When a younger woman (or man) forgets something, it is assumed that s/he has something else on her/his mind; but let an older woman (or man) make the same slip, and senility is seen as right around the corner. In fact, there is a medical term for this phenomenon: presenile cognitive slippage (PSCS). As we grow older, most of us acquire tricks to compensate for loss of short-term memory and rely more on our varied experience and improved judgment. The harm is done when we internalize the senility myth and lose faith in our own mental capacities.

According to Dr. Robert Butler, Director of the National Institute on Aging, the term is used indiscriminately, often applied by therapists to anyone over sixty with a problem. He thinks that "senility" should be discarded in favor of "emotional and mental disorders in old age," to encourage more careful diagnostic and treatment plans and to counter the notion that all mental disorders of old people are untreatable.

In some persons there is noticeable mental deterioration in old age; in many others there is not. But how much deterioration is physiologically inevitable and how much is socially induced by the label of senility, administration of drugs, and loss of dignity?

Myths are overcome in part by research, but research is stimulated by persons who clearly state from their own experience that myths are false. Women, on the whole, have successfully challenged many false conceptions about the female condition; then researchers have followed up and made it official. These myths which compound sexism with ageism are equally vincible, especially when older women speak out vigorously in their own behalf.

Some women may be in a position to influence research. Here are some questions worth pursuing related to older women and health care:

What proportion of research money is going into basic health problems of older women? For example, breast cancer is the most prevalent form of malignancy in women and usually strikes in the middle years or later. It accounts for 30,000 deaths per year, yet only 4.1 percent of cancer research funds are expended in this area. Why? Why is there no medical specialty for breast disease for that matter? What is the incidence of breast cancer of female migrant workers exposed to pesticides? Why is reconstructive surgery of the breast after mastectomy considered cosmetic? Are the sexual needs of older women less valid than for other segments of the population?

How much research money goes for studying osteoporosis (brittle bones), which occurs three to five times as often among women as men? What studies are being done on alternatives to estrogens to keep bones strong? How many research dollars are spent on arthritis, which afflicts women over sixty-five more than twice as often as men?

Is there a "gap in care" for women who no longer are served in programs related to reproduction (community health services, Planned Parenthood, etc.) and who are not eligible for Medicare? What models exist either in the U.S. or abroad for preventively oriented health care to screen for chronic diseases and offer therapies for management of such ills?

How severe is the problem of health-care access for women between the ages of forty and sixty-five? Do health-care benefits of the labor movement cover this population? Are there sex-related inequities in this age range? Do means-tested programs fill the gaps in services for middle-aged women?

How adequate are the age breakdowns in government-supported health services? The *Age Discrimination Study* noted that sufficient data were not available either nationally or by data-collecting regions to afford meaningful comparisons between the ages of participants in the community health centers program and the ages of the eligible population.

As such questions are discussed in research circles, they raise consciousness of all concerned. Occasionally a blockbuster will catch the attention of the media and help change public opinion dramatically.

One problem always leads to another. As we worked on displaced homemaker legislation, other things had to go by the board. Our "back burner" became loaded with issues awaiting action. Divorce-law reform, for example, has been more successful in improving the letter than the substance of equality. Advocacy is sorely lacking in behalf of women whose marriages of long duration are coming to an end.

Inheritance laws also have punitive effects on the homemaker. Frequently, homes and farms must be sold to pay taxes, leaving the widow who helped build these assets without shelter. Because educational curricula are still geared to younger students, creative work is needed to devise courses especially geared to the older re-entry student who has only a short time to become employable; and scholarships for this age group must somehow be provided. Housing has its special ramifications for older women as well, especially development of shared housing arrangements. The list goes on and will continue to expand as long as we live. The encouraging thing about a movement is that one group or individual begins to work to remedy a single ill, which then stimulates others to put their efforts to another, and so it goes until, looking back one day, you say, "We really *have* made some gains." The most rewarding part of the tedious work required by social activism is the many persons who are in turn motivated to take on an issue and run with it.

By the end of 1978, with the CETA amendment in our pocket and "displaced homemaker" acknowledged as a constituency to be reckoned with, and with the Displaced Homemakers Network firmed up at the Baltimore conference under Cindy Marano's capable leadership, the time to move on was clearly at hand. The Older Women's League Educational Fund (OWLEF), a nonprofit, tax-exempt organization, was already in place. We saw it as the midwife for an Older Women's League, as the brochure states:

> The activist founders of OWLEF know from first-hand experience that middle-aged and older women face special problems which have not been adequately addressed by either public or private agencies. To a degree not yet recognized, the major problems of aging in America are women's issues, the legacy of a lifetime of dependency and inequity. Circumstances now exist for a genuine civil rights struggle to rectify many of these ills, in conjunction with the women's movement and aging activism. To help bring such a movement to the fore, OWLEF is dedicated to public education and consciousness raising. Its function is to lay a foundation for the emergence of a significant advocacy organization for middle-aged and older women. . . .

What does OWLEF do? We explore issues, publish "gray papers," which are analyses of policy questions such as Social Security, pensions, health care, SSI, etc. We prepared an advocacy manual, *How to Tame the CETA Beast,* to help implement the displaced homemaker provisions of CETA. Now the time has come to make OWL really fly; recruiting members, building chapters all over the country, mobilizing our growing numbers into an effective grassroots voice for older women. The founding meeting of the Older Women's League will be held October 19, 1980, following the national mini-conference called to prepare materials on older women's issues for the 1981 White House Conference on Aging. When women ask, "What can I do to help?", we answer, pitch in to build OWL in your own communities. Readers, too, are invited to join the web of concerned and active older and "honorary older" women.

Whatever number of years are ahead, we must all take responsibility for the rest of our lives. We will be stronger if we work together. We've said it before; we'll say it again:

DON'T AGONIZE. ORGANIZE!

Appendices

VOLUNTEER
CONTRACT

VOLUNTEER: AGENCY:

DATE: JOB TITLE:

JOB DESCRIPTION: (Use extra sheet if necessary)

RESPONSIBILITIES OF VOLUNTEER:

1. Fulfillment of time commitment, as listed below.
2. Evaluation of supervision, training, and volunteer policy.
3. Evaluation of assigned duties.

WORK HOURS:

Mon: Tue: Wed: Thu: Fri: Other:

DURATION OF VOLUNTEERED SERVICES (In-kind contribution):

DURATION OF VOLUNTEER CONTRACT: To be reviewed in ____ months

RESPONSIBILITIES OF AGENCY:
1. Training and supervision: (Clarify in space below)
2. Personnel record (contract, time sheets, work evaluation, other)
3. Future work references
4. Recommendations for further responsibilities
5. Expenses, if agreed
6. Other: (Clarify in space below)

SUPERVISOR(S):

_____

Volunteer   Volunteer Coordinator or
                                   Agency Representative

USING THE VOLUNTEER CONTRACT

I INITIAL INTERVIEW

To clarify expectations and goals of both agency and volunteer, an informal discussion should precede filling out of the contract. Specifically, both should agree on the actual position, weekly time involved, length of job, purpose of volunteering (job experience leading to paid employment, college credit, general work experience, or other). The contract should be as specific and clear as possible.

II JOB TITLE

1. If work is same or similar to a paid position, state that title.
2. If work is advisory, consultant or apprenticeship, state that with identification of area involved: Legal Counselor, Volunteer Coordinator, Funding Consultant. If work is a training position, state this (e.g., Volunteer Coordinator Trainee).

III JOB DESCRIPTION

1. Specific duties: job content in detail (e.g., coordinator of

a particular workshop, administrative functions, attendance at staff meetings, supervision of clerical person, or whatever will clearly define job).
2. General duties: community outreach, legal research, answering phones, etc.
3. Future projects: to be determined by certain date.
4. Projects with a deadline: project to be accomplished by a certain date.

IV RESPONSIBILITIES OF VOLUNTEER

1. Fulfillment of time commitment; agency and volunteer must have clearly specified work hours and days, and give notice of absence.
2. Evaluation of supervision and training; volunteer's evaluation of supervision and training she is receiving; agency policy toward volunteers; can be informal or written feedback.
3. Evaluation of assigned duties: This ought to be written; it is a record for agency use when the job is assigned to another; relevance of the position, and possible improvements.

V WORK HOURS

1. Be as specific as possible: If change in hours is contemplated for the future, note time to re-evaluate.
2. If a number of hours are to be spread over a certain amount of time, try to average time on a weekly basis. If work is done outside of agency, note that.

VI VALUE OF VOLUNTEERED SERVICES

1. Determine what salary the job would command in paid employment in the area. Remember to consider previous experience. Can be an hourly wage or rate based on a specific project.
2. In-kind contribution: List the actual money amount as stated above, considering hours committed and duration of project.

VII DURATION OF VOLUNTEER CONTRACT

1. If work has a specific termination date, state it.

2. If work does not have a termination date, state a time at which to evaluate position and update the contract or end it, or rewrite contract.

VIII   RESPONSIBILITIES OF AGENCY

1. Training and supervision: Volunteer should become familiar with basic structure of agency, then be given specific training for her position. A supervisor is to be assigned to oversee the work, answer questions, and evaluate the work with the volunteer. This includes initial and ongoing training and supervision.
2. Personnel record: Agency should keep all documents concerning the volunteer and her work record in a file; evaluations should be done at specified times. Remember, this is vital in validating volunteer experience. Recordkeeping should be mandatory and consistent with agency policy re: paid personnel. Volunteer may be responsible for submitting records.
3. Recommendations for further responsibilities; within its own structure, the agency can recommend the volunteer for a more responsible position. Proper individual files will facilitate this process.
4. Future work references: Through the use of the volunteer file and supervisor evaluation, plus increase in responsibilities at the volunteer agency, the supervisor will be adequately prepared to write a job reference for a volunteer seeking paid employment.
5. Expenses: Appropriate volunteer expenses are mileage, bridge tolls, any out-of-pocket expenses (telephone, conference fees, etc.). If agency agrees to pay these, method of submitting expense forms should be discussed.
6. Other: Room for clarification—could be arrangements for specific meetings with supervisor, validation of college credit, arrangements for training, documentation of specific skills, employment possibilities.

IX   SUPERVISORS

1. Immediate supervisor
2. General supervisor
3. Special project supervisor

CHAPTER 1063

DISPLACED HOMEMAKERS

7300. The Legislature hereby finds and declares that there is an ever-increasing number of persons in this state who, having fulfilled a role as homemaker, find themselves "displaced" in their middle years through divorce, death of spouse, or other loss of family income. As a consequence, displaced homemakers are very often without any source of income; they are ineligible for categorical welfare assistance; they are subject to the highest unemployment rate of any sector of the work force; they face continuing discrimination in employment because they are older and have no recent work experience; they are ineligible for unemployment insurance because they have been engaged in unpaid labor in the home; they are ineligible for Social Security because they are too young, and for many, they will never qualify for Social Security because they have been divorced from the family wage earner; they have often lost their rights as beneficiaries under employers' pension and health plans through divorce or death of spouse, despite many years of contribution to the family well-being; and they are most often ineligible for Medi-Cal, and are generally unacceptable to private health insurance plans because of their age.

The Legislature further finds and declares that homemakers are an unrecognized part of the work force who make an invaluable contribution to the welfare of the society as a whole.

It is the intention of the Legislature in enacting this chapter to provide the necessary counseling, training, jobs, services, and health care for displaced homemakers so that they may enjoy the independence and economic security vital to a productive life and to improve the health and welfare of this ever-growing group of citizens.

7301. As used in this chapter, "displaced homemaker" is an individual who:

(a) Is over 35 years of age;

(b) Has worked without pay as a homemaker for his or her family;

(c) Is not gainfully employed;

(d) Has had, or would have, difficulty finding employment; and

(e) (1) Has depended on the income of a family member and has lost that income; or

(2) Has depended on government assistance as the parent of dependent children, but who is no longer eligible for such assistance.

7302. The Secretary of Health and Welfare shall establish a pilot multipurpose service center for displaced homemakers in the County of Alameda. To the greatest extent possible the secretary shall make grants to nonprofit agencies or organizations to carry out the various programs of the centers, as enumerated in Sections 7304 to 7310, inclusive. The service center shall be designed and staffed as follows:

(a) The multipurpose service center shall be designed to provide displaced homemakers with the necessary counseling, training, skills, services, and education to become gainfully employed, healthy, and independent.

(b) To the greatest extent possible, the staff of the service center, including supervisory, technical, and administrative positions, shall be filled with displaced homemakers. Where necessary, potential staff members shall be provided with on-the-job training by independent contractors or volunteer agencies.

7303. The secretary shall explore all possible sources of funding and in-kind contributions from federal, local, and private sources in establishing the service center, including building space, equipment, and qualified personnel for the training programs.

7304. The multipurpose service center shall be a job-counseling program for displaced homemakers. Job counseling shall be specifically designed for the person reentering the job market after a number of years as a homemaker. The counseling will take into account, and build upon, the skill and experiences of a homemaker. Peer counseling and job readiness as well as skill updating and development shall be emphasized.

7305. The multipurpose service center shall have a job-training program for displaced homemakers. The staff at the center shall work with local government agencies and private employers to develop training programs for available jobs in the public and private sectors. The job-training programs shall provide a stipend for trainees.

7306. The service center shall include, but not be limited to, the following job-training programs:

(a) Lay advocates. This program shall be directed toward developing skills in counseling and advising on administrative procedures in government programs such as Social Security, supplemental security income, welfare, and unemployment, in order that such trainees will be trained for employment in social service agencies on a community level, such. as senior citizen centers and legal aide offices.

(b) Home health technicians. This program shall be directed toward developing skills in nutrition, basic health care, and nursing for the disabled and elderly, in order that such trainees will be trained for employment by persons who are homebound through illness or disability and unable to care for themselves and their own households.

(c) Health care counselors. This program shall be directed toward developing skills in counseling techniques and in basic health care, especially for middle years individuals, in order that such trainees will be trained for employment in community and hospital outpatient health clinics.

7307. Each of the job-training programs enumerated in Section 7306 shall have as a goal for the first year, training and placing displaced homemakers, some of whom could be employed in the service programs specified in Section 7309. In addition, the service center staff shall develop with the Employment Development Department plans for including more displaced homemakers in existing job-training and placement programs.

7308. Service center staff shall be responsible for assisting the trainee in finding permanent employment. To this end, the secretary and the service center staff shall work with the Employment Development Department and the prime sponsors under the Comprehensive Employment and Training Act of 1974 in the area of the center to secure employment for displaced homemakers.

7309. The multipurpose service center shall include, but not be limited to, the following service programs for displaced homemakers:

(a) A well-woman health clinic. Based on principles of preventative health care and consumer health education, the clinics shall be staffed to the greatest extent possible by displaced homemakers and serve the health needs of older women in particular. The functions of the clinic shall include:

(1) Basic physical and gynecological examinations with emphasis on screening for common health problems of older women. The examinations may be conducted by nurse practitioners. Emphasis of such a program shall be on explanation and education about health care and physical well-being.

(2) Information and referral to physicians and clinics.

(3) Discussion and activity groups on menopause, aging, weight, and nutrition.

(4) Alcohol and drug addiction programs designed specifically to deal with the social and physical causes of addiction among displaced homemakers and other middle years women.

(b) Money management courses, including information and assistance in dealing with insurance programs (life, health, home, and car), taxes, mortgages, loans, and probate problems.

(c) Outreach and information for government programs, including concrete information and assistance with supplemental security income, Social Security, Veterans Administration benefits, welfare, food stamps, unemployment insurance, and Medi-Cal.

(d) Educational programs, including courses offering credit through community colleges or leading toward a high school equivalency degree. These courses shall be designed to supplement the usual academic course offerings with classes geared toward older persons to improve their self-image and abilities.

7310. The secretary, in consultation with the director of the service center, shall establish regulations concerning the eligibility of persons for the job training and other programs of the multipurpose service center, the level of stipends for the job training programs described in Section 7205, a sliding fee scale for the service programs described in Section 7309, and such other matters as the secretary deems necessary.

7311.

(a) The secretary shall require the director and staff of the multipurpose service center to evaluate the effectiveness of the job training, placement and service components of the center. Such evaluation shall include the number of persons trained, the number of persons placed in employment, follow-up data on such persons, the number of persons served by the various service programs, and cost effectiveness of the various components of the center.

(b) There shall be a first-year evaluation in accordance with the requirements of this section filed by the director with the secretary no later than February 1, 1977; and there shall be a second-year evaluation filed by the director with the secretary no later than January 1, 1978.

7312. The secretary shall delegate any or all of the authority granted him by this chapter to whatever department within the Health and Welfare Agency which he deems appropriate.

7313. Two years after this act goes into effect the Secretary of the Health and Welfare Agency and the Legislative Analyst shall report to the Legislature on the effectivenss of this program.

7314. This chapter shall only remain in effect until January 1, 1978, and as of such date is repealed, unless a later enacted statute, which is chaptered on or before January 1, 1978, deletes or extends such date.

Sec. 2. The sum of two hundred thousand dollars ($200,000) is hereby appropriated from the General Fund to the Secretary of Health and Welfare for the purpose of carrying out the provisions of this act. Such appropriation shall be available for expenditure until January 1, 1978.

RESOURCES

Older Women's League Educational Fund, a nonprofit organization providing public information on issues of concern to mid-years and older women. Newsletter subscription and Gray Papers which explore issues in depth, $10. Newsletter only, $3. 3800 Harrison Street, Oakland, CA 94611, (415)658-8700.

Displaced Homemakers Network, Inc., a national nonprofit organization which serves as a clearinghouse and advocate for DH programs throughout the country. The Network regional representatives are:

REGION I   Pat Wallace
             Project Second Wind
             113 Union Street
             Natick, MA 01760

REGION II   Florence Leon
             Volunteer Bureau of Bergen County
             389 Main Street
             Hackensack, NJ 07601

REGION III   Millie Jones
Displaced Homemakers Project
Villa Julie College
Brainspring Valley Road
Stevenson, MD 21153

REGION IV   Beatrice Ettinger, Director
Center for Continuing Education
Valencia Community College
P.O. Box 3028
Orlando, FL 32802

REGION V   Ruth Fossedal
Women's Development Center
Waukesha County Technical Institute
800 Main Street
Pewaukee, WI 53072

REGION VI   Jan P. Ortego, Supervisor
Displaced Homemaker Services
P.O. Box 44064
Baton Rouge, LA 70864

REGION VII   Shirley Sandage, Director
The Door Opener
215 N. Federal Avenue
Mason City, IA 50401

REGION VIII   Jerri Brown
Phoenix Institute
383 South 600 East
Salt Lake City, UT 84102

REGION IX   Joan Suter, Director
Displaced Homemakers Center
Career Planning Center
2260 W. Washington Blvd.
Los Angeles, CA 90018

REGION X   Barbara Crawford
P.O. Box 2386
Seattle, WA 98111

DISPLACED HOMEMAKERS PROGRAM DIRECTORY

A LISTING OF CENTERS, PROGRAMS, AND PROJECTS
PROVIDING SERVICES TO DISPLACED HOMEMAKERS

ALABAMA

•Displaced Homemakers Project
Women's Center
Enterprise State Junior College
Enterprise, AL 36330
Linda C. Wilson, Project
   Director
(205) 347-7881

ALASKA

•Displaced Homemaker Project
Alaska Women's Resource
   Center
P.O. Box 188
Anchorage, AK 99510
Sharon White, Project
   Coordinator
(907) 278-9047
•Displaced Homemaker Program
   of Fairbanks
Regional Adult Learning
   Center
P.O. Box 74278
Fairbanks, AK 99707
Gene Kingrea, Program
   Director
(907) 456-8473

•Inner Dimensions: Homemaker
   Re-Entry Program
South East Regional Resource
   Center
538 Willoughby Avenue
Juneau, AK 99801
Twyla Coughlin, Project
   Director
(907) 586-6806

ARIZONA

•Arizona Action for Displaced
 Homemakers, Inc.
607 N. Third Avenue
Phoenix, AZ 85003
Joann Phalen, Coordinator
(602) 252-0918

•PHASE — Project for
 Homemakers in Arizona
 Seeking Employment
University of Arizona —
 Continuing Education
1717 E. Speedway, Room 3212
Tucson, AZ 85719
Lynn O'Hern-Williams,
 Director
(602) 626-3902

•Women in Transition
Arizona Western College
2098 Third Avenue
Yuma, AZ 85364
Gail Ross, Coordinator
(602) 726-1000

ARKANSAS

•Displaced Homemakers in
 Transition
Home Economics Education
210 Home Ec. Bldg.
University of Arkansas
Fayetteville, AR 72701
Reba Davis, Director
(505) 575-4308

•Displaced Homemaker
Crowley's Ridge Development
 Council
P.O. Box 1497
Jonesboro, AR 92401
Judy Fleming, Director
(501) 932-1086

•Displaced Homemaker Program
Pulaski Vocational Technical
 School
3000 West Scenic Drive
North Little Rock, AR 72118
Kathleen P. Peek
(501) 771-1000

CALIFORNIA

•Women's Center
Chaffey Community College
5885 Haven Avenue
Alta Loma, CA 91701
Jeanne Hamilton, Director
(714) 987-1737

•Displaced Homemaker Project
Women's Resources for Work
517 Third Street
Eureka, CA 95501
Judy Wood, Project
 Coordinator
(707) 442-3773

•Displaced Homemakers
Project of Older Americans
Organization
431 E. Olive Avenue
Fresno, CA 93728
Gay L. Kennedy, Director
(209) 485-7908

•YWCA Women's Center for
New Directions
1600 M Street
Fresno, CA 93721
Betty True-Gruen, Director
(202) 237-4701

•Displaced Homemaker Program
Career Planning Center, Inc.
2260 W. Washington Blvd.
Los Angeles, CA 90018
Joan Suter, Program Director
Eleanor Hoskins, CPC Director
(213) 735-1325 or 273-8123

•Displaced Homemaker Project
Merced College — Continuing
Education
3600 M Street
Merced, CA 95340
Lynn D. Moock, Coordinator
(209) 723-4321 x291

•Displaced Homemakers Center,
Inc.
Mills College
P.O. Box 9996
Oakland, CA 94613
Milo Smith, Director
(415) 632-3205

• Crossroads Program
Cosumnes River College
8401 Center Parkway
Sacramento, CA 95823
Alleen Murdoch, Director
(916) 421-1000 x381

•Displaced Homemaker Project
Fremont School for Adults
2420 N Street
Sacramento, CA 95816
Virgil Price, Project
Administrator
(916) 454-8748

•Homemakers Employment
Re-entry Program
Inland Area Urban League
498 W. Court Street
San Bernardino, CA 92401
Mikki Pallottelli, Program
Director
(714) 884-5343

•Displaced Homemaker Project
PROVEN Seniors Program
San Diego KIND
Corporation
927 C Street
San Diego, CA 92101
Rhetta Alexander, Director
(714) 239-7751

•Displaced Homemakers Service
San Diego Community College
District
5350 University Avenue
San Diego, CA 92105
Phyllis Cooper, Project Leader
(714) 280-7610 x286

•Employment Program for
Mature Women
South Orange County YWCA
1411 N. Broadway
Santa Ana, CA 92706
Lois Morgan, Program
Coordinator
(714) 542-3577

•Displaced Homemaker Project
924 Anacapa/Lobero Bldg.,
    Suite 4-BC
Santa Barbara, CA 93101
Evelyn Ouellette, Director
(805) 966-5530

•Displaced Homemaker Project
406 N. McClelland Street
Santa Maria, CA 93454
(satellite — see Santa Barbara)
(805) 925-7817

•Working Women, Inc.
P.O. Box 7038
Santa Rosa, CA 95401
Sandra Sweitzer/Linda
    Lindsay, Co-Directors
(707) 523-3167

COLORADO

•Boulder County Women's
    Resource Center
1406 Pine Street
Boulder, CO 80302
Susan Milner, Program
    Director
(303) 447-9670

•Displaced Homemaker Program
Women's Resource Agency
25 N. Spruce Street, #309
Colorado Springs, CO 80905
Ethel Tamblyn, DH
    Coordinator
(303) 471-3170

•Mi Casa Women's Resource
    Center
1045 W. Tenth Avenue
Denver, CO 80204
Janelle Martin, Director
(303) 573-1302

•Women in Transition
    Community Programs
Center for Self-Reliant
    Education
De Anza College/Sunnyvale
808 W. McKinley Avenue
Sunnyvale, CA 94086
Celeste Brody, Project Director
(408) 737-9212

•Displaced Homemakers
    Resource Center
Victor Valley YMCA
P.O. Box 1249
Victorville, CA 92392
Margaret Jensen, Director
(714) 245-0171

•Displaced Homemaker Project
Elizabeth Stone Resource
    Center
340 E. Mountain Avenue
Ft. Collins, CO 80524
Marilyn Boyer/Elaine
    Courtney, Directors
(303) 484-1902

•Displaced Homemaker Program
Colorado Mountain College —
    Community Ed.
526 Pine
Glenwood Springs, CO 81601
Dave Beyer, Project Director
(303) 945-9196

•Women's Center
Community College of Denver,
    Red Rocks
12600 W. Sixth Avenue
Golden, CO 80401
Joyce Forney, Coordinator
(303) 988-6160 x213

•Displaced Homemaker Program
Women's Resource Center
1059 Rood Avenue
Grand Junction, CO 81501
Phyllis Carpenter, Program
  Coordinator
(303) 243-0190

•Women's Resource Center
Arapahoe Community College
5900 S. Santa Fe Drive
Littleton, CO 80123
Merna Saliman, Director
(303) 794-1550 x410

•Virginia Neal Blue Women's
  Resource Center
238 Main Street, #25
Montrose, CO 81401
Lael Van Riper, Director
(303) 249-7733

•Displaced Homemaker Program
Pueblo Vocational Community
  College
Administration Bldg., Room
  108
900 West Orman Avenue
Pueblo, CO 81004
Vera Estrada, Coordinating
  Director
(303) 549-3213

•Pueblo Women's Career
  Development Center
330 Lake Avenue
Pueblo, CO 81004
(303) 544-2192 or 2193

•Displaced Homemaker Project
Women's Center
Community College of Denver,
  North
3645 W. 112th Avenue
Westminster, CO 80030
Dixie Darr, Project Director
(303) 466-8811 x466

•Emerge — Displaced
  Homemaker Program
Colorado Northwestern
  Community College
P.O. Box 9010
Steamboat Springs, CO 80477
Janet Carlson, Project
  Administrator
(303) 879-3288

CONNECTICUT

•Women Helping Women
  Program
YWCA
1862 E. Main Street
Bridgeport, CT 06610
Swarna Raghuvir, Program
  Director
(203) 334-6154

Women's Center/Cooperative
  Education
Asnuntuck Community College
P.O. Box 68
Enfield, CT 06082
Joan Reuter/Hank Bennett,
  Directors
(203) 745-1603 x26 or x42

•The Counseling Center
Hartford College for Women
1283 Asylum Avenue
Hartford, CT 06105
Mary Merritt, Director
Sharon T. Shepela, Director of
   Research
(203) 236-5838

•Displaced Homemaker Program
YWCA
135 Broad Street
Hartford, CT 06105
Norma Cobbs, Dir. Y
Ruthie Bush Matthews, Project
   Director
(203) 525-1163

•Displaced Homemaker Program
New Haven Urban League
1184 Chapel Street
New Haven, CT 06511
Surverne Miller, Director
(203) 624-4168

•Women's Employment
   Resource Center
384 Whalley Avenue
New Haven, CT 06511
Ruth Cohen, Administrator
(203) 624-2331 or 787-0540

DELAWARE

•Delaware Displaced
   Homemakers Center
James Williams Service Center
805 River Road
Dover, DE 19901
Theresa del Tufo, Coordinator
(302) 678-4540 or 4510

•Displaced Homemakers
   Program
New London OIC
106 Truman Street
New London, CT 06320
Cathy Hampton (temporary
   Contact)
(203) 447-1731

•Center for Displaced
   Homemakers
Stamford Area CETA
422 Summer Street
Stamford, CT 06901
Norma Abrahams, Director
(203) 348-4263 x265

•Displaced Homemaker Program
(WISE Program—Women
   Involved in Securing
   Employment)
Women's Center
Mattatuck Community College
60 Harvester Road
Waterbury, CT 06706
Maureen O'Leery
(203) 574-6971

•Delaware Displaced
   Homemakers Center
New State Office Building
820 N. French Street, 6th floor
Wilmington, DE 19801
Theresa del Tufo, Coordinator
(302) 571-2714 or 2715

DISTRICT OF COLUMBIA

•Displaced Homemaker Program
Wider Opportunities for
  Women
1649 K Street, NW
Washington, DC 20006
Janet Silverman, Coordinator
(202) 638-4868

•Hannah Harrison Career School
4470 MacArthur Blvd., NW
Washington, DC 20007
Anne K. Milkes, Director
(202) 333-3500

FLORIDA

•Manatee County Displaced
  Homemaker Program
405 Sixth Avenue, East
Bradenton, FL 33508
Margot Joynes, Director
(813) 748-2761 or 747-4611

•Department of HRS Displaced
  Homemaker Program
1100 Cleveland Street, 7th
  floor
Clearwater, FL 33515
Rebecca Stutchin, Coordinator
(813) 461-1616 x271

•Fresh Start for Displaced
  Homemakers
Daytona Beach Community
  College — Women's Center
P.O. Box 1111
Daytona Beach, FL 32015
Sue Rollins, Project Director
(904) 255-8131 x326

•Rediscovery — Displaced
  Homemaker Program
Lee County CETA
3800 Michigan Avenue
Fort Myers, FL 33905
Emma Dunmire, Program
  Administrator
(813) 334-8184

Challenge: The Displaced
  Homemaker
Florida Junior College at
  Jacksonville
101 W. State Street
Jacksonville, FL 32202
Elaine R. Smith, Coordinator
(904) 633-8316 or 8319

•Displaced Homemaker Center
YWCA
210 N. E. 18th Street
Miami, FL 33132
Carol Klopfer, Project Director
(305) 377-8161

•Displaced Homemakers
  Resource Center
Adult/Community Education
  Program
Collier County Public Schools
3710 Estey Avenue
Naples, FL 33942
Jacquelin I. Fleming, Program
  Director
Linda M. Milone, Center
  Coordinator
(813) 774-3460

•Displaced Homemaker Program
Center for Continuing
   Education for Women
Valencia Community College
P.O. Box 3028
Orlando, FL 32802
Beatrice Ettinger, Center
   Director
Virginia Stuart, Program
   Coordinator
(305) 299-5000 x526

•Department of HRS Displaced
   Homemaker Program
240 N. Washington Blvd., #704
Sarasota, FL 33577
Ellen K. Simpson, Coordinator
(813) 366-1707

•Women's Living and Learning
   Program
St. Petersburg Junior College —
   Continuing Ed.
P.O. Box 13489
St. Petersburg, FL 33733
Jane Maddox, Director
(813) 546-0011 x289

•Displaced Homemaker Program
Adult Home Econmics
St. Petersburg, Voc.-Tech.
   Institute
901 34th Street, South
St. Petersburg, FL 33711
Judith Smith, Coordinator
(813) 895-3617, x270

•Center for Creative
   Employment
P.O. Box 1326
Tallahassee, FL 32302
Pat Schwallie, Director
(904) 222-3824

•Women's Survival Center, Inc.
305 Hyde Park Avenue
Tampa, FL 33606
Janet Schapper, Executive
   Director
(813) 251-8437

GEORGIA

•Displaced Homemaker Project
Atlanta Area Technical School
   — Home Ec. Dept.
1560 Stewart Avenue, SW
Atlanta, GA 30310
Irene Rose, Supervisor
(404) 758-9451

•Displaced Homemaker Program
Augusta Area Technical School
1688 Broad Street
Augusta, GA 30904
Frances Yeargan, Coordinator
(404) 738-3010

•Career Center
DeKalb Community College
555 N. Indian Creek Drive
Clarkston, GA 30021
Ann M. Castricone, Director
(404) 292-1520 x304

•Displaced Homemakers
   Program
Columbus Area Vocational –
   Technical School
928 45th Street
Columbus, GA 31904
Connie Hebb, Coordinator
(404) 322-1425

•DH Program
Department of Home
 Economics
110 Herty Bldg.
Georgia Southern College
Stateboro, GA 30458
Cindy Thomas, Acting
 Coordinator
(912) 681-5345

HAWAII

•Displaced Homemaker Project
YWCA of Oahu
P.O. Box 337
Honolulu, HI 96809
Barbara Dykes, Project Director
(808) 538-7061

•Divorce Clinic/Divorce
 Experience
217 S. King, Room 211
Honolulu, HI 96813
Marybeth Webster, Director
(808) 523-1776

IDAHO

•YWCA Women in Transition
 Project
720 Washington Street
Boise, ID 83702
Vicki Jo Riggins, Program
 Coordinator
(208) 343-3688

•YWCA Women in Transition
 Project
300 Main Street
Lewiston, ID 83501
Lydia Bodah, Project
 Coordinator
(208) 746-9205

•Displaced Homemaker Program
 — Women's Center
College of Southern Idaho
P.O. Box 1238
Twin Falls, ID 83301
Cherri Briggs, Program
 Coordinator
(208) 733-9554

ILLINOIS

•Displaced Homemaker Program
321 S. Main Street
Benton, IL 62812
(satellite — see Carbondale)
(618) 439-9720

•Displaced Homemaker Program
Carbondale Women's Center
408 W. Freeman Street
Carbondale, IL 62901
Rosemary Hawkes, Coordinator
(618) 529-2412

•Project New Start/Displaced
  Homemakers Center
Chicago City-Wide College
185 N. Wabash Avenue, 8th
  floor
Chicago, IL 60601
Carol R. White, Coordinator
(312) 977-2538

•Horizons Unlimited — The
  Displaced Homemaker
  Project
Richland Community College
2425 Federal Drive
Decatur, IL 62526
Diana Meister, Director
(217) 875-7200 x234

•Project Turning Point
Harper College — Women's
  Program
Algonquin & Roselle Roads
Palatine, IL 60067
Rita Michalak, Coordinator
Anne Rodgers, Counselor
(312) 397-3000 x536

INDIANA

•Fort Wayne Women's Bureau,
  Inc.
P.O. Box 554
Fort Wayne, IN 46801
Harriet Miller, Executive
  Director
(219) 424-7977

IOWA

•The Door Opener
106 N. Moore Street
Algona, IA 50511
(satellite — see Mason City)
(515) 295-2256

•Displaced Homemaker Program
Community Service Council of
  N. Will County
759 Luther Drive
Romeoville, IL 60441
Rose P. Lee, Director
(815) 886-5000

•Displaced Homemakers Project
Student-Counseling Center
Lincoln Land Community
  College
Shepherd Road
Springfield, IL 62708
Jean Shuman
(217) 786-2226

•Displaced Homemaker Project
College of Continuing
  Education — Women's
  Programs
Drake University
Des Moines, IA 50322
Rita Kingkade, Project Director
(515) 271-2011 (operator)

•The Door Opener
215 N. Federal Avenue
Mason City, IA 50401
Shirley Sandage, Executive
Director
(515) 424-9071

KANSAS

•Displaced Homemakers
Program
College of Education
Holton Hall
Kansas State University
Manhattan, KS 66506
Debra L. Olson

KENTUCKY

•Center for Displaced
Homemakers
Talbert Continuing Education
Center
1018 S. Seventh Street
Louisville, KY 40203
Bettye Ferguson, Coordinator
(502) 584-5194

•DH Program
Creative Employment Project —
YWCA
608 S. Third Street
Louisville, KY 40202
Susan Reid, Program Director
Betsy Jacobus, Director
(502) 585-5550

LOUISIANA

•Displaced Homemakers Center
Louisiana Bureau for Women
2441 Government Street
Baton Rouge, LA 70806
Mary Boyd, Director
(504) 342-2728

•Project for Displaced
Homemakers and Others
Indian Hills Community
College
Ottumwa, IA 52501
Loretta Hudson, Coordinator
(515) 682-8081

•Displaced Homemakers Center
YWCA
350 N. Market Street
Wichita, KS 67202
Virginia Moss, Center Director
(316) 263-7501

•Displaced Homemaker Center
Owensboro Public Schools
1212 W. 11th Street
Owensboro, KY 42301
Marilyn Fentress, Director
(502) 685-4964

•Center for Displaced
Homemakers
414 Louisiana Avenue
Lake Charles, LA 70601
Patricia Dowe, Director
(318) 433-6525

• Center for Displaced
  Homemakers
  4747 Earhart Blvd., Suite 205
  New Orleans, LA 70125
  Rebecca Ripley
  (504) 483-4664

MAINE

• In Transition: Displaced
  Homemaker Project
  Stoddard House
  University of Maine at Augusta
  Augusta, ME 04330
  Gilda Nardone, Project Director
  (207) 622-7131 x338 or x334

MARYLAND

• Career Resource Center
  YWCA Women's Center
  1153 Tyler Avenue
  Annapolis, MD 21403
  Lea Price, Director
  (301) 268-4393

• Center for Displaced
  Homemakers
  Baltimore New Directions for
  Women
  2435 Maryland Avenue
  Baltimore, MD 21218
  Barbara Turner, Director
  (301) 243-5000

• Open Doors: A Career
  Counseling Center
  YWCA
  2023 Emmorton Road — Rt. 24
  Bel Air, MD 21014
  Louise Kennard, Program
  Coordinator
  (301) 838-1480 or 879-9627

• Candance Pickering
  City of Shreveport
  P.O. Box 31109
  Shreveport, LA 71130
  (318) 226-5848

• CASA, Inc. — New Directions
  for Women
  100 N. Potomac Street
  Hagerstown, MD 21740
  Vicki Sadehvandi, Program
  Coordinator
  (301) 739-4990

• New Phase: Career Readiness
  for Women
  50 Monroe Street, Room B-06
  Rockville, MD 20850
  Lavonne Hurd, Program
  Manager
  (301) 279-1800

• New Alternatives
  601 Addison Road, South
  Seat Pleasant, MD 20027
  Doris McGuffey, Director
  (301) 350-0843

•Displaced Homemakers
  Program
Villa Julie College
Greenspring Valley Road
Stevenson, MD 21153
Millie Jones, Director
(310) 486-7353

MASSACHUSETTS

•Widening Opportunity
  Research Center (WORC)
Middlesex Community College
P.O. Box T
Bedford, MA 01730
Susan Capon, Coordinator
(617) 275-8910 x291

•Math & Electronics for
  Displaced Homemakers
120 Pembroke Street
Boston, MA 02118
Ferol Breymann, Director
(617) 423-4630

•Project Re-Entry
Civic Center and Clearing
  House, Inc.
14 Beacon Street
Boston, MA 02108
Phyllis Adelberg/Sandra Kahn,
  Co-Directors
(617) 227-1762

•Women's Job Re-entry Center
34 Follen Street
Cambridge, MA 02138
Sheila Cook
(617) 547-1123

•Homemaker Re-entry Program
545 Westminster Street
Fitchburg, MA 01420
Winnie Deibert, Senior Trainer
(617) 342-7919

•Displaced Homemakers
  Re-entry Center
Chesapeake College
Wye Mills, MD 21679
Mary Jane Meyers, Director
(301) 758-1537

•Second Wind/Displaced
  Homemaker Project
196 Fountain Street
Framingham, MA 01701
Patricia Wallace, Coordinator
(617) 872-4661

•Clerical/Office Skills for
  Displaced Homemakers
Holyoke Community College
303 Homestead Avenue
Holyoke, MA 01040
Judy Edwards/Jane Provost,
  Coordinators
(413) 538-7000 x308 or x310

•Homemaker Re-entry Program
57 Jackson Street
Lawrence, MA 01840
Gloria Bernheim, Director
(617) 687-6607

•Multi-Skills Program for
  Displaced Homemakers
WINNERS, Inc./Roxbury
  Community College
134 Warren Street
Roxbury, MA 02119
Marguerite Goodwin, Executive
  Director
Karen Blake, Program
  Coordinator
(617) 442-9150

•Hamden County Women's
Center
347 St. James Avenue
Springfield, MA 01109
Janis DiMonaco, Director
(413) 739-4775

MICHIGAN

•Soundings: A Center for
Continuing Growth
602 Oswego Street
Ann Arbor, MI 48104
Glenora Brown, Director
(313) 665-2606

•Displaced Homemaker Program
Bay County Women's Center
P.O. Box 646
Bay City, MI 48707
Maureen Almond

•Women's Resource Center
Henry Ford Community
College
5101 Evergreen Road
Dearborn, MI 48128
Grace B. Stewart, Director
(313) 271-2750

•Displaced Homemaker Center
806 Ludington Street
Escanaba, MI 49829
(satellite — see Marquette)
(906) 228-9400

•Displaced Homemaker Center
Women's Resource Center
226 Bostwick, NE
Grand Rapids, MI 49503
Joyce Puls, Director
(616) 456-8571

MINNESOTA

•Displaced Homemaker Program
Fairmont CETA Center
932 E. Kent Street
Fairmont, MN 56031
(satellite — see New Ulm)
(507) 238-4214

•Displaced Homemaker Center
Women's Center
N. Michigan University
Marquette, MI 49855
Marilyn Marshall, Executive
Director
(906) 227-2219 or 228-9400

•Women Reaching Out/CETA
Program
Everywoman's Place, Inc.
23 Strong Avenue
Muskegon, MI 49441
Althea Stevens, Program
Coordinator
(616) 726-4493

•Displaced Homemaker Project
Community Resources/
Women's Center
Macomb County Community
College
14500 Twelve Mile Road
Warren, MI 48093
Ruth Anne Ziegler, Project
Coordinator
(313) 779-7417

•Displaced Homemaker Program
Mankato CETA
709 N. Front Street
Mankato, MN 56001
(satellite — see New Ulm)
(507) 389-6073

•Mainstay, Inc.
700 N. Seventh Street
Marshall, MN 56258
Ruthann Wefald, Coordinator
(507) 537-7166

•Metropolitan Center for
  Displaced Homemakers
Working Opportunities for
  Women
2344 Nicollet Avenue, South
  Suite 240
Minneapolis, MN 55404
Marita Heller, Project Director
(612) 874-6636

•Displaced Homemakers
  Program
CETA Center
1200 S. Broadway
New Ulm, MN 56073
Pamela Brumbaugh,
  Coordinator
(507) 359-2031

MISSISSIPPI

•Displaced Homemaker Project
  — Program Services
Itawamba Junior College
653 Eason Blvd.
Tupelo, MS 38801
Bill T. Lowry, Coordinator
(601) 842-5621

MISSOURI

•New Directions Center
200-A Austin Avenue
Columbia, MO 65201
Marci Lower, Coordinator
(314) 443-2421

•Metropolitan Center for
  Displaced Homemakers
Working Opportunities for
  Women
2233 University Avenue, Suite
  340
St. Paul, MN 55114
Project Director — see
  Minneapolis
(612) 647-9961

•Displaced Homemaker Project
  — Program Services
Vocational-Technical Center
Mississippi Delta Junior
  College
Moorhead, MS 38761
Matha Woodall, Coordinator
(601) 246-8802

•Project SEARCH
Displaced Homemakers
  Program
Central County School, Room
  134
10900 Ladue Road
Creve Coeur, MO 63141
(314) 432-4865

●People Employable — CETA
  Project
University of Missouri at
  Kansas City — Truman
600 Mechanic
Independence, MO 64050
Jo Ellen Lightle, Coordinator
(816) 254-8739

●Project Transition
Kansas City Technical
  Education Center
1215 Truman Road
Kansas City, MO 64106
Joe Perez, Director
(816) 471-3568 x30

●Re-entry/Displaced
  Homemakers Program
560 Westport Road
Kansas City, MO 64111
Karen Herzog, Director
(816) 756-0220, x330

●Project Re-entry
Moberly Junior College
College & Rollins
Moberly, MO 65270
Dr. Jeanne Lee, Coordinator
(816) 263-4110

MONTANA

●Women's Center
YWCA
909 Wyoming Avenue
Billings, MT 59101
Sally Weinschrott, Center
  Director
Jean Bradford, YWCA
  Executive Director
(406) 245-6879

●Displaced Homemaker Program
Department of Human Services
299 E. Commercial Street
Springfield, MO 65803
Mary Schaeffer, Administrator
(417) 864-1800

●Displaced Homemaker Program
University of Missouri — St.
  Louis
8001 Natural Bridge Road
St. Louis, MO 63121
Jean S. Berg, Project Director
(314) 453-5621

●New Directions — Displaced
  Homemaker Center
Buder School
5319 Lansdowne Avenue
St. Louis, MO 63109
Dorothy O. Survant,
  Coordinator
(314) 352-4343

●Women in Transition/
Displaced Homemaker Center
Missoula YWCA
1130 W. Broadway
Missoula, MT 59801
Jo Waldbillig, Center Director
Arlene Ward Braun, YWCA
  Executive Director
(406) 543-6768

NEBRASKA

*Displaced Homemakers
Program
YWCA
222 E. Third Street
Grand Island, NE 68801
Glenda Brown, Coordinator
(308) 384-8170

•Displaced Homemaker Program
Omaha YWCA
3929 Harney Street, Room 100
Omaha, NE 68131
Holly Alexander, Coordinator
(402) 342-2748

NEVADA

•Divorced and Widowed
Adjustment Groups, Inc.
P.O. Box 5861
Las Vegas, NV 89102
Park Baker, Director
(702) 382-8243

•Displaced Homemaker Center
Clark County Community
College
3200 E. Cheyenne Avenue, Rt.
2204
N. Las Vegas, NV 89110
Fern Lea Latino, Director
(702) 643-6060 x272

•Women's Resource Center
Reno-Sparks YWCA
1301 Valley Road
Reno, NV 89512
Nadine Phinney, Program
Director
(702) 322-4531

NEW HAMPSHIRE

•Displaced Homemaker Program
YWCA
72 Concord Street
Manchester, NH 03101
Susan Littlefield

•Project PLACE
Adult Learning Center
27 Burke Street
Nashua, NH 03060
Shelley Barsanti, Project
Coordinator
(603) 882-9080

NEW JERSEY

•Alternatives for Women Now
517 Penn Street
Camden, NJ 08102
Carlette Robert, Program
Director
(609) 964-8033 or 8034

•Displaced Homemaker Project
Women's Career Information
Center
Middlesex County College
Edison, NJ 08817
Bonnie Dimun, Center Director
(201) 548-6223

• Women Working
Bergen County Community
Action Program, Inc.
17-25 DiCarolis Ct.
Hackensack, NJ 07601
Judy Murphy, Coordinator
(201) 487-3400 x26 or x44

• Women's Services
YWCA of Burlington County
15 W. Main Street
Moorestown, NJ 08057
Janet Tegley, Program
Development
(609) 235-6697

NEW MEXICO

• Displaced Homemakers Office
New Mexico Commission on
the Status of Women
Plaza del Sol Bldg., Room 811
600 Second Street, NW
Albuquerque, NM 87102
Tasia Young, Executive
Director
(505) 842-3286 or 3141
(800) 432-9168 (toll free — in
state)

NEW YORK

• Displaced Homemaker Program
Nassau BOCES
Adult Occupational Education
Center
One Albertson Avenue
Albertson, NY 11507
Doris Peppard, Project
Coordinator
(516) 484-1900

• Project WHY — Women Help
Yourself
Essex County College
Newark, NJ 07102
Carolyn Miller, Director
(201) 877-3370

• Douglass Advisory Services for
Women
Rutgers Women's Center
132 George Street
New Brunswick, NJ 08903
Viola Van Jones, Director
(201) 932-9603 or 9274

• Displaced Homemakers
Program
Bronx Community College of
CUNY
University Avenue and W.
181st Street
Bronx, NY 10453
Margaret Hunt, Project
Director
(212) 367-7300

• Displaced Homemaker Program
of Park Slope
WISH — Women in Self Help
421 Fifth Avenue
Brooklyn, NY 11215
Carol McVicker, Program
Director
(212) 768-9700 or 9714

• Fresh Start Training Program
Agudath Israel of America
813 Avenue H
Brooklyn, NY 11230
Risa Schmookler, Director
(212) 434-8098 or 8099

• Displaced Homemaker Center
of Western New York
Everywoman's Opportunity
Center, Inc.
1407 Genesee Bldg.
Buffalo, NY 14202
Betsy Hopkins, Director
(716) 847-8850

• "Suddenly Single" Project
YWCA
211 Lake Street
Elmira, NY 14901
Betsy Boland, Executive
Director
(607) 733-5575

• Displaced Homemakers Center
5 East Main Street
Fredonia, NY 14063
(satellite — see Buffalo)
(716) 673-1388

• Displaced Homemakers
Program
Action Council of Central
Nassau, Inc.
Farmedge Road, Island Trees 1
Levittown, NY 11756
Phyllis Borger, Director
(516) 579-7616

• Displaced Homemaker Program
— Women's Center
YWCA of New York
610 Lexington Avenue
New York, NY 10022
Chris Filner, Program Director
(212) 755-4500 x15

• Displaced Homemaker Project
— Women's Center
National Council of Negro
Women
198 Broadway, Suite 200
New York, NY 10038
Henrietta Whitcomb, Project
Coordinator
Merble Reagon, Center
Director
(212) 964-2727

• Displaced Homemakers Center
1317 Portage Road
Niagara Falls, NY 14301
(satellite — see Buffalo)
(716) 282-8472

• Displaced Homemakers
Program
Rockland County Guidance
Center for Women
10 N. Broadway
Nyack, NY 10960
Margaret T. Anderson
(914) 358-9390 or 9391

• Displaced Homemakers Center
149 Broad Street
Tonawanda, NY 14150
(satellite — see Buffalo)
(716) 692-4268

NORTH CAROLINA

•Displaced Homemaker Center
YWCA
809 Proctor Street
Durham, NC 27707
Julia Slabos, Project Director
(919) 682-9671

•Displaced Homemakers Center
Center for Continuing
Education
Fayetteville State University —
Newbold Station
Fayetteville, NC 28301
Barbara Ragland Jones,
Director
(919) 486-1221

•Career Development Center for
Displaced Homemakers
Wilcar Executive Center
223 W. Tenth Street
Greenville, NC 27834
Nan Cheek, Director
(919) 752-0642

•Homemaker Entry Program
YWCA Women's Center
112 Gatewood Avenue
High Point, NC 27260
Muriel M. Gruen, Program
Coordinator
(919) 882-4126

•Career Development Center
Project for Displaced
Homemakers
139 College Street
Oxford, NC 27565
Chris Amerling, Director
(919) 693-1342, 693-6027

•Career Development Center
Council on the Status of
Women
526 N. Willmington Street
Raleigh, NC 27604
(919) 733-2455

•Career Development Center for
Displaced Homemakers
Old Post Office Bldg.
Roxboro, NC 27593
Darlene Wells, Director
(919) 599-9865

•Career Development Center for
Displaced Homemakers
Cleveland Tech Annex
North Washington Street
Shelby, NC 28150
Pat Evans, Director
(704) 487-1901

•Displaced Homemaker Project
Women's Center
Southeastern Community
College
P.O. Box 151
Whiteville, NC 28472
Nancy A. Merson, Coordinator
(919) 642-8700

•Displaced Homemaker Program
Cape Fear Technical Institute
411 N. Front Street
Wilmington, NC 28401
Robin Lewis, Coordinator
(919) 343-0481

NORTH DAKOTA

•Bismarck-Mandan Displaced
Homemakers League
704 Mandan Street
Bismarck, ND 58501
Bonnie Palacek/Bette
Hildebrand, Coordinators
(701) 258-3597

OHIO

•Four County JVS
Archbold, OH 43502
(419) 267-3331

•Career Advancement Program
— Women's Network
Peoples Federal Bldg., Suite 502
39 E. Market Street
Akron, OH 44308
Elizabeth Wettach-Ganocy,
Program Director
(216) 376-7852

•Ohio Hi-Point JVS
Bellefontaine, OH 43311
(513) 599-3010

•Pickaway-Ross JVS
Chillicothe, OH 45601
(614) 642-2550

•Displaced Homemaker Program
McMillan Adult Center
608 E. McMillan
Cincinnati, OH 45206
Sandra L. Hendricks,
Coordinator
(513) 241-7090 or 221-5052

•Scarlet Oaks JVS
3254 E. Kemper Road
Cincinnati, OH 45241
(513) 771-8810 x203

•Montgomery County JVS
Clayton, OH 45315
(513) 837-7781

•Displaced Homemaker Program
CAP—Region VII
2105 Lee Avenue
Bismarck, ND 58501
(701) 258-2240

•Displaced Homemaker Program
Cuyahoga Community College
11000 Pleasant Valley Road
Cleveland, OH 44130
Roslyn Talerico, Director
(216) 845-4000 x250 or 241-5966
x437

•Dayton Public Night School
118 E. First Street
Dayton, OH 45402
(513) 222-6301

•Re-entry Women Program
Career Development Center
Wright State University
140 E. Monument Avenue
Dayton, OH 45402
Syd Golub, Coordinator
(513) 223-6041

•Vanguard Vocational Center
Fremont, OH 43420
(419) 332-2626

•Ashtabula County JVS
Jefferson, OH 44047
(216) 576-6015

•Apollo JVS — State Coord.
Office
2225 Shawnee Road
Lima, OH 45806
Carol Bodeen, Program
Developer
(419) 999-3015

•Columbiana County JVS
Lisbon, OH 44432
(216) 424-9561

•New Directions for Women
Project
The Grail — Grailville
Loveland, OH 45140
Mary Gindhart, Coordinator
(513) 683-2962

•Tri-Rivers JVS
Marion, OH 43302
(614) 389-4681

•Tri-County JVS
Nelsonville, OH 45763
(614) 753-3511 x23

•Buckeye JVS
New Philadelphia, OH 44629
(216) 339-2288

•Upper Valley JVS
Piqua, OH 45356
(513) 778-1980

•Guernsey-Noble JVS
Senecaville, OH 43780
(614) 685-2518

•Springfield Clark JVS
1901 Selma Road
•Springfield, OH 45505
(513) 325-8347

•Laurel Oaks JVS
Wilmington, OH 45177
(513) 382-1411

•Green County JVS
2960 Enon Road
Xenia, OH 45385
(513) 372-6941

•Youngstown City Schools
200 E. Wood Street
•Youngstown, OH 44503
(216) 743-2187

OKLAHOMA

•Displaced Homemakers Project
YWCA
525 S. Quincy
Enid, OK 73701
Ethel Mae Payne, Project
Director
(405) 234-7581

•Center for Displaced
Homemakers
Moore-Norman Area
Vocational-Technical School
4701 12th Avenue, NW
Norman, OK 73069
Jan Womack, Director
(405) 364-5763

•Displaced Homemaker Services
— University Extension
137 Home Economics West
Oklahoma State University
Stillwater, OK 74074
Beulah Hirschlein, Director
(405) 624-6570

•YWCA Employment/Personal
Counseling Service
1920 S. Lewis
Tulsa, OK 74105
Karen Griffith, Project Director
(918) 749-2519

OREGON

•Displaced Homemakers/
  Widowed Services Program
1609 Agate Street
Eugene, OR 97403
Hazel M. Foss, Director
(503) 686-4220

•Solo Center
1832 N.E. Broadway
Portland, OR 97232
Betty Daggett, Director
(503) 287-0642

•Displaced Homemakers
  Program
Salem YWCA
768 State Street
Salem, OR 97301
Diane Clayton, Program
  Coordinator
(503) 581-9922

PENNSYLVANIA

•Displaced Homemaker Program
Butler County Community
  College
College Drive, Oak Hills
Butler, PA 16001
Sue R. Bennitt, Coordinator
(412) 287-8711

•Women's Career Alternative
  Program
Continuing Education
Cheyney State College
Cheyney, PA 19319
Priscilla Farmer, Program
  Coordinator
(215) 758-2406

•Displaced Homemakers
  Program
Central Pennsylvania
  Community Action
650 Leonard Street, Box 792
Clearfield, PA 16830
Kay Selner, Coordinator
(814) 765-1551

•Steppin Stones
Bucks County Community
  College
Swamp Road
Newtown, PA 18940
Kathleen Torzala
(215) 968-5861 x358
(215) 672-5505

•Women in Transition, Inc.
4025 Chestnut Street, Room 305
Philadelphia, PA 19104
Linda Resnick/Sarah Lynne
  McMahon, Co-Directors
(215) 387-5556 or 386-4900
  (hotline)

•Job Advisory Service
Chatham College
Woodland Road
Pittsburgh, PA 15232
Kathryn McGregor, Director
(412) 441-6660 or 6661

•Women in Transition Project
Community College of
  Allegheny County — North
1130 Perry Highway — 111
  Pines Plaza
Pittsburgh, PA 15237
Mary Lane Salsbury,
  Coordinator
(412) 366-7000 x35

•Women's Career Development
  Center for DH
Reading Area Community
  College
Box 1706
Reading, PA 19603
Belinda Gutwein, Coordinator
(215) 372-4721 x288

•WORC Project
64 S. Beeson Blvd.
Uniontown, PA 15401
Marilyn McDaniel, Project
  Director
(412) 438-1470

•Iris Freiman, Project
  Coordinator
West Chester YWCA
123 N. Church
West Chester, PA 19380
(215) 692-3737

RHODE ISLAND

•Displaced Homemaker Center
Department of Community
  Affairs
150 Washington Street
Providence, RI 02903
Elaine Roberts, Coordinator
(401) 277-2862

SOUTH CAROLINA

•Opening Doors for the
  Displaced Homemaker
Center for Continuing
  Education for Women
Greenville Technical College
P.O. Box 5616
Greenville, SC 29606
Harriet Kessinger, Director
(803) 242-3170 x500

•Transition Resources, Inc.
P.O. Box 512
Orangeburg, SC 29115
Jean Lipscomb, Project
  Coordinator
(803) 536-5972

•Center for Displaced
  Homemakers
YWCA of Wilkes-Barre
40 W. Northampton Street
P.O. Box 1283
Wilkes-Barre, PA 18703
Marianne Mebane, Director
(717) 823-7758 or 0181

•Displaced Homemaker Project
Beaufort-Jasper Career
  Education Center
Route 1, Box 127
Ridgeland, SC 29936
Mary Lou Cordray,
  Coordinator
(803) 726-8107

SOUTH DAKOTA

•Displaced Homemaker Project
Center for Women
Sioux Falls College
Sioux Falls, SD 57101
Jan DeWitt, Director
(605) 336-2850 x161

•Displaced Homemaker Project
Resource Center for Women
620 S.E. 15th Avenue
Aberdeen, SD 57401
Mary Hayenga, Project Director
(605) 226-1212

TENNESSEE

•WORK Program
Knoxville Women's Center
406 Church Street
Knoxville, TN 37902
Cheryl Fowler, Director
(615) 524-0716

•Displaced Homemakers
Project
YWCA
1608 Woodmont Blvd.
Nashville, TN 37215
Gail Kopcsak, Director
(615) 385-3952

•Second Start
East Tennessee Human
Resource Agency
4711 Old Kingston Pike, #112
Knoxville, TN 37919
Jo Rutherford, Director
(615) 584-0244

•Career Directions for Displaced
Homemakers
Kingsbury Vocational-
Technical Center
1328 N. Graham Street
Memphis, TN 38128
Laura Lea Terrill/Ruth Ann
Wright, Coordinators
(901) 454-5586

TEXAS

•Displaced Homemakers
Program
Amarillo College — Office of
Women's Programs
P.O. Box 447
Amarillo, TX 79178
Michele Gilmour, Director
(806) 376-5111 x319 or x320

•Displaced Homemaker Program
Henderson County College
Athens TX 75751
Cora Govan, Coordinator
(214) 675-6379

•Redirected Homemakers
  Program
Community Education Office
Independent School District
1607 Pennsylvania
Austin, TX 78702
Ann Finch, Director
(512) 476-4661

•New Dimensions — DH
  Training Program
Texas Engineering Extension
  Service
Texas A&M University System
F.E. Drawer K
College Station, TX 77843
Pam Horne, Project
  Coordinator
(713) 845-4814 or 4815

•Mountain View College
4849 W. Illinois Avenue
Dallas, TX 75211
Carol Flannery, Project Director
(214) 746-4180

•El Paso Community College
El Paso, TX 79905
Yolanda Sitters, Coordinator
(915) 594-2636

•New Beginnings — DH
  Program
Ft. Worth Ind. School District
705 S. Henderson
Ft. Worth, TX 76104
Johnny Sue Reynolds,
  Coordinator
(817) 332-7544

•Houston Community College
2720 Leeland
Houston, TX 77003
Carol Cresswell
(713) 237-1040

•Displaced Homemaker Project
Houston Community College
  System
22 Waugh Drive
Houston, TX 77007
Patricia Davis, Administrator
(713) 869-5021

•Displaced Homemakers
  Program
North Lake College
2000 Walnut Hill Lane
Irving, TX 75062
Sharon Tuck, Coordinator
(214) 659-5370

•Displaced Homemaker Project
Central Texas College
Highway 190 West
Killeen, TX 76541
Rhetta Flemming, Project
  Coordinator
(817) 525-1291

•Displaced Homemaker Program
Laredo Junior College
Laredo, TX 78040
Stella McKinnis
(512) 724-3611

•Displaced Homemaker Project
Paris Junior College
Paris, TX 75460
Vicki Oglesby, Coordinator
(214) 785-7661 x169

•Displaced Homemaker Program
Bexar County Women's Center
2300 W. Commerce
San Antonio, TX 78207
Rosemary Stauber, Executive
  Director
(512) 225-4387

•Displaced Homemaker Project
San Jacinto College — Central
Pasadena, TX 77505
Pricilla Wake
(713) 476-1501 x297

•Ranger Junior College
Ranger, TX 76470
JoAnne Moore, DH
  Coordinator
(817) 653-2350

•Homemakers Education/
  Employment Re-entry
  Program
San Antonio College —
  Continuing Education
1300 San Pedro Avenue
San Antonio, TX 78284
Kay Moore, Coordinator
(512) 734-7311 x212

UTAH

•Alternative Job Options for
  Women
Phoenix Institute
383 South 600 East
Salt Lake City, UT 84102
Jerri Brown, Program
  Development Director
(801) 532-5080

VERMONT

•YWCA Referral Project
278 Main Street
Burlington, VT 05401
Suzanne Ferland, Coordinator
(802) 862-7520

VIRGINIA

•Re-entry Women's Employment
  Center
7620 Little River Turnpike
Annandale, VA 22003
Eieanor Lent, Director
(703) 750-0633

•Displaced Homemaker Project
McLellan Community College
1400 College Drive
Waco, TX 76708
Marylea Henderson
(817) 756-6551 x213

•New Directions Career
  Development Program
North Texas Skills Center
300 Third Street
Wichita Falls, TX 76301
Shirley Woods, Coordinator
(817) 322-1197

•Displaced Homemaker Project
FOCUS
P.O. Box 3365
Charlottesville, VA 22903
Susan Fischer, Project
  Coordinator
(804) 293-2222

WASHINGTON

•Women's Center Displaced
  Homemaker Program
Bellevue Community College
3000 Landerholm Circle, SE
Bellevue, WA 98007
Catherine Taskett, Coordinator
(206) 641-2279

•Displaced Homemakers
  Program
Lower Columbia Community
  Action Council
P.O. Box 2126
Longview, WA 98632
Marilyn Melville/Judi Raiter,
  Co-Directors
(206) 425-3430

•Rural Access
Edmonds Community College
20000 68 West
Lynwood, WA 98036
Ruth McCormick, Program
  Coordinator
(206) 775-4444

•Displaced Homemaker Program
  — Women's Center
Highline Community College
Midway, WA 98031
Betty Colsaurdo, Coordinator
(206) 878-3710 x365

•Displaced Homemaker Program
YWCA of Seattle-King Co.
1118 Fifth Avenue
Seattle, WA 98101
(206) 447-4851

•Displaced Homemaker Project
  — Human Development
  Center
Seattle Central Community
  College
1701 Broadway
Seattle, WA 98122
Diane Wolman, Program
  Director
(206) 587-3852

•Displaced Homemaker Program
Shoreline Community College
16101 Greenwood North Drive
Seattle, WA 98133
Diane Dailey, Coordinator
(206) 546-4606

•Displaced Homemaker Program
  — Women's Programs
Spokane Falls Community
  College
3410 W. Fort George Wright
  Drive, W 3410
Spokane, WA 99204
Shirley Michaelsen, Director
(509) 456-3275

•Action Based Clinic for
  Displaced Homemakers
Fort Steilacoom Community
  College — Career Ed.
9401 Farwest Drive, SW, Room
  6022
•Tacoma, WA 98498
Marty Lind, Coordinator
(206) 964-6712

•Pierce Co. Women's Transition
Re-entry Program
Clover Park Vocational-
Technical Institute
4500 Steilacoom Blvd.
Tacoma, WA 98499
Dorothy Doss, Coordinator
Carol Mooney, Program
Supervisor
(206) 584-7611

WEST VIRGINIA

•Wider Opportunities for
Women Program
West Virginia Northern
Community College
College Square
Wheeling, WV 26003
Scotty David, Program
Coordinator
(304) 233-5900 x280

WISCONSIN

•Displaced Homemaker Service
Center
Beloit YWCA
246 W. Grand Avenue
Beloit, WI 53511
Joan Okray, Coordinator
(608) 364-4438

•Passages Homemakers Center
Skilled Jobs for Women, Inc.
2095 Winnebago Street
Madison, WI 53704
Andrea Graff, Director
(608) 244-5181

•Career Orientation and
Women's Bureau
Milwaukee Area Technical
College
1015 N. Sixth Street
Milwaukee, WI 53203
Marion I. Medley, Director
(414) 278-6672

•Displaced Homemaker Project
YWCA Job Bank
1115 Ester Street
Vancouver, WA 98660
Maxine Seljack, Director
(206) 696-0167

•Displaced Homemakers Support
Groups
Women's Coalition
2211 E. Kenwood Blvd.
Milwaukee, WI 53211
Cheryl Kader, Coordinator
(414) 964-6117

•YWCA of Greater Milwaukee
610 N. Jackson
Milwaukee, WI 53202
Emily Erickson, Program
Director
(414) 271-1030 x14

•Women's Development
Program
Wisconsin Indianhead
Technical Institute
1019 S. Knowles
New Richmond, WI 54017
Kathy Johnson, Program
Coordinator
(715) 246-6561

•Women's Development Center
Waukesha County Technical
    Institute
800 Main Street
Pewaukee, WI 53072
Ruth Fossedal, Director
(414) 548-5400

•Women's Bureau
Gateway Technical Institute
1001 S. Main Street
Racine, WI 53403
Ann Timm, Director
(414) 637-9881 x35

•DH Program
Women's Resource Bureau
Nicolet College & Technical
    Institute
Box 518
Rhinelander, WI 54501
Laurie Schmidt, Director
(715) 369-4410

WYOMING

•Exploring Opportunities for
    Women Program
Women's Center
Western Wyoming College
P.O. Box 428
Rock Springs, WY 82901
Connie Neunaber, Program
    Coordinator
(307) 382-2121 x192

•Life/Work Planning Center
607 S. Water Street
Sheboygan, WI 53081
Judy Fedler, Administrator
(414) 452-1803 or 693-8211

•Women on the Move to
    Employment Now
    (WOMEN)
Central Wisconsin Community
    Action Council, Inc.
211 Wisconsin Avenue
Wisconsin Dells, WI 53965
Louise Stewart, Program
    Supervisor
(608) 254-8353

Reprinted with permission of Displaced Homemaker Network, Inc.

These programs are all so new, even in 1980, that it is possible some will be added by the time this book appears. For additional information contact:

Displaced Homemakers Network
755 Eighth Street, NW
Washington, DC 20001

HELPFUL

PUBLICATIONS

Coverletter and Gray Papers on issues for action ($10). Older Women's League Educational Fund, 3800 Harrison St., Oakland, CA 94611.

Network News. Displaced Homemakers Network, Inc., 755 Eighth St., NW, Washington, DC 20001. Detailed information for programs seeking CETA funding for displaced homemakers. Also: *Displaced Homemakers: Program Options.* Manual on setting up displaced homemaker programs ($13.25); *Displaced Homemaker Program Directory.* Lists all such programs as of August 1979 ($1.50).

Jacobs, Ruth Harriet. *Life After Youth: Female, Forty—What Next?* Boston: Beacon Press, 1979.

Berman, Eleanor. *Re-Entering: Successful Back-to-Work Strategies for Women Seeking a Fresh Start.* New York: Crown Publishers, Inc., 1980.

Michelozzi, Betty Neville. *Coming Alive from Nine to Five: The Career Search Handbook.* Palo Alto, California: Mayfield Publishing Co., 1980.

Tenenbaum, Frances. *Over 55 Is Not Illegal: A Resource Book for Active Older People.* Boston: Houghton Mifflin Company, 1979.

Rubin, Lillian. *Women of a Certain Age: The Midlife Search for Self.* New York: Harper & Row, 1979.

Wax, Judith. *Starting in the Middle.* New York: Holt, Rinehart and Winston, 1979.

Meier, Gretl S. *Job Sharing: A New Pattern for Quality of Work and Life.* Kalamazoo, Michigan: W.E. Upjohn Institute for Employment Research, 1978.

How to Tame the CETA Beast: an Advocacy Manual for Older Women. Prepared by OWLEF to help implement the new CETA legislation. Older Women's League Educational Fund, 3800 Harrison Street, Oakland, CA 94611 ($2.50 individuals; $5.00 institutions; add $1 for 1st-class mail).

The Age Discrimination Study. U.S. Commission on Civil Rights, January 1979. Part II of the study documents age discrimination in a number of areas, including CETA (pp. 117–170).

Report on Single Heads of Households. National Commission for Employment Policy, June 1979. Useful statistical study of particular relevance to older women. Also indicates the huge gap between persons eligible and available employment and training slots. 1522 K St., NW, Suite 300, Washington, DC 20005.

Obstacles & Opportunities for Employment of Older Persons in California. Tish Sommers, California Commission on Aging, 1978. For free copy, write CCOA, P.O. Box 350, Sacramento, CA 95802. Documents issues and proposed solutions which emerged from statewide hearings. Applicable to other states. 56 pages.

A Guide to Coordinating CETA/Vocational Education Legislation Affecting Displaced Homemaker Programs, May 1979. Women's Bureau and Bureau of Occupational & Adult Education in the U.S. Office of Education provides a "matrix" which summarizes and compares provisions of the two bills and discusses relevant sections for displaced homemaker programs.

Women's Bureau kit for women's organizations, April 1979. Contains final regs of pertinent CETA titles; sections of rules of particular significance for women's organizations and businesses owned by women; Prime Sponsor planning schedule for FY 1980; review of CETA Reauthorization (Public Law 95-254); summary of participation of women in CETA decision making; directory of state employment and training services councils.

Tables Pertinent to Women and Displaced Homemakers by Selected Characteristics, July 13, 1979. Provides such data as is currently available on the target population, displaced homemakers, by age groups. Women's Bureau, D.O.L.

Shortchanged and Slighted: An Assessment of the D.O.L.'s National Response to Women's Employment and Training Needs, January 1979. Women's Work Force (Advocacy Network for Women's Employment Programs), 1649 K St. NW, 4th floor, Washington, DC 20006. Documents some of the shortcomings of CETA in regard to women and makes recommendations.

CETA Monitoring Memo. League of Women Voters Education Fund, 1730 M St. NW, Washington, DC 20036. June 1978. Useful information for groups interested in monitoring CETA on state or local level.

Age Audits in Employment: Data and Instruments. Michael D. Batten. Clearinghouse on Employment for the Aging, 80 Reid Ave., Port Washington, NY 11050, 1977. Excellent methodology for accurate data gathering on older unemployed.

CETA Litigation Kit. National Employment Law Project, 475 Riverside Drive, New York, NY 10027. Kit includes summary of 1978 amendments, model complaint and model interrogatories. The Project also offers various support services.

Employment Services for Older Job Seekers. Human Resources Research Organization, 300 N. Washington St., Alexandria, VA 22314. A study of employment services available to older workers, funded by the AOA. Includes usable statistics, charts and documented supportive materials for advocacy. June 1978, 225 pages.

Survey of Working Women. National Commission on Working Women, 1211 Connecticut Ave., NW, Suite 400, Washington, DC 20036. 1978. Summarizes 150,000 questionnaires, from "the 80% of women in the labor force concentrated in lower-paying lower-status" jobs ($2.00).

The People's Guide to a Community Work Center. Sidney Brown, New Ways to Work. A basic "how-to" for setting up and running an employment-oriented center. Includes job finding and creation as well as the nuts and bolts. 1977, 50 pages ($4.75 inc. postage). Other resources include: *Adjusting Work Time*, A New Ways to Work position paper, September 1978; *Working Less but Enjoying It More*, a description of the job-sharing process. For publications list, write New Ways to Work, 149 Ninth St., San Francisco, CA 94103.

Older Americans: An Untapped Resource. National Committee on Careers for Older Americans. Good background material on why and how to employ older persons. 1979, 87 pages ($8.50). Write NCCOA, 1414 22nd St. NW, Washington, DC 20037.

SER 1978 Annual Report: Building Human Resources. SER-Jobs for Progress, Inc. is an example of a nonprofit community-based organization, with emphasis on the Hispanic population, which has become a community development corporation of national scope. Concerned with displaced homemakers. For information, write Josephine Segura, Women's Division Adm. SER-Jobs for Progress, 9841 Airport Blvd., Los Angeles, CA 90045.

Film:
Who Remembers Mama? A provocative film documentary exploring the economic and emotional devastation experienced by millions of middle-aged women when they lose their roles as homemakers through divorce. Available in 16mm film, $550 to purchase, $75 to rent. Also in video cassettes, $200 to purchase, $60 to rent. This prize-winning production by Cynthia and Allen Mondell is available through Media Projects Incorporated, 5215 Homer, Dallas, Texas 75206; phone: 214-826-3863.

INDEX

ACTION, 152, 164
Actuarial reduction, Social Security, 203
ADH (*see* Alliance for Displaced Homemakers)
Administration on Aging, 191
AFDC (*see* Aid to Families with Dependent Children)
Age Discrimination in Employment Act, 32
Age Discrimination Study, 211, 213
Agee, Irene, 179–180, 187
Aging, ageism, XIII, XIV, 4, 12–16, 19, 20–22, 24, 25–27, 31–32, 36, 46, 112, 126, 137–146, 157, 181, 185, 188, 190–192, 215
  and public policy, 200–202
  beauty of aging, 197, 210
  some myths, 208–212
  (*See also* Demographic changes)
Aid to Families with Dependent Children (AFDC), 19, 86, 114, 204
Alameda County Center (*see* California Displaced Homemakers Center)
Alexander, Holly, 93
Alliance for Displaced Homemakers

(ADH), XI, 46, 47, 48, 71, 75, 76, 122, 131, 170, 176, 183, 191
American Bar Association, Silver Gavel Award, 166
American Vocational Association, 160
Anderson, Jack, 115
Anderson, Wendell, 139
Area Agency on Aging, 200
Arthritis, 213
Assertion and aggression, 180
Assertiveness training, 89
"Assessment of need," 198
Associated Press, 55
Attractiveness, 210

Babysitting, babysitters, 16–17, 81, 88, 207
Bacon, Francis, 189
Baltimore Center for Displaced Homemakers, 62, 76–79, 82–84, 87–90, 128, 136, 173–174, 179
  and job training, 104–111
Baltimore Displaced Homemakers Conference, 162–176, 214
Baltimore New Directions for Women, 77, 136, 163
Balzar, John, 18

Barter centers, non-profit, 199
Batterton, Richard, 136
Bayh, Birch, 123, 138–139, 140
Bennett, Tony, 32
Berglin, Linda, 64
Bergmann, Barbara, 156
Bernheim, Gloria, 178
Blackwell, Alice, 189
Boston Civic Center and Clearing
    House, 153
Brown, Jerry (Edmund G., Jr.),
    50–62
Brown, Pat (Edmund G.), 50
"Brown Throat," 125–127, 137–138,
    139, 145
Burke, Yvonne B., 47, 118, 119–120,
    123–125, 138, 142
Burns, James MacGregor, 26–27
Burton, Sandra, 178
Business and Professional Women's
    Clubs, 177
Butler, Robert, 211–212

California Career Planning Center,
    178
California Displaced Homemakers
    Act, XI, 35–36, 39, 46, 47,
    50–62, 64, 71
    (See also Displaced homemakers
    bills and centers)
California Displaced Homemakers
    Center, 61–62, 71, 77, 78,
    90–91, 100–104, 119–120, 128,
    152–153, 173–174
    comprehensive, multiservice,
    71–76
    Los Angeles, 79–82, 93, 166–167
California Manufacturers
    Association, 18
Cardin, Benjamin, 76
Career Planning Center (CPC), 82
Carter, President Jimmy; Carter
    administration, 87, 91, 193 and
    Displaced Homemakers Act,
    121–123, 127, 143–144
Carter, Rosalynn, 87, 127, 189
Catania, Susan, 136

Catch-22, 15
CETA (see Comprehensive
    Employment Training Act)
Chacon, Estelle and Philip, 51
Chance, Dick, 184–186
"Change of life," 208–209
Charles, Manuel, 181–183
Chemical workers, 18
Cherkin, Arthur, 18
Chicago, First National Bank of,
    Temporary Work Force, 151
Child, Julia, 150
Churches, and jobs for women,
    63–64, 129, 130–131
Cicero, Marcus Tullius, 72
Clauss, Carin, 31, 34
Clay, William ("Bill"), 119–120
"Closure," 147–148, 190
Community Block Grant, 200
Community organizers, 195
Comprehensive Employment
    Training Act (CETA), XI, 15,
    78, 87, 100, 121, 125, 126–127,
    128, 129, 138, 144, 178,
    180–187, 193–194, 197, 200,
    214, 215
Congressional Record, 115
Congressional staff and aides,
    115–117, 129, 136, 143–144
Conservation, 85–87, 195–196
Costanza, Midge, 122–123
CPC (see Career Planning Center)
Cranston, Alan, 139, 140
Crisp, Mary, 121–122

Daley, Richard, 145
Davis, Marguerite, XIII
Demographic changes, 10–11
Demosthenes, 72
Department of Education, 156
Department of Health, Education
    and Welfare (HEW), 12
Department of Human Resources,
    200
Department of Labor (DOL), X, 12,
    14, 31, 128, 143, 145, 150, 156,
    176, 178, 184–186, 191

Dependency, XIV, 22–23, 30, 46, 114
  and Social Security, 204, 205, 215
Depression, the, 193, 195, 199
Desertion, deserted wives, 147, 149
Dietrick, John, 181, 182–183
Disability insurance, XIV, 14–15, 30, 190, 204
Discrimination against older women (*see* Aging, ageism)
Displaced Homemakers Act, federal, 113–146, 178, 194
  Bastille Day hearing, 127–129
  Congressional attitudes and workings, 113–117, 126–129, 136–137, 140–142, 143–145
  in House, 118–121, 123–129
    Carter administration, 121–123, 127
  in Senate, 129, 135–146
  intent of bills, 113–114
  opposition, 129–135
  special-interest lobbyists, 115, 117
Displaced homemakers bills and centers, 28–31, 35–36, 46, 47–64, 123, 178, 190–191, 202
  California, 50–62, 64, 71, 73, 79–82, 90–91, 93, 100–104, 119–120, 128, 152–153, 166–167, 173–174
    text of bill, 223–228
  Florida, 62–63
  Illinois, 136
  Iowa, 84–87
  Maryland, 62, 76–79, 82–84, 87–90, 104–111, 128, 136, 163, 173–174, 179
  Minnesota, 64
  Montana, 124, 128
  Nebraska, 93–94, 136
  New York, 94–100, 123
  Oregon, 63, 128, 168–170
  Texas, 170
  (*See also* Displaced Homemakers Programs Directory)
Displaced homemakers, definition, characteristics, modes,

  IX–XIV, 35, 124–125, 141–142, 185
  skills of, XI, 12, 30, 35, 69–70, 140–141, 142–143, 150–154, 161, 173–174
  (*See also* Job training)
Displaced Homemakers Network, 177–189, 193–194, 214, 229
Displaced Homemakers Programs Directory, 231–260
"Displaced Homemakers Speak-Out," 165–176
Dissolution (Eisler), 6–8
Distinguished Rural Service Award, 84n
Divorce, divorced women, IX, 5–10, 11, 15, 20, 25–26, 29, 30, 79, 86, 94, 95, 97, 102, 103, 147, 148, 149, 166
  alimony, 15, 55, 97
  and health insurance, 206–207
  and pensions, 205, 206
  and Social Security, 204
  divorce law reform, 214
  judge's statement, 8–10
DOL (*see* Department of Labor)
Domestic service, workers, 87–90, 207
Donahue, Phil, TV show, 121
Door Opener, The (Iowa), 84–87
Douglass, Frederick, XIV
Dudley, Barbara, 34–35, 37, 38, 45, 47, 48, 49, 60, 61, 71, 72, 73, 74, 82, 161, 187, 191
Durand, Agnes, 90–91

Eagle Forum, 130, 132
Early retirement, 198, 203
Education Development Center, 160
Educational TV, 198–199
Eisenhower, Dwight D. ("Ike"), 40
Eisler, Rianne Tennenhaus, 6–8
Ekstrom, Ruth B., 160–161
Employment Training Agency (ETA), 127, 186–187
Endings and beginnings, 190, 208–209

Environmental Protection Agency, 86
Equal Opportunity Commission, 155
Equal pay, 155–156
ETA (*see* Employment Training Agency)
Eugene Displaced Homemakers Center (Oregon), 63, 128, 168–170
Evers, Ben, 183–184, 186
Exon, J. James, 136
Exploitive jobs, 16–17, 203

Fadeley, Nancie, 63, 128
Fairmont Caper, 31–34
Family structure, changing, IX, 201
Feit, Rona, 92
Felmley, Jenrose, 177
Feminists, feminism, 3–4, 22–23, 26, 27–28, 37, 42–43, 46, 98, 126, 130, 133, 165, 175–176, 189, 191, 215
    and age discrimination, 24, 26–27
Fitzgerald, William, 136, 137
Fonseca, Estel, 96, 98–99
Ford, Gerald Rudolph, 33, 121
Friedan, Betty, 4
Full Employment Act, 118

Gardner, Robert, 8–10
Garfield, James Abram, XI
Garvue, Margaret, XIII, 62
General Accounting Office, 196
Geriatric revolution, XIV, 18–19, 33–34, 84
Geriatric specialists, 196
Ginsburg, Scott, 142, 143
Goetze, Mandy, 77–78, 136, 137
Goodin, Joan, 155
Goodman, Ellen, XII
Governor's Office of Employment and Training Administration, 181
Gray Panthers, 18, 33
    Seattle, 200

Green, Ernest, 127, 144
Gresham, Martha, 37–38, 42–43, 162–163, 165
Griffin, Florence, 171

Handel, George Frederick: *The Messiah*, 148
Harding, Jim, 83–84
Harralson, Margaret, 103
Hatch, Orin, 137
Hathaway, William, 139
Hawkins, Augustus, 117–118, 119, 127–128, 130, 143
Health care, home, 196, 207
Health care and insurance, 5, 11–12, 17, 25–26, 28–29, 35, 176, 190, 200–201, 206–208, 210–211, 213, 215
Hisquierdo (Supreme Court Decision), 206
Hite Report, 209–210
Hitler, Adolf, 31
Home cleaning, 89–90
Homemaking a viable occupation, XIV, 23–24, 30, 35, 135, 160–161, 205, 207
Home-sharing expeditors, 199–200
Hoskins, Eleanor, 82
House Select Committee on Aging, 188
Housekeepers, live-in, 15–17
Housing, shared, 199–200, 214
How to Tame the CETA Beast (Sommers), 78, 215
Humphrey-Hawkins bill, 118

Illinois Commission on the Status of Women, 136
"In Stitches," 91
Income security programs, federal, IX–X
    (*See also* Disability; Retirement; Social Security; Unemployment; Welfare)
Independent Cleaning Contractor Training Program, 89

Inheritance laws, 214
Interagency Committee on
    Women's Business Enterprise,
    92
International Personnel
    Management Association, 151
International Women's Year (IWY),
    131, 132
Iowa Lakes Community College, 85
IWY (*see* International Women's
    Year)

Jackson, Terri, 172
Jacobs, Ruth, 180
James, Willy, 119–120
Javits, Jacob, 141
Jensen, Joan, 53–54
Job-training programs, 13–15,
    35–36, 52, 72–75, 77, 82,
    94–100, 103–112, 123–124, 138,
    151–153, 186–187, 194
    and creation of jobs, 73–74, 76,
        82–87, 93–94, 113–114,
        173–174
    lessons learned, 194–200
    small businesses, 87–92
    at Baltimore center, 104–111
    conference, 162–176
Jobs for Older Women Action
    Project, 31–36, 39, 45, 55–56,
    73
Jordan, Barbara, 172–173
JOW (*see* Jobs for Older Women)
June, 167–170

Keating, Joyce, 83, 104, 111
Kirby, Ellen, 63
Knight, Thelma, 166–167
Koss, Helen, 62, 76–77, 78
Krucoff, Carol, 155–156

LaVerne, Opal, 172–174
Leadership (Burns), 26–27
Leahy, Joan, 56, 61
Leary, Mary Ellen, 50
Legal services, 197–198

Lessing, Doris, 24
Libra, Al, 18
Life After Youth (Jacobs), 180
Life Focus, 100–104
Lincoln, Abraham, 41
Lobbyists, special interest, 115, 117
Loeser, Herta, 153–154
Los Angeles Center for Displaced
    Homemakers, 79–82, 93,
    166–167
Los Angeles Commission on the
    Status of Women, 118

MAC (*see* Mobile Ag Company)
Male displaced homemakers, 90
Marano, Cynthia (Cindy), 78,
    82–83, 128, 163–164, 176–177,
    214
Marriage an economic partnership,
    23–24
Marshall, Ray, 21, 127, 144
Maryland Department of Human
    Resources, 77, 136
Maslow's hierarchy, 19
Maxey, Jo Ann, 136, 137
McAtee, Doris, XIII
McCarthy, Fran, 85
McGovern, George, 139
McLaughlin, Diana, 87–88
McVicker, Carol, 96, 98–99
Medicaid, 207
Medical records technicians,
    107–108
Medicare, 11, 26, 196, 207, 213
Melvin, Alice, 75–76
Menopause, 208–209
Middle age, 208–209
Milhous, Barbara, 90–91
Mobile Ag Company (MAC), 86–87
Moore, Marjorie, 157
Moore, Sandra Smith, 19
Motherhood and Social Security,
    203
Mowry, Jan, 164, 165
Murphy, Judy, 158
Mutual-aid projects, 194–195

Myths, and challenging of, 208–212

National Commission on Working Women, 155
National Council of Catholic Women, 129
National Institute on Aging, 211
National Observer, 170
National Rural Center, 84n
National Science Foundation, 196
National Urban League, 157, 160
National Women's Political Caucus, 33
Nelson, Gaylord, 126, 135–137, 140–141, 144
Network News, 178
New Directions (*see* Baltimore)
New life, organization of, 147–189
  and "closure," 147–150
  getting work, 150–189
    and education, 155–161, 176–177
    CETA plan, 182–187
    national clearinghouse, 177–189
    training conference, 162–176
New York Times, The, 55
Nollen, Stanley, 150
Norton, Eleanor Holmes, 155–156
Not So Helpless Female, The (Sommers), 27–28
NOW (National Organization of Women), 4, 27, 33, 44, 48, 49, 56–57, 59, 62, 64, 76, 152
Nuclear cleanup teams, 18

Older Americans Act, 197, 198
Older Women's Advocates, 215
Older Women's League Educational Fund (OWLEF), 176–177, 215–216, 229
Omaha YWCA displaced homemaker program, 93–94
Osteoporosis, 213
OWLEF (*see* Older Women's League Educational Fund)

Paid peers, 197
Paraprofessionals, 197–198
Part-time work, 150–151, 164
"Pedestal principle," 23
Peer counseling, 70
Pensions (*see* Retirement benefits)
Phantom Politics (Leary), 50
Planned Parenthood, 213
Poche, Marc, 58, 59–61
Politics and women, 114–115, 145–146, 196
  activism, 191–193
Poverty, 12–13, 202–205
Power and concession, XIV
Prime Life Styles, 197
Procurement Automated Source System, 92
Project ACCESS, 161
Project Re-Entry, 153–154
Public Health Service Act, 211
Public policy and older women, 200–202
Public relations training, 89
Public Service Employment positions, 186–187
Publicity, 195–196, 197

Quie, Albert, 142–143
Quinlan, Alice, 83, 177, 178

Railroad Retirement, 205, 206
Reagan, Ronald, 50, 51, 58
Reasoner, Harry, 179
Reproductive function, accent on, 208–209, 211, 213
Research, influencing, 212–213
Research Center for Women (Alverno College), 19
Resource Conservation Recovery Act of 1976, 85
Resources, organized, list of, 229–231
Retirement benefits, 5, 8, 17, 29, 30, 35, 176, 190, 201, 205–206, 215
Rickler, Marsha, 80–82

Riegle, Don, 136, 137, 139, 140–141, 142, 145, 178
Roach, Jane, 179
Rockefeller Foundation (*see* Winthrop)
Roosevelt, Franklin Delano, 40
Rosie the Riveter, 5, 38

St. Paul, 5
San Francisco Chronicle, 18
San Francisco Poverty Program, 152
San Francisco Volunteer Bureau, 152
Sandage, Shirley, 84–87
SBA (*see* Small Business Administration)
Scanlon, Priscilla, 178
Schlafly, Phyllis, 130–133, 135
Scully, Michael Andrew, 117, 145
Self-employment and self-help, 87–92, 150, 154–155, 194–200
Self-starters, 23
Senility, 211–212
Service-field jobs, 17–18, 87–90, 93, 197
Sexism, 20, 25–27, 31–32, 36, 46, 112, 155–157, 203, 205, 212
and medical theorists, 208–209
Sexuality of older women, 209–210, 212
Sherwood, Geri, 56
Shields, Arthur, 43, 67, 148, 150
Shields, Christine, 148
Shields, Laurie, 191, 192
and ADH, 47–48, 161–162
and California bill, 49–70
and feminism, 42–46, 165, 175–176
and national bill, 113–146
and Network, 171–189
and training conference, 161–176
and widowhood, 148
awakening interest in politics, 39–42
Sim, Ellen, 6

Sister Terence, 40–43
Sisters of the Good Shepherd, 95
Skills tests, 154
Small Business Administration (SBA), 91–92
Smith, Jerry, 51, 52, 56, 75
Social Security, X, XIV, 8, 12, 14, 17, 25, 26, 29, 30, 88, 90, 176, 193, 198, 201, 204–205, 206, 215
and cause of poverty, 202–205
Sommers, Tish, IX–XII, 24, 36, 37, 42–44, 47–48, 56, 161–165, 176, 180
and California center, 70–75, 77–78, 82, 100–104
and federal Act, 118, 120–121, 137, 138
and volunteerism, 152–153
Fairmont Caper, 31–34
founding movement for older women, 25–39, 45–46, 57–60, 61
SSI (*see* Supplemental Security Income)
State Commissions on the Status of Woman, XI
Statistics, nature and use of, 78
Stein, Aliyah, 100, 102, 153
Steinem, Gloria, 46
Steirn, Wally, 54–55, 58
Stevenson, Adlai, 72
Stewart, Charlotte, XIII, 165–166, 170–171, 178
Stress management, 89
Suicide rate, 22
Supplemental Security Income (SSI), 90, 198, 215
Survey of Income and Education, X
Suter, Joan, 79–81
Synanon, 33

Task Force on Older Women, 27
Tenner, Hallie, 118
Terence, Sister, 40–43

Thompson, Liz, 86
Thompson, Marian, 135–137
Tinkers, Paul, 181–184, 186
Tobin, Paula, 91
Toxic Substances Control Act, 85
"Trouble with Women, The" (TV
    Program), 179–180
TV, closed circuit, 198–199

Ulbinsky, Nancy, 83–84
Unemployment, hidden, 198
Unemployment insurance, X, XIV,
    14, 35
U. S. Civil Rights Commission,
    13–14, 21, 211
U. S. Commission on the
    Observance of International
    Women's Year, 131, 132
U. S. News and World Report, XII
U. S. Office of Education, 160

Vasconcellos, John, 56, 61
Veterans Administration, 196
Vista, 169
Vocational Education Amendments
    of 1976, 138
Vocational training, 158–160
Volunteer work, 151–154, 161, 195
    specimen contract, 219–222
Voorsanger, Caroline, 152

Waldron, Steve, 128
Walter, Tanis, 35
Washington Post, 117, 155–156
Weddington, Sarah, 189
Weiss, Robert, 5
Weiss, Ted, 142–143, 144
Welfare assistance, X, 12, 79, 95, 97,
    129, 201
Wellesley Center for Research on
    Women, 160
Who Remembers Mama? (film), 166
Widows, 11–12, 15, 29, 65–70, 79,
    83–84, 95, 147, 148, 149, 151,
    167–170, 179–180, 204
    and health insurance, 207
    and pensions, 205
    and Social Security, 203–204

Wigman, Mary, 31
WIN, 138
Winthrop Rockefeller Foundation,
    84n
WISH (see women in Self-Help)
Women, black and white, 79–82
Women in Self-Help (WISH),
    94–100
    Aurelia, 97–98
    Carmen, 95–97
Women's Affairs Labor, Education
    Advancement Program
    (National Urban League), 157
Women's Bureau (Department of
    Labor), X–XI, 164
Women's Equity Action League
    (Los Angeles), 198
Women's movement (see Feminism)
"Women's work," 155–160
Women's Work Force Network
    Conference, 156
World War II, 195–196
    (See also Rosie the Riveter)

Yeats, William Butler: "The Land
    of Heart's Desire," 13
Youth, America's enchantment
    with, 13, 112, 197, 210
Youth Project, 93